Companion Volumes

The companion volumes in this series are

Ethics and Research in Inclusive Education
Values into practice
Edited by Kieron Sheehy, Melanie Nind, Jonathan Rix and
Katy Simmons

Curriculum and Pedagogy in Inclusive Education
Values into practice
Edited by Melanie Nind, Jonathan Rix, Kieron Sheehy and
Katy Simmons

This Reader is part of a course: *Researching Inclusive Education Values into Practice* that is itself part of the Open University MA programme.

The Open University MA in Education

The Open University MA in Education is now firmly established as the most popular postgraduate research degree for education professionals in Europe, with over 3,500 students registering each year. The MA in Education is designed particularly for those with experience of teaching, the advisory service, educational administration or allied fields.

Structure of the MA

The MA is a modular degree, and students are therefore free to select from a range of options the programme which best fits in with their interests and professional goals. Specialist lines in management, applied linguistics and lifelong learning are also available. Successful study in the MA programme entitles students to apply for entry into the Open University Doctorate in Education Programme.

Policy and Power in Inclusive Education

The movement towards inclusive education is undoubtedly an international phenomenon, and it has resulted in the development of policy initiatives impacting on schools in all nations.

This informative, wide-ranging text brings together key illustrative material from an international field. It adopts a critical perspective on policy issues, but goes beyond this by making explicit the assumptions that drive policy development. Readers will be encouraged to develop their own framework, allowing them to conduct policy analysis and evaluation within their own educational context.

Students and researchers interested in how principles of inclusive education are being translated into educational practices around the world will find this book an enlightening read.

Jonathan Rix, **Katy Simmons**, and **Kieron Sheehy** are all lecturers in Inclusive and Special Education at the Centre for Curriculum and Teaching Studies, The Open University.

Melanie Nind was formerly a Senior Lecturer in Inclusive and Special Education at the Centre for Curriculum and Teaching Studies, The Open University, but is now Reader in Education at the University of Southampton.

Open University supported learning

The MA in Education programme provides great flexibility. Students study at their own pace, in their own time, anywhere in the European Union. They receive specially prepared study materials, supported by tutorials, thus offering the opportunity to work with other students. The University also offers many undergraduate courses. Within the area of Inclusive Education there is an undergraduate second level course *Inclusive Education: Learning from each other.*

The Doctorate in Education

The Doctorate in Education is a part-time doctoral degree, combining taught courses, research methods and a dissertation designed to meet the needs of professionals in education and related areas who are seeking to extend and deepen their knowledge and understanding of contemporary educational issues.

How to apply

If you would like to register for this programme, or simply find out more information about available courses, please write for the *Professional Development in Education* prospectus to the Course Reservation Centre, PO Box 724, The Open University, Walton Hall, Milton Keynes MK7 6ZW, UK (Telephone +44 (0) 1908 653231). Alternatively, you may visit the Open University website http://www.open.ac.uk where you can learn more about the wide range of courses offered at all levels by the Open University.

Policy and Power in Inclusive Education

Values into practice

Edited by
Jonathan Rix, Katy Simmons
Melanie Nind and Kieron Sheehy

 RoutledgeFalmer
Taylor & Francis Group

LONDON AND NEW YORK

 The Open
University

First published 2005
by RoutledgeFalmer
2 Park Square, Milton Park, Abingdon, Oxon OX14 4RN

Simultaneously published in the USA and Canada
by RoutledgeFalmer
270 Madison Ave, New York, NY 10016

RoutledgeFalmer is an imprint of the Taylor & Francis Group

© 2005 Compilation, original and editorial matter,
The Open University

Typeset in Bembo by
Newgen Imaging Systems (P) Ltd, Chennai, India
Printed and bound in Great Britain by
MPG Books Ltd, Bodmin

British Library Cataloguing in Publication Data
A catalogue record for this book is available
from the British Library

Library of Congress Cataloging in Publication Data
A catalog record for this book has been requested

ISBN 0–415–35209–6 (hbk)
ISBN 0–415–35210–X (pbk)

#55633964

Contents

Acknowledgements   x

1   Introduction: a world of change   1
    JONATHAN RIX AND KATY SIMMONS

PART I
**The struggle for an inclusive agenda: national
perspectives**   11

2   Excluding the included: a reconsideration of inclusive
    education   13
    ROGER SLEE AND JULIE ALLAN

3   Inclusion in Norway: a study of ideology in
    practice   25
    ANNLAUG FLEM AND CLAYTON KELLER

4   School choice and the pressure to perform: déjà vu for
    children with disabilities?   36
    KENNETH R. HOWE AND KEVIN G. WELNER

5   From 'special needs' to 'quality education for all': a
    participatory, problem-centred approach to
    policy development in South Africa   47
    NITHI MUTHUKRISHNA AND MARIE SCHOEMAN

PART II

The struggle for an inclusive agenda: local perspectives   57

6   In the name of inclusion: 'we all, at the end of the day,
    have the needs of the children at heart'   59
    JOHN SWAIN AND TINA COOK

7   Parents, professionals and special educational needs
    policy frameworks in England and Scotland   72
    SHEILA RIDDELL, ALASTAIR WILSON, MICHAEL ADLER AND
    ENID MORDAUNT

8   Comparison of a traditional and an inclusive secondary
    school culture   85
    SUZANNE CARRINGTON AND JOHN ELKINS

9   Exclusions from school: different voices   96
    JEAN KANE

10 Inclusion, exclusion and children's rights: a case study
    of a student with Asperger syndrome   107
    AUDREY OSLER AND CHAY OSLER

PART III

Alternative systems and policies   119

11 Special needs education as the way to equity: an
    alternative approach?   121
    ALAN DYSON

12 Early interventions: preventing school exclusions
    in the primary setting   130
    MEG MAGUIRE, SHEILA MACRAE AND LINDA MILBOURNE

13 Inclusive education in accelerated and professional
    development schools: a case-based study of two school
    reform efforts in the USA   144
    SUSAN PETERS

14   Building-based change: one school's journey toward
      full inclusion   160
      ROBERTA F. SCHNORR, EDWARD MATOTT, MICHELE PAETOW
      AND PRISCILLA PUTNAM

PART IV
Challenging perspectives   173

15   'Valuing diversity': a cliché for the twenty-first century?   175
      SHEREEN BENJAMIN

16   Migrant worker children: conceptions of homelessness
      and implications for education   191
      RICHARD H. KOZOLL, MARGERY D. OSBORNE AND
      GEORGIA EARNEST GARCÍA

17   'What are we doing this for?' Dealing with lesbian
      and gay issues in teacher education   202
      KERRY H. ROBINSON AND TANIA FERFOLJA

18   The creation of learner identities as part
      of social inclusion: gender, ethnicity and social space   213
      SUE CLEGG AND KATIE MCNULTY

      Index   223

Acknowledgements

The following chapters are reproduced with the permission of Taylor & Francis Group (www.tandf.co.uk/journals):

Chapter 3
Inclusion in Norway: a study of ideology in practice
Annlaug Flem and Clayton Keller

European Journal of Special Educational Needs (2000), 15, 2, 188–205

Chapter 5
'From special needs' to 'quality education for all': a participatory, problem-centred approach to policy development in South Africa
Nithi Muthukrishna and Marie Schoeman

International Journal of Inclusive Education (2000), 4, 4, 315–335

Chapter 8
Comparison of a traditional and an inclusive secondary school culture
Suzanne Carrington and John Elkins

International Journal of Inclusive Education (2002), 6, 1, 1–16

Chapter 12
Early interventions: preventing school exclusions in the primary setting
Meg Maguire, Sheila Macrae and Linda Milbourne

Westminster Studies in Education (2003), 26, 1, 45–62

Chapter 13
Inclusive education in accelerated and professional development schools: a case-based study of two school reform efforts in the USA
Susan Peters

International Journal of Inclusive Education (2002), 6, 4, 287–308

Chapter 15
'Valuing diversity': a cliché for the twenty-first century?
Shereen Benjamin

International Journal of Inclusive Education (2002), 6, 4, 309–323

Chapter 16
Migrant worker children: conceptions of homelessness and implications for education
Richard H. Kozoll, Margery D. Osborne and Georgia Earnest García

Qualitative Studies in Education (2003), 16, 4, 567–585

Chapter 17
'What are we doing this for?' Dealing with lesbian and gay issues in teacher education
Kerry H. Robinson and Tania Ferfolja

British Journal of Sociology of Education (2001), 22, 1, 12–133

Chapter 18
The creation of learner identities as part of social inclusion: gender, ethnicity and social space
Sue Clegg and Katie McNulty

International Journal of Lifelong Learning (2002), 21, 6, 572–585

The following chapters are reproduced with the permission of Sage Publications Ltd:

Chapter 6
In the name of inclusion: 'we all, at the end of the day, have the needs of the children at heart'
John Swain and Tina Cook

Critical Social Policy (2001), 21, 2, 185–207

Chapter 10
Inclusion, exclusion and children's rights: a case study of a student with Asperger syndrome
Audrey Osler and Chay Osler

Emotional and Behavioural Difficulties (2002), 7, 1, 35–54

The following chapter is reproduced with the permission of Blackwell Publishing Ltd:

Chapter 11
Special needs education as the way to equity: an alternative approach?
Alan Dyson

Support for Learning (2001), 16, 3, 99–104

The following chapter is reproduced with the permission of The Policy Press:

Chapter 7
Parents, professionals and special educational needs policy frameworks in England and Scotland
Sheila Riddell, Alastair Wilson, Michael Adler and Enid Mordaunt

Policy and Politics (2002), 30, 3, 411–425

The following chapter is reproduced with the permission of PRO-ED:

Chapter 4
School choice and the pressure to perform: déjà vu for children with disabilities?
Kenneth R. Howe and Kevin G. Welner

Remedial and Special Education (2002), 23, 4, 212–221

The following chapters are reproduced with the permission of the authors:

Chapter 2
Excluding the included: a reconsideration of inclusive education
Roger Slee and Julie Allan

International Studies in the Sociology of Education (2001), 11, 2, 173–191

Chapter 9
Exclusions from school: different voices
Jean Kane

Paper presented at BERA 2003, Herriot Watt University

The following chapter is reproduced with the permission of National Middle School Association.

Chapter 14
Building-based change: one school's journey toward full inclusion
Roberta F. Schnorr *et al.*

Middle School Journal, January, 44–52

Chapter 1

Introduction

A world of change

Jonathan Rix and Katy Simmons

Whatever the debates around definitions of inclusive education – and there are many – inclusive thinking and action has become 'a central component of social and educational policy' on a 'consistent and widespread global canvas' (Daniels and Garner, 1999, p. xiii). While international agencies working in the majority world increasingly focus on the development of inclusive education as the way to extend education to all learners, national governments in industrialised countries focus on inclusion policies as a response to perceived national needs for greater social cohesion. At national and at international levels, inclusive practice is increasingly seen as a strategy for responding to diversity. In Peter Mittler's words, 'Inclusion is now a world-wide movement' (Mittler, 2000, p. 13).

This volume reflects national and international perspectives on inclusive education, the policies that have encouraged its development and the shifts of power that these emergent policies involve. It draws on material from industrialised countries ('countries of the North') and from the majority world ('countries of the South'). The challenges faced in each area, though very different, have much in common, as writers with experience of both, such as Hazel Bines and Tony Booth have pointed out (Booth, 1999; Bines, 2001). Tony Booth writes of the 'vast exclusionary pressures' experienced in contexts where there is no mass education and low rates of literacy (Booth, 1999, p. 165). Hazel Bines, working as an education adviser in Pakistan, writes about the development of policies to include 'the poorest people, in a country with many demands on its limited resources and with some of the lowest human development indicators in the world' (Bines, 2001, p. 93). Both write of the challenges of removing barriers for all learners and this perspective is one we have sought to adopt in this volume.

The barriers may be very different in different contexts: in the UK they may be the persisting processes that result in Black Caribbean children continuing to have the highest rate of exclusion from school (Parsons, 2003), in South Africa, as Tony Booth has recorded, they may be the lack of safe routes for girls to school (Booth, 1999, p. 167). But while experience may be different, in terms of the processes of analysing the challenges and working towards solutions, countries of North and South have much to share. In addition, countries of the North have much to learn. As Susie Miles, of the Enabling Education Network, has pointed out, the industrialised North has had a long-term commitment to segregated education, with a long history of institutionalised separate provision for different 'categories' of children. This legacy of separate provision has created an entrenched bureaucracy as well as attitudinal barriers to inclusion. By contrast, '(t)here is little or no legacy of segregation in Africa and Asia and inclusive education programmes are often more successful at being fully inclusive and community-based than countries in the North' (Miles, 2004, p. 2).

While the Report of the 1998 Agra Seminar records that countries of the South do have traditions of segregated provision and categorisation of impairment, even so it points out that

> the 'three quarters of the world known as the so-called "developing countries" have many examples of excellent practice in inclusive education, despite large class sizes, few material resources and limited access to information', because they can draw on community solidarity and have expertise in utilising existing local resources.
>
> (EENET, 1998, p. 2)

The Agra Seminar was entitled 'Lessons from the South': it brought together practitioners from countries of the South to exchange ideas and experience and to identify common ground. The Report of the Seminar records that 'Participants were helped to think through their own situations and to work out their own context-specific solutions' (EENET, 1998, p. 3).

This volume takes a similar position. In it, we present a range of different experiences of these inclusive policies, drawn from a global context and reflecting the struggle for inclusion from a range of different perspectives: the individual, the school and the national level in countries of the North and of the South. Inclusive education is a contested area, as these chapters show individually and as a whole.

Insights into practice

None of the chapters is held up as an exemplar of 'how to do inclusion', since the cultural contexts of many of the chapters may be very different from the one experienced by the reader. Rather, in compiling the volume, we have borne in mind Alan Dyson's idea of 'a multiplicity of inclusions' (Dyson, 1999, p. 46). Dyson's argument is that instead of seeking a 'single form' of inclusive practice, we should rather look for 'a wide range of practice and organization, which needs constantly to be interrogated in terms of different notions of inclusion that are available' (Dyson, 1999, p. 46). Such a perspective enables us to use the chapters, not as exemplars, but rather as insights into other practices. Tony Booth has described how to approach comparative study of inclusion:

> It requires taking the anthropological perspective into the 'villages' of others and bringing it back to one's own. My view of comparative study is not about the search for 'good practice' but about finding instructive lessons in all practice.
>
> (Booth, 1999, p. 165)

It is these 'instructive lessons' that we have looked for while selecting the chapters. For, while the chapters reflect varied geographical and political settings, they share a concern for fundamental social issues of access to justice, equity and citizenship.

We are concerned too that promises of entitlement can often become merged with notions of equity, so that those who create policies can suggest, and sometimes believe, they have provided genuine opportunity of access when they have only created a right of access. As Corbett (2001) described in a case study of a French skills training course for North African immigrants, equity is not about providing the minimum. In this instance, she describes how equity involved much more than skills training. Staff saw the importance of talking with students about prejudices they would face, helping them to build pride in their identity despite this and to counterbalance the social inequities they would have to deal with when on work placement.

Within this book are a number of chapters that explore the gaps between entitlement and equity of access, and ways in which the gaps could be filled. We also acknowledge that for many the policy that generates entitlement is still lacking. In a number of instances inclusive education initiatives are filling this gap, and are being used to respond to diversity and to improve educational experiences for all. The *Times Educational Supplement* reported an Indian initiative with disabled children. The article records that 'The Indian government is to abandon separate education for disabled pupils and has asked all states to integrate such pupils into mainstream schools by the next academic year' (Behal, 2001, p. 16).

But 'separate education' for many disabled children actually meant no education: the article goes on to report that 98 per cent of Indian disabled children did not attend school at all. So the Indian inclusive education initiative was actually a movement towards the broader goal of education for all.

Education for all

Accounts by Peter Mittler (Mittler, 2000) and Peter Evans (Evans, 1999) give details of the work of the United Nations and other international bodies in promoting globally the inclusive agenda of 'education for all'. The UN Convention on the Rights of the Child, agreed in 1989, demands, in Article 28, that primary education should be 'compulsory and available free to all' (UNICEF, 2004). Article 23 covers the rights of disabled children and includes their right to education that is responsive to their individuality. Evans comments that 'while inclusive education in the sense of mainstreaming is not specifically covered', the Article is not 'incompatible with such an interpretation' (Evans, 1999, p. 230).

Following the Convention, the Education for All by 2000 programme was a global initiative launched in 1990 at a United Nations conference, held in Jomtien, Thailand and sponsored by a range of United Nations organisations, as well as the World Bank. The Jomtien Conference 'placed education at the top of the international agenda' and was 'an attempt to halt the decline in basic education which had taken place during the 1980s when many countries were forced to cut down on expenditure in education due to debt repayments and lower export earnings'. (Peresuh, 2000, p. 1). Ministers from 155 governments committed themselves at this Conference to the principle of universal access to primary education: 'In essence, Jomtien marked the emergence of an international consensus that education is the most single vital element in fighting against poverty, empowering women, promoting human rights and democracy, protecting the environment and controlling population growth' (Peresuh, 2000, p. 1).

The 1994 Salamanca conference followed on from Jomtien and 'succeeded in reminding governments that children with difficulties and disabilities must be included within EFA' (Mittler, 2000, p. 17). Representatives of 92 governments and 25 international organisations agreed the Salamanca statement on the education of all disabled children and adopted a new Framework for Action. Although focused on the education of children with disabilities, the Framework saw these children as part of a much larger marginalised group:

> The guiding principle that informs this **Framework** is that schools should accommodate all children, regardless of their physical, intellectual, social, emotional, linguistic or other conditions. This should include disabled and gifted children, street and working children, children from remote or nomadic populations, children from linguistic, ethnic or cultural minorities and children from other disadvantaged or marginalized areas or groups.
>
> (UNESCO, 1994, p. 6)

The Statement thus went beyond the limitations of 'special education needs', with its focus on learner deficits, to look at children marginalised socially, geographically or linguistically. It took a rights-based perspective:

> We believe and proclaim that
>
> • every child has a fundamental right to education, and must be given the opportunity to achieve and maintain an acceptable level of learning...
> • those with special educational needs must have access to regular schools which should accommodate them within a child-centred pedagogy capable of meeting these needs.
>
> (UNESCO, 1994, p. ix)

The Statement took a clear position on where education should take place:

- Regular schools with this inclusive orientation are the most effective means of combating discriminatory attitudes, creating welcoming communities, building an inclusive society and achieving education for all; moreover, they provide an effective education to the majority of children and improve the efficiency and ultimately the cost-effectiveness of the entire education system.

(UNESCO, 1994, p. viii)

It also acknowledged the multiple identities of some learners and the consequent additional marginalisation that they experience:

It is particularly important to recognize that women have often been doubly disadvantaged, bias on gender compounding the difficulties caused by their disabilities.... Special efforts should be made to encourage the participation of girls and women with disabilities in educational programmes....

(UNESCO, 1994, p. 14)

Several kinds of ambiguity

Dyson points to the powerful impact of the Salamanca Statement and its influence in stimulating change at national and international level, even in countries such as the UK, which generally has had little interest in 'international proclamations'. (Dyson, 1999, p. 37). At the same time, while acknowledging its impact, Dyson describes the Salamanca Statement as 'a deeply ambiguous document', and goes on to analyse the way in which it maintains its rights-based tone across, as he sees it, areas that would be better seen as subjects of debate or research. He attributes this ambiguity to the fact that the Statement is the outcome of political processes and therefore is subject to compromise between fundamentally different discourses.

Such an observation could be made of attitudes to inclusive education policies both at local and national levels. Croll and Moses, for example, in their research in the UK with head teachers and classroom teachers, showed that many teachers readily identified children with emotional and behavioural difficulties, in particular, as candidates for exclusion from mainstream into segregated settings. However, when they were asked about particular children in their classes, teachers generally supported mainstream placements. Croll and Moses point to the contrast between teachers' professed ideological position and their actual classroom practice:

There is no commitment among the teachers in the survey to inclusion as generalized educational ideology, and there is strong awareness of the pragmatic case for special schools.... But, at the same time, there is a good deal of inclusive practice in the classrooms in the study, with teachers committed to meeting very considerable levels of educational needs in the mainstream.

(Croll and Moses, 1999, p. 9)

Such ambiguities and contradictions exist perhaps even more strikingly at national level. In 1997, campaigners for inclusive education welcomed the UK Government's affirmation of its support for the Salamanca Statement. They were later disappointed that increasing inclusion of disabled pupils remained slow. That disappointment turned to outrage in 2003 when, on the publication of a report by the Special Schools Working Group, Baroness Ashton, the Minister responsible for the report, wrote in its preface of the importance of special schools and of the government's continuing commitment to such schools. Campaigning organisations accused the Government of 'breaking its promises' (Alliance for Inclusive Education *et al.*, 2003).

Such ambiguities lie at the heart of a number of the chapters in this volume. Whether they should be viewed as 'broken promises' or 'mixed messages', the inevitable gap between political rhetoric and practical reality or the jagged edges between different competing discourses will depend on the perspective of the reader. Further sources of ambiguity lie in the persistence of older discourses within emerging alternatives. Sometimes, as Susie Miles has pointed out, as inclusive practice emerges, different discourses co-exist, albeit uncomfortably:

> Sometimes this is from a rights perspective: 'Disabled children and other marginalised groups have a right to be educated alongside their peers'. And sometimes this comes from an economic perspective: We cannot afford or sustain segregated 'special' education, and so inclusion is the only option.
>
> (Miles, 2004, p. 2)

Not only do different discourses compete, but different perspectives on inclusion may be accorded different weight. At the Agra seminar, there was deliberate emphasis on the practical experiences of practitioners from countries of the South:

> ... practitioners from the South have very few opportunities to attend the many so-called 'international' conferences which tend to be held in the North and to be dominated by Northern agenda. Token representation of people from the South at international conferences rarely leads to a genuine exchange of ideas and experience taking place.
>
> (EENET, 1998, p. 2)

In this volume, we hope that insights from unfamiliar settings will be valued as the basis for fresh thinking about more familiar locations.

Structure of this volume

The first part of this volume looks at national perspectives on the struggle for inclusive education and draws on material from the highly industrialised North, countries from the OECD and a country of the South, post-apartheid South Africa. The chapters share a sense of the emergent nature of inclusive education and of the struggle to maintain new perspectives in a climate where old ideologies remain strong influences and where there are other, pressing political imperatives. Roger Slee and Julie Allan look at the persistence of existing discourses within the language of official documentation in Australia and the UK. They deconstruct official documentation and suggest that inclusive education should be seen as an entirely new discourse. Annlaug Flem and Clayton Keller look at the gap between intention and reality in Norway, showing how inclusion is 'work in progress' rather than a steady state, while Kenneth Howe and Kevin Welner look at competing political perspectives that threaten the integrity of the inclusion movement in the USA. They explore the underlying tension and 'jagged edges' between the inclusion agenda and the parental choice agenda, showing their basic incompatability. The writers warn that the ground gained by the inclusion movement may well be lost. Nithi Muthukrishna and Marie Schoeman describe the efforts made in post-apartheid South Africa to break away from deficit-based definitions of disability to a broader awareness of exclusionary pressures that marginalise particular groups of learners. They contrast the principled way that policy was driven with the actual outcomes that were shaped by political necessity.

The second part of this volume considers the contested ground at local level, focusing on schools and regional organisation and at the impact of policies on families and young people. The section highlights the need to listen to members of the local community and the struggle that organisations face to do this. John Swain and Tina Cook explore the development of an inclusive policy in one English Local Education Authority. They show that, despite changing names and structures, old discourses die hard. The chapter emphasises the imperative of rights-based, participatory policy development. Sheila Riddell, Alastair Wilson, Michael Adler and Enid Mordaunt look at the way that parents in England and Scotland engage with policies and policy makers and at the attitudes of professionals whose job it is to implement policies. Suzanne Carrington and John Elkins contrast the beliefs, values and practices in two Australian high schools, highlighting the significant conflict between negative attitudes and inclusive goals. Jean Kane examines how Scottish policy is attempting to deal with issues of exclusion and the responses of pupils and professionals who are affected by the process of exclusion. This part ends with another exploration of the impact of exclusion on families and young people. In this chapter, Audrey Osler and her nephew Chay, a young man with Asperger Syndrome, describe how policy is implemented by schools. Their chapter explores the tension between the 'standards' agenda and the inclusion agenda in one high-performing comprehensive school in the UK.

The third part of this volume considers some possible ways of moving the inclusive agenda forward across the contested ground. It draws upon models that can serve as a starting point and upon specific examples of schools moving forwards. The part opens with Alan Dyson's challenge to both the individual focus of 'special needs provision' and some inclusionists' rejection of any framework for individual support. He suggests there is a need to be clear about the form and purpose of learning and participation, and to acknowledge that specific interventions can be recommended for individuals within mainstream settings. The next three chapters consider school attempts to implement inclusive policy. Meg Maguire, Sheila Macrae and Linda Milbourne examine three UK primary schools' attempts to generate effective strategies for overcoming the pressures to exclude pupils, while Susan Peters explores the development of two school reform efforts in the USA which focus on reflective practice and creating a collaborative, responsive learning community. The part concludes with the chapter by Roberta Schnorr, Edward Matott, Michele Paetow and Priscilla Putnam, in which they describe the creation and implementation of a policy in a US school to increase student diversity, with an emphasis on whole school change and collaboration.

The fourth part of this volume starts from the premise that inclusion must never be reified by policy and systems and is not a static but an evolving state. Inclusion is a constant reminder that we must start our search again for increasing involvement of individuals in their own learning. This part raises questions about current widely held preconceptions and in so doing challenges the education system to examine itself from a wider variety of perspectives. Shereen Benjamin opens this examination with an exploration of the competing discourses that surround the notion of diversity, demonstrating that language in the education system may have changed but underlying power relationships may not have. Richard Kozoll, Margery Osborne and Georgia Earnest Garcia then present a case study of migrant workers that encourages us to question our notions of home and family, raising questions about the types of experiences on which schools can draw and about which they must come to understand. This chapter is followed by Kerry Robinson's and Tania Ferfolja's analysis of the resistance in individuals and systems to questioning of values and attitudes towards sexuality and other hidden biases. It highlights the need for such issues to be confronted in the training of teachers going into inclusive settings. This part concludes with an examination by Sue Clegg and Katie McNulty of what counts as learning with adult learners and the degree to which they view education as useful. It encourages us to question how we can re-engage individuals with learning.

We began this introduction by stating that there are many definitions of inclusive education. The very notion of inclusion encourages such a debate, requiring us to consider issues from a variety of perspectives. Ironically, this often means that we are faced with opinions and views that do not make creating inclusion any easier. Inclusion and exclusion are, of course, fundamentally tied up with notions of power. They are active consequences of human relations. In creating inclusive policies and systems we attempt to direct the power and maximise its positive benefit. Since policies exist across time, there will, however, always be a fundamental tension between them and the experience of power and inclusion in the moment. At best we can attempt to examine tensions that are prevalent in the initiation and implementation of inclusive policies and systems, and to highlight areas in which there is still much to be done. We hope that this book goes some way towards achieving these aims.

References

Alliance for Inclusive Education, Bolton Institute of Higher Education, Centre for Studies on Inclusive Education, Disability Quality in Education and Parents for Inclusion (2003) 'Government breaks promises on inclusion for disabled children' (press release), London, Parents for Inclusion. Available at http://www.parentsforinclusion.org/pressrel.htm (Accessed July 2003).

Behal, Suchitra (2001) 'Disabled to make the mainstream', *Times Educational Supplement*, May 18, p. 16.

Bines, H. (2001) 'A longer road to inclusion', *Support for Learning*, 16(2), 92–93.

Booth, T. (1999) 'Viewing inclusion from a distance: gaining perspective from comparative study', *Support for Learning*, 14(4), 164–168.

Corbett, J. (2001) 'Is equity compatible with entitlement? Balancing inclusive values and deserving needs', *Support for Learning*, 16(3), 117–121.

Croll, P. and Moses, D. (1999) 'Mainstream primary teachers' views of inclusion', paper presented at the Annual Conference of the British Educational Research Association, 2–5 September.

Daniels, H. and Garner, P. (1999) 'Introduction to the paperback edition Inclusive Education: challenges for the new millennium', in Daniels, H. and Garner, P. (Eds) *Inclusive Education: Supporting Inclusion in Education Systems*, Kogan Page, London.

Dyson, A. (1999) 'Inclusion and inclusions: theories and discourses in inclusive education', in Daniels H. and Garner, P. (Eds) *Inclusive Education: Supporting Inclusion in Education Systems*, Kogan Page, London.

EENET (1998) Lessons from the South: Making a Difference. Report of an International Disability and Development Consortium (IDDC) Seminar on Inclusive Education, Agra, India, 1–7 March 1998, www.eenet.org.uk/reports/agra/agra.htm (Accessed 21 March 2004).

Evans, P. (1999) 'Globalization and cultural transmission: the role of international agencies in developing inclusive practice', in Daniels, H. and Garner, P. (Eds) *Inclusive Education: Supporting Inclusion in Education Systems*, Kogan Page, London.

Miles, S. (2004) 'Creating conversations: the Evolution of the Enabling Education Network (EENET)' www.eenet.org.uk/about/evolutn.shtml (Accessed 21 March 2004).

Mittler, P. (2000) *Working Towards Inclusive Education: Social Contexts*, David Fulton, London.

Parsons, C. (2003) Minority Ethnic Exclusions and the Race Relations (Amendment) Act 2000: Interim Summary, London, DFES.

Peresuh, M. (2000) 'Early Childhood Education Programmes: Focus on Developing Countries on setting the pace for Learning', http://www.isec2000.org.uk/abstracts/papers_p/peresuh_1.htm (Accessed 21 March 2004).

UNESCO (1994) 'The Salamanca Statement: Framework for Action', http://www.unesco.org/education/pdf/SALAMA_E.PDF (Accessed 21 March 2004).

UNICEF (2004) 'UN Convention on the Rights of the Child', http://www.unicef.org/crc/crc.htm (Accessed 26 March 2004).

Part I

The struggle for an inclusive agenda

National perspectives

Chapter 2

Excluding the included

A reconsideration of inclusive education

Roger Slee and Julie Allan

Introduction

This chapter explores the adhesion of the traditional special and regular educational imperative to the development of inclusive education. The distinction between a traditional special educational paradigm[1] and disability studies will be considered in the context of inclusive education policies in Australia and England. We then examine the role of deconstruction in inclusive educational policy making and provide an example of a deconstructive reading of the United Kingdom Quality Assurance Agency's Code of Practice on Disability in Higher Education. The purpose of such a reading is to explore how texts 'get into trouble, come unstuck, offer to contradict themselves' (Eagleton, 1993, p. 134). Deconstruction is thus intended to operate as playful, positive and generative: 'it's not a question of calling for the destruction of such institutions, but rather of making us aware of what we are in fact doing when we are subscribing to this or that institutional way of reading' (Derrida, 1983, p. 125). The final part of the chapter contains a number of themes that emerge as a series of openings for the kinds of dialogue we see as important.

[...]

A recent evaluation of the progress of the inclusion programme in the Australian state of Western Australia (Tuettemann *et al.*, 2000) confirms continuing anxiety about the resilience of traditional forms of special education (Brantlinger, 1997) and its appropriation of inclusion in order to maintain unreconstructed notions of schooling and educational defectiveness (Skrtic, 1995; Corbett, 1996; Allan, 1999; Barton and Slee, 1999).

[...]

As Barton has asserted, 'special educational needs' is a euphemism for the failure of schooling to meet the needs of all children, a discursive tactic to de-politicise school failure (Barton, 1987) and legitimise the professional interest of special education workers (Tomlinson, 1996). The reconstruction of traditional special education as inclusive education is a manifestation of what Brantlinger

(1997) refers to, borrowing from Thompson (1984), as 'meaning in the service of power' (p. 7).

[. . .]

Ways of knowing are intensely political (Hammersley, 1995; Troyna, 1995; Ball and Gewirtz, 1997; Tooley, 1997; Oakley, 2000). This remains the challenge for inclusive education, which must position and declare itself as a project in the cultural politics of knowledge formation. It is the continuing struggle of the politics of identity and difference. Hence this chapter is about the production and deployment of meaning in education, and about the politics of knowledge and research. Here we are concerned with how the field of disability studies makes meaning of disability and impairment and also how the non-disabled person comes to know about disability.

[. . .]

Inclusive education needs first to deconstruct traditional forms of knowledge lurking behind codes of practice in the UK and inclusion programmes in Australia to signal the possibility for 'thinking otherwise' (Ball, 1998, p. 81) and to avoid re-runs of old theatre.

This might be achieved in two ways. First, by sponsoring critical research that deconstructs disability and disablement (Oliver, 1990) and exposes potentially oppressive educational settlements (Corbett and Slee, 2000). Second, by supporting hitherto silenced or marginalised voices to enter and lead the conversation about educational exclusion and inclusion (Booth, 1995; Clough and Barton, 1995).

[. . .]

Inclusive education is not self-evident, nor can it be a seamless progression from the past or present. We are suspicious of descriptions of present policy that posture as a necessary step towards inclusive schooling. In other words, when considering models of co-location[2] and people are calling for patience because this is a first step to making it different, we become restive. Or when psychologists and special educators tell us that they must do the lectures on inclusive education because they have the knowledge on the special needs children who will be the inclusive education kids, we are appalled.

[. . .]

Beyond special educational needs

Here we make a number of key points in an attempt to shift education research and policy beyond the special educational needs straightjacket. First, inclusive education is not a linear progression of the discursive practices of 'special educational needs'.

Inclusive education represents a fundamental paradigm shift (Kuhn, 1970) and needs to be presented and recognised as such. Taking up the observations of Ballard (1997), Ainscow (1999, p. 218) suggested that inclusive education was elusive, a continuing struggle against the processes and practices of schooling that erect barriers which compromise the participation of some students. We would underline their observations and add a cautionary note. The deconstruction of these barriers is only made possible by a refutation of the liberal reforming project of submerging disabled students in the unreconstructed culture of regular schooling. Inclusive education is not just about disabled students, about those we describe as having 'special educational needs'. It is about all students. Inclusive schooling is a social movement against educational exclusion.

Exclusion is structural and cultural (Levitas, 1998). The racialisation of special education, as Tomlinson (1982) argued two decades ago, is not accidental. Nor is it a relic from the past as research on the exclusion of black pupils from schools in England confirms (Gilborn and Gipps, 1996; Gilborn, 1997; Sewell, 1997; Parsons and Castle, 1998; Wright et al., 2000).

We need, as Booth (1995) argues, to establish our understanding of inclusive schooling by analysis of the pervasive and pernicious forms and impacts of exclusion. Bauman (1997, p. 17) reflects upon the capacity of societies to produce strangers: 'people who do not fit the cognitive, moral or aesthetic map of the world'. The construction and adjudication of people as strangers is a moveable feast. The extension of schooling has been a significant force for disablement. Schools are cartographic police. Exclusion proceeds through deep structural and broad cultural mechanisms to invigilate a shifting spectrum of diversity. Generally speaking, the boundaries in this sub-map are sharpest along the lines of disability, race, gender, class, sexuality, bilingualism, ethnicity and geographic position.

[...]

Our second point is about dissembled, as opposed to 'joined up', thinking in the field, to borrow a UK political expression. The dissembling takes two major forms. Initially there is a characterisation of disability as a characteristic of individual pathology. People and their complex sets of identities are reduced to anatomical shorthand.

The development of sociologies of special education and disability studies provides powerful critiques of the epistemological foundations of disability and, more recently, impairment and of medical and special education knowledge. Based upon a medical model of individual pathological defectiveness, the discursive practices of special education proceed from essentialising views of normality and abnormality. As such they represent powerful discourses that establish hierarchies of those who are included in regular social life and those who are dispersed to the margins and beyond. At the centre of these discourses are particular forms of knowledge that construct the world. Inclusive education for many has simply meant that people have altered their geography (Armstrong, 2000), without being reflexive about the integrity and implications of the knowledge.

The other form of dissembling or reductionism to which we refer is that of contextual disconnection. There is a tendency to speak in one breath about inclusive education, but to fail to acknowledge the policy context that presses us relentlessly towards educational exclusion in the other. Here we refer to the marketisation of schooling; national curriculum, based upon a notion of curriculum as museum; standardised testing; published league tables; a pernicious regime of inspection and the incorporation of pupil referral units as an accepted part of the educational landscape.

Our third point is about professional interest. In her powerful descriptions of her experience of special educational practice as a disabled student, Walsh (1993, p. 243) describes the closing down of opportunity as professionals worked towards their perception of her 'as different and needing exceptional handling'. Others have charted the deployment of professional discourses in individual educational programme meetings (Marks, 1993) and the manoeuvring of testing instruments to reify and entrench the work of special educators (Gartner and Lipsky, 1987). Reporting on earlier research by Galloway *et al.* (1994), Tomlinson concludes that

> in practice, the bureaucratization of the professional–parent relationship and of the assessment process has led to a situation in which the primary function of parental involvement is to legitimize professional decisions.
>
> (Tomlinson, 1996, p. 182)

The collapse of so-called inclusion policy into a crude model of distributive justice has resulted in financially driven educational settlements. Tomlinson (1996, p. 182) argues that in England, following the 1981 Education Act, 'LEAs attempted to use psychologists as gatekeepers to resources'. In the Australian states of Queensland and Western Australia, elaborate ascertainment schedules have been created in which statements about the nature and severity of disability are used to calculate the resource provision for regular schools in which disabled students are seeking enrolment. Consequently, inclusive schooling is reduced to pitched battles for apparently scarce resources.

[...]

Deconstruction: daring to think otherwise?

Mythologising the past contributes partly to the maintenance of unreconstructed notions of schooling and educational defectiveness. There is also a tendency to mythologise the present as progressing towards some idealised inclusive state, with statements like 'not yet there' or simply moving 'towards inclusion'. This seems to create its own inertia, or at least removes the imperative for 'thinking otherwise' (Ball, 1998, p. 81).

Here, we explore the possibilities offered by deconstruction for daring to think otherwise and envisioning more inclusive educational settlements.

[. . .]

The example here is the UK Quality Assurance Agency's (QAA) Code of Practice for Students with Disabilities. The QAA document can be read constructively as an attempt to assure 'the quality of learning opportunities for students with disabilities in UK institutions' (QAA, 1999, p. 1). On the other hand, it can be read as yet another example of missing the point about inclusion, evidenced in the language and the assumptions about practice. A deconstructive reading, however, suggests not so much an absence of inclusion, but rather a ghostly presence, since inclusion appears to be both there and not there.

[. . .]

The quality assurance of disability

The QAA's Code of practice was established in response to the UK wide National Committee of Enquiry into Higher Education (the Dearing and Garrick reports). The Code is intended to 'identify a comprehensive series of system wide expectations' (p. 1) and to provide 'authoritative reference points for institutions as they assure, consciously, actively and systematically, the academic quality and standards of their programmes, awards and programmes' (ibid.). Within section three, relating to students with disabilities, 24 'precepts' (ibid.) have been established with the expressed aim of providing quality assurance 'safeguards' (p. 2). These precepts, the QAA insists, are neither a charter, nor a blueprint, but merely offer 'some pointers towards good practice' (p. 3). In the four precepts considered briefly here, the apparition of inclusion is both conjured and expelled. First, however, it is worth noting how the QAA has constructed its constituency of disabled students.

Who is disabled?

'There are many different ways of defining who is disabled' (p. 5), according to the Code, which claims to follow no particular model, but instead goes for coverage, listing the various impairments including medical conditions and health problems. The fluctuating nature of disability, arising, for example, from illness or injury or needs changing during the course of study, is highlighted, with the goal of 'developing an environment within which individuals feel able to disclose their disability' (p. 11). The under representation of disabled people is reflected upon and attributed, in part, to problems of access, teaching methods and attitudes and in this move, inclusion is conjured as a wish to be more 'welcoming' to disabled students. But it is also banished by the very notion that disabled students need to be welcomed, like some guest who would otherwise not be there. The document claims that it 'recognises that disabled students are an integral part of the academic

·community' (p. 3). It also acknowledges their problematic status, however, and by naming this, expels inclusion once again:

> It may appear that the needs of disabled students are not central to institutional survival and should therefore give way to issues of 'higher' priority.
>
> (ibid.)

The quotation marks around 'higher' are intriguing and suggest possibly that the QAA is daring institutions to consider anything of greater significance than the needs of disabled students. This is followed immediately by a clear threat:

> When setting their priorities, however, institutions will want to take into account that the quality of their overall provision will be measured, in part, on how well they meet the expectations of this code.
>
> (ibid.)

Inclusion is swiped twice here, first of all by the insistence on demonstrating measurable outcomes, then by an unspecified threat of a negative QAA report. The effect is not to remove inclusion entirely, but to leave a trace which amounts to a set of technical solutions to personal troubles (Wright Mills, 1959). Inclusion as 'an unabashed announcement, a public and political declaration and celebration of difference' (Corbett and Slee, 2000, p. 134) is silenced.

> Precept 1: general principles
> Institutions should ensure that in all their policies, procedures and activities, including strategic planning and resource allocation, consideration is given to the means of enabling disabled students' participation in all aspects of the academic and social life of the institution.
>
> (p. 6)

This precept calls up inclusion, in terms of enabling disabled students' 'participation in all aspects of . . . academic and social life' (ibid.), yet also banishes it, by inviting institutions merely to 'consider' (ibid.) the means of achieving this. What follows this precept in the document is a series of active verbs: 'implementing' (procedures); 'ensuring' (information and understanding of the legal framework); and 'providing' (staff development) (pp. 6–7). Again, however, institutions are only asked to 'consider' (p. 6) enacting these.

> Precept 4: information for applicants, students and staff
> The institution's publicity, programme details and general information should be accessible to people with disabilities and describe the opportunities for disabled students to participate.

Disabled students, according to this precept, are only supposed to participate where there are 'opportunities', and only when these are 'described' to them (p. 9). Institutions are asked, in this case, to 'consider implementing arrangements which ensure that' (ibid.) information is clear, accurate and accessible. Again, the verb to 'consider' (ibid.) cancels out any requirement to 'ensure' (ibid.) and simultaneously cancels out inclusion.

> Precept 10: learning and teaching
> The delivery of programmes should take into account the needs of disabled people or, where appropriate, be adapted to accommodate their individual requirements.
>
> (ibid., p. 13)

The undecidability within this precept is striking. It offers an either/or scenario: either the needs of disabled people are taken into account, or the 'delivery' of programmes is adapted 'where appropriate' (ibid.). It is difficult to envisage doing the latter without the former, but the presentation of these two options in this way leads to a displacement of responsibility, or a license to do nothing. Inclusion does not even exist here as an apparition; it remains uninvited by inertia. Yet, it makes a rare appearance, of sorts, in the subsequent enjoinder to institutions to ensure staff 'plan and employ teaching and learning strategies which make the delivery of the programme as inclusive as is reasonably possible'. The question of how much inclusion is reasonably possible (ibid.), together with the recommendation that staff 'know and understand the learning implications of any disabilities of the students whom they teach' (ibid.), allows inclusion, once again, to be spirited away.

> Precept 13: Examination, assessment and progression
> Assessment and examination policies, practices and procedures should provide disabled students with the same opportunity as their peers to demonstrate the achievement of learning outcomes.
>
> (p. 15)

This particular precept appears relatively unproblematic and is potentially inclusive. Again, however, in the recommendations, institutions are asked only to 'consider implementing procedures for agreeing alternative assessment and examination arrangements' (p. 15) and only 'when necessary' (ibid.). Institutions are asked both to be flexible in their conduct of assessment, and to apply procedures 'consistently across the institution' (ibid.). 'Rigour and comparability' (ibid.) must also be upheld. These points of guidance are, of course, only what institutions 'should consider' (ibid.). An apparently subsidiary set of recommendations, relating to the provision of extra time, equipment and alternative assessment formats is provided and flexibility is mentioned once again, but these suggestions are given as those which institutions 'may wish to consider' (p. 16). So, inclusion is ghosted out of the assessment process out of respect for institutional preferences.

Inconclusive policy?

The QAA document claimed to be inclusive, yet managed to avoid this in ways which appeared, on the surface, to be rational and well intentioned. In asking why once again, had the point about inclusion been so spectacularly missed, it did not seem sufficient to complain about the obstructive and obscure nature of policy, since this has already been well documented (Ball, 1998; Barton and Slee, 1999). More importantly, the clear steers on what needs to be done in order to achieve inclusion, given by many disabled and non-disabled writers, appears to have gone unheard. The prospect of an indefinite period ahead spent proselytising, coupled with the frustration of apparent inertia, is unacceptable to us. The QAA document, however, seemed to reveal itself as speaking of inclusion as if it was already present....

Inclusion, it appeared, was the particular blind spot which was both enunciated and denied by the QAA. Because enunciation and denial were both partial, inclusion appeared to be still there, allowing for the displacement of authority. Thus, inclusion was avowed as being *in place*, yet remained outside, a spectator in its own wake. Inclusion is like the piece of grafitti which reads 'do not read me' (Derrida, 1979, p. 145), an order that has to be transgressed in order to be obeyed....

Openings for dialogue

Inevitably, a chapter of this kind, in which we propose deconstruction as a principal methodology, cannot easily be concluded, and indeed closure is something we are anxious to avoid. We offer a series of questions that are intended as openings for the kind of dialogue that seems to be necessary.

The relationship between ideas and politics – a theory of activism?

We have suggested that deconstruction can be used as a tool for helping to read policy documents against themselves and to understand how we have got to where we are. This might then help us to decide how to move on. But how do the ideas produced by deconstruction relate to the kinds of politics that are necessary in order to make such moves? Is there a need for a theory of activism which enables ideas about inclusion to be enacted? If so, how is this initiated and by whom?

New forms of research for new aspirations – a new politics of research?

What kinds of research will provide us with appropriate forms of educational settlement for young disabled people? This implies a new politics of research (Gitlin, 1994) which raises further questions about the relations of research production (Clough and Barton, 1995); identity and the privileging of particular values (Oliver, 1996; Moore *et al.*, 1998; Corker and French, 1999). The partisan research (Troyna, 1995) genre to which we have signed up is one aspect of the general call to activism. The politics of research relationships and the role of non-disabled researchers and activists are at the heart of this discussion of new educational relationships.

Forms of schooling? Envisioning and stipulating inclusion that eschews the modernist blueprint?

This chapter has raised questions about the nature of policy that ties itself to the existing assumptions about regular and special education. Regular schooling was never meant for all comers. Its constitution reflects this fact. Many children find that schooling does not serve them well and placing more children into the current system of schooling will exacerbate failure for increasing numbers. Assimilation appears to be flawed on all levels . . . . Inclusive schooling may well imply an array of offerings; the key issues will revolve around the authenticity of choice and destination.

Reflexivity

Our discussions about the writing of this chapter suggested a greater need for reflexivity. Interrogating the form and acquisition of knowledge about disability is essential and this needs to be set against the work of disabled researchers in particular and disability studies in general. We would suggest that such a process of reflecting upon knowledge formation would refract the research process and make new forms of research production possible.

Teaching inclusion

Earlier we mentioned our disdain for the practice of allowing faculties of special education to change their nomenclature as they move into the fertile fields of inclusion. Throughout Australia, faculties of education are using special educators to train the emerging teacher workforce to be inclusive. This is no different from the practice of bureaucracies as they bring unreconstructed psychologists and special educators into the inclusion policy forums. Inclusive education foreshadows a reconstruction of regular education and those who work in and with it.

Notes

1 In this chapter, we use the term traditional special education following Ellen Brantlinger's (1997) characterisation of the field of special education in her strident critique of Kauffman and Hallahan's (1995) rejection of inclusive education as ideological.
2 Co-location refers to the growing practice of re-locating a special school inside the grounds of a regular school and encouraging some shared activity.

References

Ainscow, M. (1999) *Understanding the Development of Inclusive Schools*. London: Falmer Press.

Allan, J. (1999) *Actively Seeking Inclusion*. London: Falmer Press.

Armstrong, F. (2000) Space, place: the production of the other. A study of differ-ence, disability and policymaking in England and France. PhD Thesis, University of Sheffield.

Ball, S. (1998) Educational studies, policy entrepreneurship and social theory, in R. Slee, G. Weiner and S. Tomlinson (Eds) *School Effectiveness for Whom?* London: Falmer Press.

Ball, S.J. and Gewirtz, S. (1997) Is research possible? A rejoinder to Tooley's 'On School Choice and Social Class', *British Journal of Sociology of Education*, 18, pp. 575–586.

Ballard, K. (1997) Researching disability and inclusive education: participation, construction and interpretation, *International Journal of Inclusive Education*, 1, pp. 243–256.

Barton, L. (Ed.) (1987) *The Politics of Special Educational Needs*. Lewes: Falmer Press.

Barton, L. and Slee, R (1999) Competition, selection and inclusive education, *International Journal of Inclusive Education*, 3, pp. 3–12.

Bauman, Z. (1997) *Postmodernity and its Discontents*. Oxford: Basil Blackwell.

Booth, T. (1995) Mapping inclusion and exclusion: concepts for all?, in C. Clark, A. Dyson and A. Millward (Eds) *Towards Inclusive Schools?* London: Fulton.

Brantlinger, E. (1997) Using ideology: cases of non–recognition of the politics of research and practice in special education, *Review of Educational Research*, 67, pp. 425–459.

Clough, P. and Barton, L. (1995) Conclusion: many urgent voices, in P. Clough and L. Barton (Eds) *Making Difficulties: Research and the Construction of SEN*. London: Paul Chapman.

Corbett, J. (1996) *Bad Mouthing: The Language of Special Needs*. London: Falmer.

Corbett, J. and Slee, R. (2000) An international conversation on inclusive education, in F. Armstrong, D. Armstrong and L. Barton (Eds) *Inclusive Education: Policy, Contexts and Comparative Perspectives*. London: David Fulton.

Corker, M. and French, S. (Eds) (1999) *Disability Discourse*. Buckingham: Open University Press.

Derrida, J. (1979) Border lines, in H. Bloom, J. Derrida, G.H. Hartman and J.H. Miller (Eds) *Deconstruction and Criticism*. New York.

Derrida, J. (1983) Deconstruction and the other, interview, in R. Kearney (Ed.) *Dialogues and Contemporary Continental Thinkers: The Phenomenological Heritage*. Manchester.

Eagleton, T. (1993) *Literary Theory: An Introduction.* Oxford: Blackwell.

Galloway, D., Armstrong, D. and Tomlinson, S. (1994) *The Assessment of Special Educational Needs: Whose Problem?* Harlow: Longman.

Gartner, A. and Lipsky, D.K. (1987) Beyond special education: toward a quality system for all students, *Harvard Educational Review,* 57, pp. 367–395.

Gilborn, D. (1997) *Racism and Antiracism in Real Schools.* Buckingham: Open University Press.

Gilborn, D. and Gipps, C. (1996) *Recent Research on the Achievement of Ethnic Minority Pupils.* London: Her Majesty's Stationery Office.

Gitlin, A. (Ed.) (1994) *Power and Method: Political Activism and Educational Research.* New York: Routledge.

Hammersley, M. (1995) *The Politics of Social Research.* London: Sage.

Kauffman, J.M. and Hallahan, D.P. (Eds) (1995) *The Illusion of Full Inclusion: A Comprehensive Critique of a Current Special Education Bandwagon.* Austin: Pro-ed.

Kuhn, T.S. (1970) *The Structure of Scientific Revolutions.* Chicago: The University of Chicago Press.

Levitas, R. (1998) *The Inclusive Society? Social Exclusion and New Labour.* London: Macmillan.

Marks, G. (1993) Contests in decision making at the school level, in R. Slee (Ed.) *Is There a Desk with my Name on it? The Politics of Integration.* London: Falmer Press.

Moore, M., Beazley, S. and Maelzer, J. (1998) *Researching Disability Issues.* Buckingham: Open University Press.

Oakley, A. (2000) *Experiments in Knowing: Gender and Method in the Social Sciences.* Cambridge, Polity Press.

Oliver, M. (1990) *The Politics of Disablement.* London: Macmillan.

Oliver, M. (1996) *Understanding Disability: From Theory to Practice.* London: Macmillan.

Parsons, C. and Castle, F. (1998) The cost of school exclusion in England, *International Journal of Inclusive Education,* 2(4), pp. 277–294.

Quality Assurance Agency for Higher Education (1999) *Code of Practice for the Assurance of Academic Quality and Standards in Higher Education: Students with Disabilities.* Gloucester: QAA.

Sewell, T. (1997) *Black Masculinities and Schooling: How Black Boys Survive Modern Schooling.* Stoke-on-Trent: Trentham Books.

Skrtic, T. (1995) (Ed.) New *Disability and Democracy: Reconstructing Special Education for Postmodernity.* New York: Teachers College Press.

Thompson, J.B. (1984) *Studies in the Theory of Ideology.* Berkeley: University of California Press.

Tomlinson, S. (1982) *A Sociology of Special Education.* London: Routledge and Kegan Paul.

Tomlinson, S. (1996) Conflicts and Dilemmas for Professionals in Special Education, in C. Christensen and F. Rizvi (Eds) *Disability and the Dilemmas of Education and Justice.* Buckingham: Open University Press.

Tooley, J. (1997) School class and social choice: a response to Ball, Bowe and Gewirtz, *British Journal of Sociology of Education,* 18, pp. 217–230.

Troyna, B. (1995) Beyond reasonable doubt? Researching 'race' in educational settings, *Oxford Review of Education,* 21, pp. 395–408.

Tuettemann, E., Or, L.T., Slee, R. and Punch, K. (2000) An evaluation of the inclusion programme. *A report on the process and outcomes of enroling students with intellectual disabilities in regular education classes of 28 Education Department Schools in Western Australia.* Report to Education Department of Western Australia.

Walsh, B. (1993) How disabling any handicap is depends on the attitudes and actions of others: a student's perspective, in R. Slee (Ed.) *Is There a Desk with My Name on it? The Politics of Integration*. London: Falmer Press.

Wright, C., Weekes, D. and McLaughlin, A. (2000) *'Race', Class and Gender in Exclusion from School*. London: Falmer Press.

Wright Mills, C. (1959) *The Sociological Imagination*. London: Penguin.

Chapter 3

Inclusion in Norway

A study of ideology in practice

Annlaug Flem and Clayton Keller

Introduction

Context for the study

Norway's ideology of integration or inclusive education can be traced back to the 1960s and ought to be understood in the context of a broader historical and social change of the welfare state (Vislie, 1995). In most Western societies at that time, there were increased emphases on democracy, social justice, equality for all and the improvement of legal and civil rights (Befring, 1990; Vislie, 1995; Rizvi and Christensen, 1996).

[. . .]

   In Norway a reorganization of special education began in the late 1960s. Equality, integration, normalization, participation and decentralization were important principles in this reorganization. New laws clearly established the ideology of integration and adapted education. Legislation was enacted that promoted or even mandated a move away from the use of segregated to integrated educational settings. In 1975, the so-called Integration Act incorporated the Act of 1951 relating to special schools into the ordinary Education Act of 1969 ('Grunnskoleloven'). Special legislation and a special system of administration of special education were thus eliminated. In the 1980s and 1990s several White Papers appeared that proposed a reorganization of the state special schools. A system of 20 centres of competence, at both the regional and national level, was developed. These centres are expected to arrange courses and provide guidance and counselling as well as to be involved in the assessment of students with special needs. The main object of the competence centres is to give help to the local support services in districts and schools.

   The municipalities now have the responsibility for the education of all children, and the students have the right to be educated in local schools as far as it is possible and professionally justifiable (Befring, 1990; Helgeland, 1992; Dalen, 1994). The local schools, in addition to having a special education team or a special education teacher, have access to pedagogical/psychological support services provided by the municipality. These services may consist of various categories of professionals like educational psychologists, specialized teachers and pre-school teachers and social welfare workers.

Traditionally, the focus of education was more on the individual, functional disorders of pupils with special needs. The trend is now towards a more comprehensive, contextual and ecological approach. 'A common school for all' and 'inclusive education' are the terms that are used. Most of the students having special educational needs are now educated in ordinary schools. However, data from the late 1980s show that about 1 per cent of the total school population in compulsory schools in Norway is found difficult to integrate, and such students receive their education in special classes/units (0.3 per cent) or in special schools (0.7 per cent) (Helgeland, 1992).

Our study was conducted in a Norwegian city. This municipality is divided into six school districts, each having its own pedagogical/psychological support service. In the surrounding region there are two national competence centres, one for students who are deaf and one for those who are blind. Professionals from a national competence centre for children and young people with emotional and behavioural problems are connected to the university in the city. The area contains a regional competence centre for students with general learning problems and a habilitation centre. In addition, a municipality special school has been established for students in the primary and lower secondary stages (ages 6–13 and 13–16 years, respectively), who may attend as full- or part-time students.

This study

Pijl and Meijer (1997) suggest that factors affecting inclusive schooling occur on three levels: (1) the classroom level, (2) the school level and (3) the external level, consisting of factors outside the schools.

[...]

We therefore wanted to obtain information about the practice of Norway's ideology of inclusion from informants at multiple levels in the Norwegian educational system . . . . At the national level, our informants included two staff members from the competence centre for students who are deaf, two educators from the competence centre for individuals who are blind and one consultant from the competence centre for children and young people with emotional and behavioural problems. Our participants representing the regional level were an administrator from the habilitation centre and most of the professional staff from the centre for students with general learning disabilities. At the municipality level, we interviewed an administrator from the city's special education school. For perspectives from the district level, six people from the support services of five of the six districts in the city shared their thoughts with us. Our informants at the school level included two kindergarten educators (each representing different kindergarten programmes) and 12 educators from 8 different primary and lower secondary schools sampled from all 6 school districts in the city. The school-level participants included leaders or principals, general education teachers and special educators. Altogether, excluding the staff from the regional centre for students with general learning disabilities, we interviewed 27 educators.

Data collection and analysis

We used semi-structured interviews that asked the same kinds of question of all our informants. One of our major questions was 'how do you see Norway's ideology of inclusion realized in practice?'. Related to this, we talked with our informants about how inclusion is organized and about the nature and levels of integration. For instance, have the schools and communities succeeded in social and curricular integration, or do placements in separate settings still exist? We were also interested in our informants' opinions and attitudes about integration. Are fully inclusive classes a desirable solution for some students? Is there still a place for separate schools or classes? Our other major question was 'what factors work to support, and what factors hinder, the implementation of the ideology of inclusion?'.

All but one of the interviews was in English, though sometimes Norwegian was used to express a technical term or convey an idea that was difficult to present outside the informants' native language. They took place at the informants' places of work, which often allowed us the opportunity to walk around and observe the setting. Most of the time, we interviewed the educators individually, although occasionally we talked with pairs of educators and, at the regional centre for students with general learning problems, the interview took place during a staff meeting.

[. . .]

The analyses of our interview data focused on summarizing answers to our main research questions. We worked to identify commonalities or themes that were shared by multiple informants, as well as retain important points or perspectives from individuals that reflected the richness of ideas and feelings we experienced from our informants. It was the challenge of 'reconciling the tension of an individual case's uniqueness with the need to understand generic processes at work across cases' (Silverstein, 1988, in Huberman and Miles, 1994, p. 435).

How is Norway's ideology of inclusion realized in practice?

Generally all of the informants were positive towards the ideology of inclusion. Integration had become a natural part of the thinking and was thus taken for granted. One of the informants specified that the idea of inclusion was influenced by Norway's social democratic ideas. Another noted that, according to the ideology of equality, every child should have an adapted education. Several informants from different levels mentioned that inclusion should not only be restricted to schooling. One said: 'We should all be included in the society.'

The informants from both the municipality school and the competence centre for behavioural problems stressed that the aim was that the ordinary schools should manage to include all of their pupils. The municipality special school cooperated with the local school so that they could succeed in including their students. In order to learn how to handle these students, some informants stated that it was very important for teachers in ordinary schools to be in contact with and have experience of special needs students.

Many informants considered what would be best for the individual child. For instance, informants from two different support services told us: 'What is good for the child? We never ask the child', and

> Every child is an individual with different needs, and you should always plan education in the way where the need of the child is satisfied as well as possible . . . . So I think most of the children will get their needs fulfilled within the ordinary school.

Many informants at different levels stressed that inclusive education was good for the ordinary pupils, and that perhaps they benefited the most from it. For instance, they learned to be respectful and to take other people's perspectives: 'Children accept that children are different.' Some mentioned, though, that typical children did not get enough help and that children in a class who were gifted could get bored because there were not enough challenges.

There were disadvantages to having students attend separate classes or schools. Several informants at different levels mentioned that ordinary schools are better fitted to help students with disabilities become more adapted to normal life. Special schools could be too protective. As the informant from the municipality special school herself said:

> it is too easy for them to be here. Too safe for them, so that we can make them more handicapped.

Similar arguments were made by one of the informants from the deaf competence centre. Students who were deaf and attended the residential school there did not have access to a 'normal' youth group and, consequently, fewer models of behaviour; they also did not live at home and were separated from their families and neighbourhoods. The informant from the competence centre for students with behavioural problems indicated that students attending an alternative school might be stigmatized. Ordinary schools did not take any responsibility for them after admittance to the alternative school, and their return to upper secondary schools when they left the alternative schools could be difficult.

Even if our informants were positive about the ideology of inclusion, many viewed inclusive education as a challenge that is not always easy to attain. Some described it as a process that takes time: 'We are in the early phase of the process.'

Some saw a distance between the ideology and its implementation in practice. As one of the teachers said:

> We do a lot of things that are right. But it is still too much on the planning level. It takes time to come down to the concrete level.

There were some differences of opinion about how well inclusion was being implemented. Most of the informants at the kindergarten and school level seemed pleased with their efforts, and several stressed that they had competent people. Several of the educators working at other levels, though, thought that there were great differences between the schools in how well they succeeded in realizing the ideology of inclusion.

A theme related to the challenge of inclusion considered which students were the most difficult ones to include in ordinary schools. Our informants at the school and kindergarten level, in particular, mentioned that students with emotional and behavioural difficulties were a great challenge – one that posed an increasing difficulty in Norwegian schools, especially when considering, for instance, students with drug problems. Teachers might have difficulties handling such problems and the other students might suffer as well.

[...]

The biggest challenge facing the implementation of the inclusion ideology seemed to be social integration. Overall, our informants were much more concerned about social integration than curricular integration. Some saw social integration as the foundation or basis of academic learning. They felt that, although intellectual challenges were important for students in special education, teachers were more clever in planning for the academic, rather than the social, integration of students. A common refrain was that these students were isolated and felt lonely, particularly as they grew older and reached the fifth and sixth classes:

> They are alone. I think it is a pity to hear all the parents saying something like that.
> The other pupils are nice to them, but they have no friends, they are lonely.

This happened both at school and during their leisure time. Even if the other students accepted them and took care and were nice to them, students with disabilities often had neither friends nor anybody to identify with.

[...]

Probably because of these challenges, an informant from a district support service team said that in the past years there had been an increase in the use of separate special education settings.... Many stated that there will be a group of children who are best served by a special school or by attending a special class: 'The schools aren't prepared for all these pupils.'

Several informants felt that the greatest advantage of special schools or classes was the possibility of meeting peers with similar difficulties and needs. In addition to giving pupils a feeling of belonging and a better self-esteem, real friendships could be established. Students with disabilities could find someone with whom they could identify; they were among equals.

Our informants saw other advantages to separate classes and schools. Such educational arrangements have staff with competence and expertise – professional people who can give students proper challenges, intellectual as well as physical. The informant from the competence centre for students with emotional and behavioural difficulties stressed that an alternative school can give students new opportunities in a new setting for a period of time and, because of the low teacher–student ratios, they can give children something they missed in ordinary schools. Such settings can also render more project-oriented teaching. The informant from the lower secondary school that had established a special group for students with severe behavioural problems stated that the school had positive experiences with this group . . . . With regard to students who are deaf, the informants from the deaf competence centre stressed that it was important that the students become acquainted with the deaf culture and community. These students have sign language as their first language and Norwegian as their second. Sign language develops in a signing milieu. In a special school they have the opportunity to experience this milieu and deaf culture.

Factors that support or hinder inclusive education

The organization and provision of special education

[. . .]

At the school level, the offer of special education resources was organized in different ways. A common model was to have a special education team at each school, with one of the team members serving as the coordinator. Particular responsibilities of the team could vary, though, depending upon the services that the district decided to provide centrally.

The majority of students with special needs received their education, including their special education services, in ordinary classes. Most of the schools had flexible systems. For instance, students could receive their education in a special group part-time and in a regular class the rest of the time. Several schools also grouped the children in a special class at one of the schools. One of the kindergartens had established a special group for children with attention problems. Some groups, however, did not have much contact with regular classes. One of the lower secondary schools had a group of students with severe emotional and behavioural problems and this group did not have any contact with their own classes. Such students could also receive their education at a special alternative day school run by the municipality.

Because the site of our research was a large city, the municipality had also managed to establish a special day school. Some students attended this special school for five days but most went to the school for two or three days a week. The students who attended had a variety of disabilities, from individuals with multiple disabilities and severe language problems to aggressive children who were considered to have minimal brain dysfunction. Most of the students in the school, half of whom were girls, were in classes from the sixth through tenth levels. Thus it seemed that the ordinary schools could handle younger children with disabilities well.

Like the district-level services, the regional and national competence centres were also involved in guidance, counselling and the assessment of students with special needs, although with levels of expertise that usually went beyond what was commonly available in schools and district offices. The competence centres for students who are blind and deaf arranged training courses for teachers, parents and students with those disabilities.

[...]

Factors at the classroom level

Our informants identified several factors at the classroom level that pertained to teachers.

For instance, most of the informants were concerned about the characteristics of teachers. Terms that were used to describe why certain teachers succeeded in realizing inclusive schooling were 'warm-hearted teachers', 'teachers with enthusiasm', 'high level of understanding', 'personal abilities', 'climate between the teacher and the child' and 'calm'. Others stressed that teachers ought to be good models for their students and to have the ability to communicate and give attention in a positive way. Some teachers mentioned that it was important for students to have a teacher they could trust and who was able to establish clear routines, structure and stability in the classroom which could lead to predictability. Likewise, successful inclusion was dependent on the teachers' knowledge and competence; for example, a member of a support service team said teachers 'ought to have the skill of structuring the lessons and teaching'.

Our informants identified classroom environment factors that help to adapt education and promote inclusion. Several informants at different levels stressed the importance of focusing on the students' potentialities and their competence and helping them feel successful. The pupils should also be given responsibility. They should 'do the same things as the rest of the class' and 'participate in all the activities'. The children should feel safe and have a feeling of being accepted.

[...]

Even if several of the schools claimed that they had competent people, a severe problem according to other professionals was the lack of qualified teachers.

Teachers did not always have the competence needed for inclusion. They did not have the expertise to know how to adjust their teaching for children with severe learning disabilities or for students who are blind or deaf, nor did they have enough knowledge about how to prevent reading and writing problems. The education provided could be too theoretically based for many children. Many of the informants at different levels stressed that the basic teacher training was not good enough: 'I think teachers must get a better education in inclusive education.'

[. . .]

Factors at the school level

Our informants also focused on the characteristics of schools. A school's climate and its ethos influenced successful inclusion. Mostly professionals outside the school/kindergarten level claimed that successful inclusion was dependent on the principal or leadership of the school or institution. The school's organization was cited as an important factor – for instance, the flexibility with which it used the special educators and its arrangements of groups inside or outside classrooms. The need for common responsibilities for special educators and ordinary teachers was also mentioned. The informant from the competence centre for students with behavioural problems stressed the importance of changing the ordinary schools. Some schools reported that in order to meet their children's needs, they initiated different projects.

Cooperation in many forms was another theme at the school level. Good cooperation with parents was often mentioned. Cooperation among the staff was also looked upon as important . . . . A positive consequence of cooperation and changes in attitudes was that the school's staff took more responsibility for every child. Contact and cooperation between the schools/kindergartens and the different external support services and between the schools themselves helped inclusion.

Access to and support from people with knowledge and competence for educating special needs students promoted inclusion.

[. . .]

Factors at the external level

'Attitude' was a term that was greatly emphasized when describing factors important for realizing inclusive education. Most of the informants at all levels stressed the effects of teachers', parents' and students' attitudes in the success of inclusion.

[. . .]

Resources in many forms affected the success of inclusive education. School buildings and classrooms should be adapted to students with disabilities and contain the technical equipment and materials they need. Some informants thought that open schools could be a problem. The buildings should also not be too crowded.

Our informants commonly mentioned that the lack of financial resources could hinder inclusive education, though one educator stressed that it was not only a question of resources, but also a matter of how the resources were used. Fewer resources could cause problems, especially for students with less severe learning disabilities. Several educators mentioned that during past years there was less money and resources for students with special needs.

[...]

The experiences with assistants were mixed. Some of the assistants were skilful, while others were too passive or could give too much help. As one educator said: 'To put an adult together with them [the students] stops the including processes.'

Discussion

At times, there seemed to be some distance between the key principles of Norway's inclusion policy and its realization in practice. Taken together, the schools in which we collected our information presented a continuum of educational solutions for students with disabilities, ranging from regular class placement to in-class support for teachers and students to combinations of special and regular school placements to full-time special school settings.

The biggest challenge to the realization of Norway's inclusion ideology appeared not to be the academic integration of students with disabilities into their classroom milieu but rather their social integration. Many children were becoming lonely and isolated in ordinary schools by the fifth and sixth classes. The opportunities for frequent social interactions that ordinary classrooms provided were not enough. It was more difficult to find peers with whom they could communicate and share their experiences.

[...]

Our study suggests that, even in an educational system like Norway's that strongly values and emphasizes social outcomes, and with educators that accept a policy of inclusion at least partly for social reasons, it can still be difficult to achieve positive social outcomes for students with disabilities in inclusive settings.

[...]

Our informants were also concerned about the characteristics of schools, for example, their climates or atmosphere, organization and provision of special services, and the competence of their leaders. The ideology of inclusive education is about a reform of the entire educational system to meet the needs of all students (Vislie, 1995; Haug, 1996; Sugden, 1996; Dyson and Millward, 1997; Meijer *et al.*, 1997; Stangvik, 1997). Only one informant stressed the importance of changing the ordinary schools. According to Haug (1998), most of the schools in Norway have not succeeded in implementing inclusive education. Some schools have adapted the educational tradition from the special schools, while other schools have adapted the existing educational tradition from compulsory schools to special education. In compulsory schools the teaching is often collective and individual adapted teaching is thus missing in ordinary schools. In order to become a 'school for all', the compulsory (ordinary) school system has to change.

[. . .]

Conclusion

Like all such case studies, our results about how Norway's inclusion policies are realized in practice and the factors that affect the success of inclusion are bound by time and location. The changes that inevitably occur over time in a dynamic system like education will affect the responses of informants such as ours. In a complex, democratic society, inclusive education will not be realized only through laws and regulations. It involves changes in school organization, teaching methods, attitudes and values – changes that are part of an ongoing process that may never end as each district, school or classroom has to construct the policies anew, as Fulcher (1989) suggests, in each case it encounters. Mere access to or placement in ordinary school settings will not be sufficient. Thus, the development of inclusive schooling that meets the needs of all students is, as one of our informants told us, a challenge that is not easy to achieve.

References

Befring, E. (1990). 'Special education in Norway', *International Journal of Disability, Development and Education*, 37, 2, 125–136.

Dalen, M. (1994). '*Så langt det er mulig og faglig forsvarlig': Integrering av funksjonshemmede i grunnskolen* ['*As Far as it Is Possible and Professionally Justifiable': Integration of Students with Disabilities in Elementary School*]. Oslo: Universitets-forlaget.

Dyson, A. and Millward, A. (1997). 'The reform of special education or the transformation of mainstream schools?'. In: Pijl, S.J., Meijer, C.J.W. and Hegarty, S. (Eds) *Inclusive Education: A Global Agenda*. London: Routledge, pp. 51–67.

Fulcher, G. (1989). *Disabling Policies? A Comparative Approach to Education Policy and Disability*. London: Falmer Press.

Haug, P. (1996). 'Lærerutdanning til ein skule for alle' ['Teacher education towards a school for all'], *Spesialpedagogikk*, 61, 9, 3–12.

Haug, P. (1998). 'Integration and special education research in Norway', *International Journal of Educational Research*, 29, 119–130.

Helgeland, I. (1992). 'Special education in Norway', *European Journal of Special Needs Education*, 7, 2, 169–183.

Huberman, A.M. and Miles, M.B. (1994). 'Data management and analysis methods'. In: Denzin, N.K. and Lincoln, Y.S. (Eds) *Handbook of Qualitative Research*. Thousand Oaks, CA: Sage, pp. 428–444.

Meijer, C.J.W., Pijl, S.J. and Hegarty, S. (1997). 'Introduction'. In: Pijl, S.J., Meijer, C.J.W. and Hegarty, S. (Eds) *Inclusive Education: A Global Agenda*. London: Routledge, pp. 1–7.

Pijl, S.J. and Meijer, C.J.W. (1997). 'Factors in inclusion: a framework'. In: Pijl, S.J., Meijer, C.J.W. and Hegarty, S. (Eds) *Inclusive Education: A Global Agenda*. London: Routledge, pp. 8–13.

Rizvi, F. and Christensen, C. (1996). 'Introduction'. In: Christensen, C. and Rizvi, F. (Eds) *Disability and the Dilemma of Education and Justice*. Buckingham: Open University Press, pp. 1–8.

Stangvik, G. (1997). 'Beyond schooling: integration in a policy perspective'. In: Pijl, S.J., Meijer, C.J.W. and Hegarty, S. (Eds) *Inclusive Education. A Global Agenda*. London: Routledge, pp. 32–50.

Sugden, D.A. (1996). 'Moving towards inclusion in the United Kingdom?', *Thalamus*, 15, 2, 4–11.

Vislie, L. (1995). 'Integration policies, school reforms and the organisation of schooling for handicapped pupils in Western societies'. In: Clark, C., Dyson, A. and Millward, A. (Eds) *Towards Inclusive Schools?* London: David Fulton, pp. 42–53.

Chapter 4

School choice and the pressure to perform

Déjà vu for children with disabilities?

Kenneth R. Howe and Kevin G. Welner

School-choice policies are becoming increasingly accepted and implemented throughout the US educational system. These policies come in a number of different forms starting with *eased catchment areas* and building up to *magnets, charters* and *vouchers*. The underlying rationales for each policy may include parental autonomy, market competition, or forging strong school communities (Howe, 1997). Because these rationales differ along with the specific approach, drawing conclusions about the merits of school choice per se is difficult. Still, one general criticism cuts across the forms of, and justifications for, school choice: these choice schemes seriously exacerbate the stratification of school populations. This general criticism is the focus of this chapter, particularly as it applies to students with special needs.

Our analysis is divided into two general sections. In the first, we examine the tension between the principles underlying the inclusion of students with special needs and the principles underlying school choice, particularly market competition and parental autonomy. In the second section, we examine empirical findings from five states and a case study of the Boulder, Colorado, school-choice system. Taken together, these findings indicate that school choice is indeed resulting in the increased stratification and exclusion of students with special needs and that the pressure to perform on achievement tests is a significant factor. We conclude with a few observations about how the current situation resembles the period before the enactment of the Education for All Handicapped Children Act of 1975.

Conflicting principles

The primary principle underlying the Individuals with Disabilities Education Act (IDEA, 1990) is inclusion. Congress' passage of the Education for All Handicapped Children Act, the precursor legislation to IDEA, was prompted by a coordinated campaign of court cases – most prominently *Pennsylvania Association of Retarded Citizens (PARC)* v. *Commonwealth* (1972) and *Mills* v. *Board of Education* (1972; see Welner, 2001). The requirements of the *principle of inclusion* may be illustrated by distinguishing it from the weaker *principle of nonexclusion*. Inclusion places the responsibility on public schools to adjust their curricula and instructional methods to accommodate students with special needs, whereas nonexclusion merely requires permitting these students to enrol in and attend public schools. More specifically, inclusion requires public schools to take steps that affirmatively provide a 'free, appropriate public education' in the 'least restrictive environment' (LRE). It also adds a presumption in favour of *mainstreaming*, which places the burden on schools to justify why they are not including students with special needs in the general education classroom within the schools that they would otherwise attend in the absence of any disability.

School choice threatens the principle of inclusion because two principles that often underlie school-choice policies – market competition and parental autonomy – are in serious tension with it. Indeed, choice policies driven by these principles can sometimes result in an abandonment of the principle of nonexclusion.

[. . .]

Test scores are the typical measure of school success (e.g. Chubb and Moe, 1990), and the criterion of test scores creates a powerful incentive system of its own that is quite at odds with the principle of inclusion. Schools that include students who do not score well on tests will be judged as inferior and, in the extreme, will be forced by the marketplace to close. The typical market-driven choice system thus provides a strong incentive for schools to exclude low-scoring students, many of whom would be students with special needs.

When choice schools define themselves in terms of an academically rigorous curriculum they are sometimes able to exclude students with special needs by citing a 'bad fit' between the school and these students' needs (Heubert, 1997; Welner and Howe, in press). In this way, these schools employ a rationale for excluding students that ironically is based on meeting the diversity of public school students' needs.

This rationale is at complete odds with the principle of inclusion and the associated practice of mainstreaming in which schools are required to adjust their curricula and instruction to meet the special needs of individual students.

Legal analysis

Given this tension between inclusion and the market-based philosophy of education one might expect to find some resolution within the set of laws governing choice and special education (see Welner, 2001). This legal framework offers comfort to both camps, however. Although disability law expressly and strenuously favours inclusion, charter school laws favour deregulation and competition with equal clarity and strength, and choice supporters could use certain loopholes in disability law designed to protect schools from onerous mandates.

Special education is framed primarily by the federal IDEA plus state statutes that are largely dictated by IDEA. Two antidiscrimination laws also provide important protections for students with special needs: Section 504 of the Rehabilitation Act of 1973 and Title II of the Americans with Disabilities Act prohibit discrimination based on disability in the administration of public services, including education.

Section 504 and Title II contain similar language, offer similar protections, and have been interpreted in a similar manner by the courts. The following discussion thus considers the two together.

Section 504 and Title II

In a nutshell, the nondiscrimination provisions in Section 504 and Title II require that choice schools must make reasonable accommodations as necessary to serve students with disabilities. Accommodations are considered reasonable unless they would create 'undue hardship' to the local education agency (LEA) or would 'fundamentally alter the nature' of the school's services or programme. According to Heubert (1997), this means that a school with an accepted test-score admission process could exclude students who score low on the test, even if this disproportionately burdens students with disabilities. By contrast, a 'back to basics' school could not set restrictive academic criteria, such as reading at grade level, because such criteria are not necessary to fulfilling the school's mission.

As a general rule, school districts are free, pursuant to the IDEA, to create cost-saving mechanisms to concentrate special education resources at particular sites. This is allowed, however, only when the mechanisms do not deny unique educational opportunities to the child with special needs. Denial of these opportunities constitutes discrimination and violates Title II and Section 504.

IDEA

IDEA provides a uniform set of rules designed to ensure that students with disabilities are educated with their general education peers to the maximum extent appropriate given each student's special education needs. It includes provisions granting funds for special education implementation and requiring all recipient states to provide qualifying students with procedural rights and entitlements. These students should be exposed to the same curriculum, the same high academic standards, and the same opportunities for socialization. The shorthand version of this concept is taken from IDEA's language: a free, appropriate public education.

Until 1997, federal legislation did not address the relationship between charter schools and students with disabilities. The IDEA regulations did, however, broadly mandate state responsibility for guaranteeing nondiscriminatory and complete schooling of children with disabilities. According to the regulations, 'Each SEA [state education agency] shall ensure that each public agency establishes and implements a goal of providing full educational opportunity to all children with disabilities in the area served by the public agency', and 'Each public agency shall take steps to ensure that its children with disabilities have available to them the variety of educational programs and services available to nondisabled children'. These provisions, in addition to Section 504 and Title II, provided important assurances to students with disabilities that they should not be excluded from admission into charter schools.

Charter school legislation

As part of an educational reform movement that began in the 1980s, states and school districts throughout the United States now offer school-choice options among public schools. The simplest of these reforms merely allows students to attend schools in their school district but outside their usual catchment area. More complex reforms allowed students to choose schools outside the district of their residence. States have also adopted reform legislation allowing people and sometimes corporations to create contractually based charter schools that could draw students from all parts of a district without regard for their place of residence.

Although this chapter considers laws governing other choice school in general – such as magnet schools and intra-district choice schools – because of the recent appearance on the scene and rapid growth of charter schools, we have singled them out for further elaboration.

The legislation allowing for charter schools ('enabling legislation') differs from state to state, but the general framework is consistent. Charter schools are exempt from many restrictions and bureaucratic rules that govern traditional schools. Charters must nonetheless abide by all federal (and most state) laws regarding safety, health, and civil rights, including federal disability laws. As a result, the majority of their increased autonomy concerns relief from state statutes and regulations governing the areas of budgeting, curriculum and instruction, materials, schedules, facilities, and personnel. Fewer teachers in charter schools may need to be certified (depending on the state), although certification of special education teachers may be required.

The most worrisome feature concerning regulation of choice schools *vis-à-vis* inclusion is admissions criteria that permit schools to determine whether students with special needs 'fit' with their missions. Although some jurisdictions explicitly forbid exclusionary admissions criteria, many others either explicitly permit them or are hopelessly vague in the guidance they provide.

These philosophical and legal discussions should prompt considerable concern among people committed to inclusion in public schools of students with special needs. The philosophical analysis reveals a fundamental tension between the libertarian/market conception of justice that underlies school choice and the egalitarian conception that underlies inclusion. Accordingly, market-driven school-choice policies can continue to expand only at the expense of inclusion. The legal analysis in turn reveals the insufficient safeguards protecting students with special needs against the exclusion from choice schools. Choice schools can potentially base their exclusion of such students on their specialized missions claiming that the students threaten to place undue hardship on the school or to fundamentally alter the nature of their services. The grim implication for inclusion is the same. Whether these analyses signal genuine problems depends on how school choice is in fact playing out for students with special needs. We now examine that question.

The empirical evidence

Empirical evidence concerning the effects of school choice on students with special needs is relatively sparse. The most comprehensive study we could find was conducted by the US Department of Education (2000) in which data were collected on the percentage of students with disabilities enroled in charter schools in 22 states and the District of Columbia. This study found that, in general, charter schools across the nation enroled a lower percentage of special education students than did public schools. In 15 states and the District of Columbia, the percentage of special education students enroled in charter schools was less than the percentage enroled in the public schools. This group included all of the jurisdictions with the largest charter school movements relative to the number of public education students served. Against this general trend, in 7 states charter schools enroled a larger percentage of special education students than did the public schools. With the exception of New Mexico, each of the 7 states had a relatively small charter-school movement.

In addition to this large-scale survey study, more focused research concerning the effects of various state choice systems on students with special needs is beginning to accumulate – typically from states that have significant charter-school programmes under way. The findings have consistently confirmed the claim suggested in the US Department of Education (2000) survey that school choice is resulting in the stratification and exclusion of these students.

Charter schools

Several states have examined the early effects of charter schools, including their special education enrolments. In California, little difference was found in the proportion of special education students enroled in charter schools versus public schools overall. When newly formed 'start-up' charter schools were distinguished from public schools that had converted to charters ('conversion' charter schools), however, the difference was pronounced. Whereas 26 per cent of start-up charter schools had no special education students, only 6 per cent of conversion charters had none of these students (SRI, 1997, reported in the UCLA Charter School Study, 1998). These findings suggest that start-up schools market themselves so as to create a niche that excludes students with special needs.

Arsen et al. (1999) found that approximately 75 per cent of Michigan's charter schools (officially called *public school academies*) offered no special education services whatsoever in 1997–98. On average, those charter schools that did enrol special education students spent approximately 1 per cent on special education services, far less than did the typical public school. In general, charter schools in Michigan enroled far fewer students with special needs and provided fewer and less costly special education services for those students they did enrol. Arsen et al. emphasized choice schools' financial incentive for excluding these students, which was not inconsistent with the incentives for excluding students that were associated with producing high test scores (also a factor in Michigan) and creating niche schools.

Indeed, the effect of these incentives was cumulative (see Welner and Howe, in press).

Arsen *et al.* (1999) found 'strong circumstantial evidence' (p. 75) of choice schools 'skimming' students who cost less to educate. Special education students with severe disabilities are extraordinarily expensive to educate. Said Arsen *et al.*, 'For many charter schools, it would be prohibitively expensive to offer a full special education program. Consequently, they have an interest in excluding students who need these services' (p. 76).

Operating along with these financial and accountability forces is a choice school's desire to reflect a 'theme' or a community vision. Charter-school personnel often speak of these matters in terms of the 'fit' between the student and the school. According to McLaughlin *et al.* (1996), 'Charter schools are, in part, based on the premise that not all the curriculum or instructional approaches used in a given charter school work for all students; there is an assumption that students should "fit" an approach' (p. 5). Arsen *et al.* (1999) described how the very process of determining fit can function to exclude students with special needs:

> Many charter schools, for example, have adopted elaborate application pro-
> cedures for prospective students. They require parents to fill out application
> forms or participate in interviews before enrolling their children. This makes
> it at least possible for administrators to discourage applications from students
> who might disrupt the school community.
>
> (p. 75)

Garn (2000) documented how the charter school funding formula in Arizona provided incentives to exclude special education students. The state offers a flat rate supplementary payment of $174 per special education student and no allocation for transportation. The former provides a disincentive for charter schools to enrol students with special needs and the latter effectively eliminates the opportunities to participate in choice for parents of these students who have no means of providing transportation. McKinney (1996) observed that because of budgetary pressures, 'the marketplace concept that drives charter school legislation is stood on its head and proves to be a disincentive when it comes to serving children with disabilities'. He quoted an Arizona charter school principal: 'One severely disabled special ed kid would put me out of business' (p. 25).

N. Zollers (2000; see also J. Zollers and Ramanathan, 1998) found that charter schools (specifically, for-profit charter schools) in Massachusetts exclude students with special needs in three ways: overtly barring them upon discovering their disabilities, returning them to their former schools on the grounds that no suitable programme exists for them, and 'counselling out' by appealing to their alleged best interests.

Charter schools also work within the set of incentives and disincentives created by states' high-stakes accountability systems. Schools are rewarded, often financially, for students who score high on tests, and they are punished for their students who score low on these tests. Yet, these mean test scores rise and fall primarily with the entering test scores of students and only secondarily with the schooling these students subsequently receive. A choice school that recruits high-scoring students thus often gains the benefit of a state-run apparatus that financially rewards such recruitment and publicizes the test scores as demonstrating instructional excellence. The opposite holds true for choice schools that enrol students with low test scores. J. Zollers and Ramanathan (1998) pointed out that the test-score incentives are even, stronger for the for-profit management companies because if they cannot show substantial test-score gains they lose their charters.

The Boulder choice system

The school-choice ('open enrolment') system in Boulder, Colorado, is unusually comprehensive among choice systems in the United States. All students in the BVSD are free to choose enrolment in a school other than the 'neighbourhood school' to which they are assigned, and approximately 20 per cent successfully exercise choice. This level of participation is sufficient to force all schools in BVSD to compete for enrolment. Schools that fare poorly in the competition face reduced resources and, in the extreme, closure.

BVSD enrols approximately 27,000 students and operates 63 schools. Open enrolment has existed in this district since 1961, but it did not become a significant practice and source of controversy until the mid-1990s. Spurred by a concerned and vocal group of parents who were discontented with the district's implementation of the 'middle school philosophy,' coupled with a perceived lack of emphasis on academics in BVSD more generally, various choice options began to proliferate. This happened at a time when the school-choice movement also began accelerating at the state and national levels.

Several types of choice options were differentiated, and *open enrolment* became an umbrella term that in addition to the option to enrol in any district neighbourhood school on a space-available basis, now covers four other kinds of options:

1   *focus schools* – schools with a particular curricular focus that have no attendance area;
2   *neighbourhood focus schools* – focus schools that give priority for enrolment to students from within the neighbourhood attendance area;
3   *strand schools* – neighbourhood schools employing two curricular strands, one of which would be the normal BVSD curriculum while the other would be an alternative curriculum (typically Core Knowledge); and
4   *charter schools* – relatively autonomous district schools with no attendance area whose accountability to BVSD is specified in a contract. Variations also exist within these types.

Prior to the 1994–95 school year, five articulated choice options were available in BVSD. All emphasized diversity, experiential learning, integrated learning, or bilingual education, sometimes in combination. By 1999–2000, 16 additional articulated choice options were available. Half of these had adopted a new kind of mission consistent with the mood of the mid-1990s, namely, an explicit emphasis on academic rigour.

Stratification by race and by income increased substantially in BVSD between the 1994–95 and 1999–2000 school years. The simultaneous advent of choice schools with an explicit emphasis on academics and college preparation best explains this increased stratification. The demand for these elite new choice schools can in turn be partially explained by Colorado's policy shift toward high-stakes standardized exams (the Colorado Student Assessment Program, or CSAP). The elite choice schools have benefited greatly under this state accountability framework by skimming the district's highest scoring students (Howe and Eisenhart, 2000). Under these conditions, one can speculate with some justification that BVSD schools would also become more stratified with respect to special education.

Our investigation of broad BVSD trends discovered no discernible longitudinal increase in stratification by special education associated with the expansion of open enrolment. (Similar analyses did demonstrate increased stratification by race and income.) Hidden within these broad statistics, however, was compelling evidence of increased stratification among the newly created choice schools. Indeed, three choice schools – a middle school emphasizing social responsibility, a high school emphasizing vocational education, and a high school serving adjudicated youth – had the highest percentages of special education students in the district (save one school dedicated exclusively to students with severe disabilities). In 2000–01, these three schools' percentages were 23.3, 25.9, and 27.3 per cent respectively, compared to 12.1 per cent for the district overall (Boulder Valley School District, 2001).

At the other extreme, the two choice schools most notorious for 'elitism' in the district, and whose formation was at the centre of the expansion of open enrolment in the mid-1990s – Pinnacle, a Core Knowledge-focus elementary school, and Firmament, an academically oriented charter middle school – had the second and third lowest special education percentages in the district in 2000–01. At 4.3 per cent and 5.4 per cent respectively, they were well below the district average of 12.1 per cent.

There is another way in which a pattern of increased stratification by special education may be masked by crude statistics. BVSD's strand schools – and many of its focus schools – report special education statistics at the school level even though they follow the school-within-a-school model. As a result, the distribution of students between the programmes within these schools is not reflected in the statistics. Three (of 34) elementary schools and 3 (of 13) middle schools fall within this category. Masked stratification is quite likely in each case, especially for the 4 schools that employ the Core Knowledge curriculum, given the data reported previously concerning the low special education enrolment in Colorado's Core Knowledge charter schools. Furthermore, parents and teachers from these BVSD schools reported that special education students are routinely counselled out of Core Knowledge because they cannot keep up with the pace of the curriculum and therefore are not a good fit.

Participants in the Boulder choice study also reported exclusionary practices in several schools other than those employing Core Knowledge. According to one individual intimately familiar with the school, BVSD's Montessori focus school (which, incidentally, tied with Firmament for the third lowest percentage in the district in terms of students with special needs at 5.4 per cent) counsels out special education students (e.g. students with ADHD) who lack the capacities for self-control and self-direction believed to be required by the Montessori method. In BVSD's arts focus middle school, scheduling constraints were identified as having an exclusionary effect. That is, enroling in certain courses in the focus curriculum forces students to take most or all of their courses together, creating tracks that exclude and concentrate special education students. Finally, one parent of a student with special needs remarked regarding her dealings with an unidentified school: 'I . . . talked to the parents and they laid it out. "We're an aggressive school. We want the best test scores. The families are very driven; we want all the higher achieving kids."'

Additional allegations that surfaced during the BVSD study applied to even deeper layers of stratification. Critics maintained that the opportunity of choice schools to use the staffing procedure to deny enrolment to conditionally admitted students with special needs permits these schools to take the least demanding and least expensive of these students. This, the critics argued, benefits the schools in two ways. First, they report a flat percentage of special education students that makes no mention of the kinds of special needs served. Second, these schools can take advantage of the state's special education funding formula, which allocates the average cost of students with special needs into various categories. Within the 'mild needs' category, some students have greater needs, and schools gain a financial advantage by admitting only those students with the mildest of mild needs.

Conclusions

The principle of inclusion is grounded in an egalitarian conception of justice – a conception that supercedes and sometimes requires setting aside the accepted practices and perceived interests of local communities. Reliance on the latter in the distribution of public education was once the rule, but it proved woefully inadequate from the point of view of students with special needs. These students were pervasively denied access to an adequate, or even any, public education. For them, local control meant segregation and discrimination. In the face of sometimes strong local objections, parents of these students turned to the federal courts and the US Congress for help.

Now Congress and state governments are looking to a new form of local control – choice schools – to help address a variety of ills that they perceive as existing in public schools. This effort may indeed find some success. Choice schools can advance some of the most worthy goals of local control. At its best, this policy results in innovative, responsive schools that embrace the uniqueness of their community. At its worst, however, this policy becomes a tool for the short-sighted to create exclusive, private academies at the public expense. Accordingly, we contend that the policy's successes will come at the expense of many vulnerable students, including those with special needs.

The nation seems to have come full circle. The federal mandate requiring that students with special needs be included in public education was passed in recognition of the unfortunate existence of powerful incentives to exclude these students from public schools. The new law required that special education students were to be included not only formally but also in a meaningful way. After a quarter-century of progress, a different cohort of reformers is designing laws that no longer embrace inclusion. Instead, these laws wholeheartedly welcome market incentives – forces that demonstrably promote exclusion. This market-driven school choice now provides public schools with the power to exclude students with special needs on the grounds that educating such students is beyond the scope of their mission. They are in fact excluding these students. Déjà vu.

References

Arsen, D., Plank, D. and Sykes, G. (1999). *School Choice Policies in Michigan: The Rules Matter.* East Lansing: Michigan State University.

Boulder Valley School District (2001). *October Count.* Boulder, CO: Author.

Chubb, J.E. and Moe, T.M. (1990). *Politics, Markets, and America's Schools.* Washington, DC: Brookings Institution.

Education for All Handicapped Children Act of 1975, 20 U.S.C. §1400 *et seq.*

Garn, G.A. (2000, October 12). Arizona charter schools: a case study of values acid school policy [Electronic version]. *Current Issues in Education*, 3(7).

Heubert, J.P. (1997). Schools without rules? Charter schools, federal disability law, and the paradoxes of deregulation. *Harvard Civil Rights-Civil Liberties Law Review*, 32, 301–353.

Howe, K.R. (1997). *Understanding Equal Educational Opportunity: Social Justice, Democracy and Schooling.* New York: Teachers College Press.

Howe, K.R. and Eisenhart, M. (2000). *A Study of the Boulder Valley School District's Open Enrollment System.* (Tech. Rep.) Boulder, CO: Authors.

Individuals with Disabilities Education Act, 20 U.S.C. §1400 *et seq.*

McKinney, J.R. (1996). Charter schools: a new barrier for children with disabilities. *Educational Leadership*, 54(22), 22–25.

McLaughlin, M.J., Henderson, K. and Ullah, H. (1996). *Charter Schools and Students with Disabilities.* Alexandria, VA: Center for Policy Research.

Mills v. *Board of Education*, 348 F. Supp. 866 (D.D.C. 1972).

Pennsylvania Association of Retarded Citizens (PARC) v. *Commonwealth*, 343 F. Supp. 279 (E.D. Pa. 1972).

SRI International (1997). *Evaluation of Charter School Effectiveness.* Menlo Park, CA: Author.

UCLA Charter School Study (1998). *Beyond the Rhetoric of Charter School Reform: A Study of Ten California School Districts*. Los Angeles, CA: Author.

US Department of Education (2000). *The State of Charter Schools 2000: Fourth-year Report*. Washington, DC: Author. Retrieved April 12, 2002, from http://www.ed.gov/pubs/charter4thyear/

Welner, K.G. (2001). *Legal Rights, Local Wrongs: When Community Control Collides with Educational Equity*. Albany, NY: SUNY Press.

Welner, K.G. and Howe, K.R. (in press). Steering toward separation: the evidence and implications of special education students' exclusion from choice schools. In J. Scott (Ed.), *School Choice and Diversity*. New York: Teachers College Press.

Zollers, J. and Ramanathan, K. (1998, December). For-profit charter schools and students with disabilities: The sordid side of the business of schooling. *Phi Delta Kappan*, pp. 297–304.

Zollers, N. (2000). Schools need rules when it comes to students with disabilities. *Education Week*, 19(25), 46.

Chapter 5

From 'special needs' to 'quality education for all'

A participatory, problem-centred approach to policy development in South Africa

Nithi Muthukrishna and Marie Schoeman

The historical context of change

In South Africa, the history of special needs education and education support services reflects extreme neglect and lack of provision for the large majority of learners. During the apartheid era, legislation and policy pertaining to education entrenched racial segregation and inequality. There is need to understand that the apartheid system categorized and officially classified people in terms of 'race'. Four major races were identified: Whites, Indian, Coloureds and African. This racial classification of South Africans impacted every aspect of their lives . . . . Education provision and support services operated along racial lines with gross inequities between white and black learners, especially African learners. These inequities in provision resulted in highly specialized and costly provision of special needs education and support services for a limited number of learners, the majority being white and Indian learners. Currently, the inadequacy in provision for African learners, in particular those in rural areas, is extreme.

[. . .]

Special needs education was fragmented not only by the apartheid laws that enforced separation along racial lines, but also by legislation and policy that separated 'ordinary' learners from learners categorized as having 'special needs'. Learners with disabilities and those experiencing learning difficulties have been relegated to a second system of education, separated and marginalized from mainstream educational provision. In addition, they were relegated to the periphery of educational concern. The nature of support services reflected a strong focus on the medical model of diagnosis and treatment of 'learner deficits'. This approach has led to exclusionary practices in education towards learners with disabilities and those experiencing learning difficulties. There has been a history of negative stereotyping and marginalization of these learners and their exclusion from mainstream educational provision.

[. . .]

The transformation process beginning in 1994

Since 1994, the new South African Government has been committed to transforming educational policy to address the imbalances and neglect of the past and to bring the country in line with international standards of recognition of human rights. A strong voice in these processes has been that of disabled people's organizations, such as the South African Federal Council on Disability (SAFCD) and parent organizations such as Down's Syndrome South Africa (DSSA) and the Disabled Children's Action Group (DICAG). A strong human rights emphasis is evident in educational policy and legislation. In addition, education policy and legislation with respect to disability reflected a move away from a welfare to a rights and developmental approach.

The Constitution of the Republic of South Africa of 1996 sets a constitutionally binding framework for national and provincial legislative action in the field of education. The notion of a democratic society based on human dignity, freedom, and equality is entrenched in the Constitution. One of the key provisions in the Constitution is the one dealing with equality of rights.

[...]

In view of the legacy of racial discrimination, and the neglect and marginalization of various sectors of the population during the apartheid era, the new government was committed to restoring the human rights of all marginalized groups. Since 1994, education policy documents that emerged entrenched the principles enshrined in the Constitution: education as a basic human right, quality education for all, equity and redress, the right of choice, curriculum entitlement, rights of parents.

[...]

National Commission on Special Needs in Education and Training (NCSNET) and The National Commission on Education Support Services (NCESS) (1996–97)

The White Paper on Education and Training (Department of Education, March 1995) announced the intention of the Minister of National Education to appoint a National Commission on Special Needs in Education and Training (NCSNET) and a National Committee on Education Support Services (NCESS) .... The task of the Commission and Committee was to investigate and make recommendations on all aspects of 'special needs' and 'support services' in education and training ....

The Terms of Reference indicated the following key areas of focus for the investigation (Ministry of Education, 1996):

- Providing a picture of the current situation with respect to 'special needs' and 'support services'.

- Developing a conceptual framework within the context of a holistic and integrated approach.
- Developing a vision, principles and strategies for the future for provision of education with respect to 'special needs' and 'support services' with a particular focus on inclusion and the strategy of mainstreaming.
- Investigating the implications of the above for curriculum and institutional development; the organization, governance and funding of schooling, and other levels of education, including higher and further education; and the staffing of educators and education support personnel.
- Development and training of educators and education support personnel.
- Developing a strategic implementation plan.

[. . .]

The following principles guided the work of the Commission and Committee. These were developed and agreed upon by all members within the first 2 months of the process:

- The NCSNET and NCESS made a commitment to uphold democratic processes in its investigation. All the work was conducted in a participatory and transparent manner, involving all members in the decision-making and in all aspects of the investigation.
- There was a participatory approach to public involvement, and a concerted effort was made to involve relevant stakeholders in the fullest possible manner. This approach was in line with the democratic ethos of public policy development that was emerging in South Africa.
- There was a commitment to exploring an indigenous response to South Africa's needs. Although the Commission and Committee considered and debated international opinion and trends, the main strategy was a radical problem-solving and solution-seeking process to address the local needs in the country . . . .

To ensure public participation, members of the NCSNET and NCESS formed provincial teams that conducted site visits, participated in stakeholder meetings, and facilitated provincial workshops and public hearings in all nine provinces in the country.

Challenging the notion of 'special educational needs'

The first important task of the Commission and Committee was to develop a conceptualization of 'special needs' and 'education support', and to clarify the relationship between special needs and support . . . . Critical issues such as the following were raised:

- The need to challenge the values and assumptions underpinning current educational practice, in particular, exclusionary concepts from pathology, medicine, and concepts relating to normative assessment that locate learning and other difficulties within the individual.

- The concern that the notion of 'special educational needs' has become a catch phrase for all categories of learners who for various reasons do not fit into the system.

- Questions of human rights, social justice, and equality of opportunity and quality education for all learners.

- The notion of 'special needs' as reflective of an 'individual change' model which has resulted in highlighting personal inadequacies in individuals rather than on challenging social inadequacies in the system.

- The view that there are aspects of language usage in special education that have promoted educational myths and discriminatory practices. One myth particularly evident in South Africa is to view the task of educating individuals with learning difficulties and disabilities so specialized that only 'experts' can handle it.

- The need for a language that allows the system to adopt a 'problem-solving, process-focused approach' to the education of all learners.

- The need for education support to focus on the development of the system so that it can recognize and respond to diversity in the student population rather than merely focus on supporting individual learners.

- The need for a community-based approach to support that would draw on and maximize local resources, and that would reflect a move away from the traditional expert model of support.

From 'special needs' to 'barriers to learning and development'

Arising from these debates, and to address the concerns around current conceptualizations, the NCSNET and NCESS argued that a range of needs exists among learners and within the education system which must be met if effective learning and development is to be provided and sustained. Therefore, the education system must be structured and must function in such a way that it can accommodate and be responsive to diverse learner and system needs. If the education system fails to provide for and accommodate such diversity, learning breakdown and the exclusion of certain learners occurs. The NCSNET and NCESS argued that a dynamic relationship exists between the learner, the centre of learning, the broader education system, and the social, political and economic context of which they are all a part. This is particularly relevant in the lives of rural learners in the country where inadequate facilities, inadequate teacher development, poverty and other social and political factors impact on the learning process. The NCSNET and NCESS agreed that the priority of an education system should be to address those factors that lead to the inability of the system to accommodate diversity, or which lead to learning breakdown or which prevent learners from accessing educational provision. The NCSNET and NCESS conceptualized these factors as 'barriers to learning and development'....

In their investigations, the NCSNET and NCESS identified and conducted an analysis of key barriers in the South African context that render a large number of children and adults vulnerable to learning breakdown and sustained exclusion (Department of Education, 1997a, pp. 11–19).

- *Problems in the provision and organization of education*: research carried out by the NCSNET and NCESS revealed vast imbalances and disparities in provision with respect to the different bands of education, rural/urban contexts, different provinces, different race groups, and different groups of learners. For example, despite the introduction of compulsory education in South Africa, many learners continue to remain outside the formal education system, many being those with disabilities who have been prevented from entering ordinary schools....
- *Socio-economic barriers*: such as lack of access to basic services, poverty and under-development.
- *Factors that place learners at risk*: such as high levels of violence and crime, HIV/Aids epidemic and substance abuse.
- *Attitudes*: in South Africa, a critical barrier is negative and discriminatory attitudes in society towards difference with respect to race, class, gender, culture, disability, religion, ability and other characteristics.
- *An inflexible curriculum*: a serious barrier relates to the rigid and inflexible nature of the curriculum which fails to cater to the diversity in the learner population and leads to learning breakdown.
- *Language and communication*: in South Africa, teaching and learning for many learners occur in a language, which is not their first language. Teachers are often not prepared to provide adequate support mechanisms for these learners and enable them to access the curriculum.
- *Inaccessible and unsafe built environment*: in the province of Kwazulu-Natal, 181 of 5340 schools have been assessed to have buildings not suitable for education. Two hundred and eighty-five schools are without water (Statistics South Africa, 1998).
- Inappropriate and inadequate *provision of support services* to schools, parents, caregivers, families and communities.
- *Lack of enabling and protective legislation.*
- *Lack of parental recognition and involvement*: in general, parents have been given little recognition within the education and training sector. They, in particular, parents of children with disabilities, have been allowed little participation in decision-making regarding their children's education.
- *Disability*: many learners with impairments experience learning breakdown and exclusion because their learning needs are not met as a result of barriers in the learning environment and in the broader society.
- *Lack of human resource development*: in South Africa, there has been a history of inadequate on-going teacher development. This has led to insecurity, low

self-esteem, and a lack of innovative practices in the classroom to meet the needs of a diverse learner population.

Framework for the future

The central role of the NCSNET and NCESS was to make proposals regarding a vision, principles and strategies for the future . . . .
    The NCSNET and NCESS articulated a vision of

> an education and training system that promotes education for all and fosters the development of inclusive and supportive centres of learning that enable all learners to participate actively in the education process so that they can develop and extend their potential and participate as equal members of society.
>
> (Department of Education, 1997a, p. 53)

Developments since the release of the report of NCSNET and NCESS in November 1997

The Minister of National Education is currently translating the Report of the NCSNET and NCESS into legislation. It was intended that the Green Paper, White Paper and legislation phases of the policy development process should take no longer than a year. At the time of the writing of this chapter (October 1999), the process has not been completed . . . . The factors contributing to the delay in finalizing the policy may be the following:

- It is clear that the shift away from a disability focus in special needs education to the broader concept of 'barriers to learning and development' is still not accepted in all education circles as viable. On the one hand, it is felt that this would be dealing with too wide a consumer group whose needs should in a way already be addressed by the general education policies. On the other hand, there is a fear that by drawing the focus so wide, the system would once again fail to address the needs of learners with disabilities. They have been a particularly marginalized and disadvantaged group that has not had adequate access to education and services. A fear is also expressed that if the necessary support cannot be provided the prevailing process of 'mainstream dumping' will continue.
- The second factor is that the learner deficit view of special needs education is still so deeply entrenched in the education system that decision-makers at all levels have failed to change their focus to a systemic one. There are still a large number of support personnel working in the system, for example, educational psychologists and therapists who reinforce the learner deficit view in the minds of parents and teachers by conducting psychometric tests for placement purposes. Although this practice is in contradiction of the South African Schools

Act, it continues under the guise of serving a diagnostic purpose. Little evidence is, however, found of psychometric assessments resulting in meaningful curriculum support for learners. In most cases, these practices also continue to serve only learners from urban advantaged settings.

- Third, the daunting process of implementing the new national curriculum, 'Curriculum 2005' in all South African schools is at the moment the first priority in education. The introduction of transformational outcomes based education has not been without some measure of controversy. It is possible that the National Ministry of education feels that the time is not ripe to introduce yet another controversial policy that will undoubtedly be challenged from many quarters.

- There is not enough expertise within the country (or possibly anywhere with regard to the developing world) to work out the funding implications of a system with infused support. The assumption that it will be more cost-effective has in fact not been verified and would be one of the most urgent priority areas of research with regard to inclusive education in the developing world.

- It is unfortunate that not all decision-makers in education can accept that the basic principles of outcomes-based education create the framework for inclusive education. 'Curriculum 2005' reflects a learner-centred approach, allowing learners to progress at their own pace and style, making use of multidimensional assessment methods and measuring progress against previous achievements and not against those of other learners (Department of Education, 1997b). The radical nature of the curriculum transformation process has been difficult to grasp by many people involved in the implementation process. In particular, moving away from a system relying heavily on norm referenced assessment and the notion of passing and failing as a means to uphold quality education, is difficult for most people.

- Since the new government came into power in 1994, various policy documents and innovations have been introduced in education to address the imbalances and neglect of the apartheid era. It seems that the concern on the part of the Ministry is that the country is experiencing 'policy overload' and that there has been limited progress in the delivery of services.

First steps

The most recent development has been the release on 30 August 1999 of the 'Consultative Paper No. 1 on Special Education: Building an Inclusive Education and Training System: First Steps (Department of Education, 1999) to the public for comment and advice . . . .

In this Consultative Paper, the Department of Education claims to have made the shift to an inclusive system of education and training that would be responsive to the diversity in the learner population. However, if one makes an in-depth study of the document, there is a definite move away from the vision of the Report of the NCSNET and NCESS. It is very clear that various influences have resulted in the Ministry shifting the focus from a transformative inclusive education approach encapsulated in the Report of the NCSNET to a rather conservative one. The transformative view is concerned with creating learning and teaching environments that are responsive to diversity, that address barriers to learning and development, and that maximize learner participation in the learning process. A critical concern with the Consultative Paper is that the paradigm shift from 'learners with special needs' to the notion of 'barriers to learning and development' is not taken up in the Consultative Paper as a critical focus.

The Consultative Paper makes some reference to a transformative view in initial chapters. It explains that the Ministry acknowledges that a broad range of learning needs exist among the learner population, and that where these needs are not met learners may fail to learn effectively or may experience exclusion (Department of Education, 1999, chapter 1) .... The Consultative Paper agrees with the Report of NCSNET and NCESS that to address learning difficulties and exclusion there is need to locate the problem within the education and training system – the teaching and learning strategy, the classroom, the school, the district, the provincial, and national organizations and systems. The education and training system should undergo change to meet the full range of learners. The Ministry explains that this is consistent with a development approach to understanding learning difficulties and exclusion, and planning action. The Ministry states that,

> It follows that to contribute to effective learning and to ensure the inclusion of all learners in the learning process, the education and training system should he structured and function in such a way that it is able to accommodate a diversity of learner needs.
>
> (Department of Education, 1999, p. 3)

[...]

However, there appear to be numerous contradictions and a lack of clarity on various issues in the Consultative Paper. This is particularly evident in the manner in which inclusion is defined in the various sections of the document. On the one hand, there is a rather narrow, conservative focus. Inclusion is concerned with learners identified in terms of their deficits and impairments, and the establishment of alternate provision for these learners. In other instances in the document there is a focus on a wider group of vulnerable learners and an interactive view of learning and teaching with a focus on systems change. In other instances in the document, there is a strong disability focus. For example, in chapter 2 the Document states that in line with the recommendations of the Report of NCNET and NCESS, 'inclusion means the participation of people with disability in all daily activities – at school, at work, at home and in our communities' (Section 1.1.1: 9). Yet, the Report of NCSNET and NCESS takes on a far broader view of inclusion as concerned with overcoming all exclusionary pressures and practices in the system, and maximizing the participation of all learners . . . .

A serious problem in this Consultative Paper is that while it argues that it upholds an inclusive education philosophy, it seems to retain the language of the traditional, medical, deficit model that locates learning and other difficulties within the individual learner. Language such as 'learners with learning difficulties', 'remedial programmes', 'ELSEN', 'learners with severe learning difficulties' and 'learners with the most severe forms of learning difficulties' abounds in the paper. Such terminology reflects confusion and serious contradictions in terms of the paradigm shift. The Ministry attempts to justify this contradiction by stating that it has opted to retain the terminology which is 'in common use' and has 'currency' because new terminology 'may complicate and obfuscate, rather than assist the participation of education managers, educators, and the public in the discourses and processes of change' (Department of Education, 1999, p. 7).

Conclusion

The authors have been actively involved in advocacy initiatives and debates around the Consultative Paper with individuals and groups in various parts of the country . . . . Throughout this policy development process, the Ministry had been committed to a democratic, participatory approach. It is, therefore, believed that the concerns of the public about the Consultative Paper would be considered in a serious light by the Ministry. The Ministry is also aware that during the past couple of years the Report of the NCSNET and NCESS has heralded a shift in international thinking with regard to special needs education, in particular, with regard to the alignment of debates around 'special needs education' and 'education for all'. The next phase in the process will be for the Ministry to undertake an analysis of all submissions received from the public. The process will then involve the release of a draft White Paper for further public comment.

References

Central Statistics Services (1998) *Census in Brief: The People of South Africa. Population Census, 1996* (Pretoria: Statistics South Africa).

Constitution of the Republic of South Africa of 1996.

Department of Education (1995) *The Organization, Governance, and Funding of Schools.* White Paper 2. November (Pretoria: Department of Education).

Department of Education (1997a) *Quality Education for All – Overcoming Barriers to Learning and Development.* Report of the National Commission on Special Needs in Education and Training (NCSNET) and the National Committee on Education Support Services (NCESS). November (Pretoria: Department of Education).

Department of Education (1997b) *Outcomes-based Education in South Africa: Background Information for Educators.* March (Pretoria: Department of Education).

Department of Education (1999) *Consultative Paper No. 1 on Special Education: Building an Inclusive Education and Training System. First Steps.* August (Pretoria Department of Education).

Ministry of Education (October 1996) *Terms of reference of NCSNET and NCESS.* Government Gazette no. 17526 (Pretoria: Government Printer).

Part II

The struggle for an inclusive agenda

Local perspectives

In the name of inclusion

'We all, at the end of the day, have the needs of the children at heart'

John Swain and Tina Cook

Introduction

The statement, 'we all, at the end of the day, have the needs of the children at heart', was made at a public meeting by a special educational needs advisor for a local authority, which for the purposes of this chapter is called Romantown. At the time of writing, the authority was reorganizing its special educational needs provision under a policy flag of 'inclusion'.

[...]

In this chapter, we critically analyse the meaning of 'inclusion' both within education policy and in its realization within provision and practice . . . . We set the scene by summarizing some key issues and themes in the rapidly expanding literature on inclusion in education.

The notion of inclusion has, centrally, shifted the debate from product to process. Whereas integration has focused on the numbers of young disabled people attending special schools or mainstream schools, the focus for inclusion, in principle at least, has been the processes involved in making mainstream schools accessible to young disabled people in terms of curriculum and teaching, organization, management, the physical environment, ethos and culture. It would seem that the question of 'integration versus segregation', which has dominated special education policy in different guises over many years, is being replaced by a struggle for children's right to be included (Vlachou, 1997; Thomas *et al.*, 1998).

[...]

An inclusive school is not a mainstream school into which some disabled students have been integrated. Indeed, it could be argued that there would be no such thing as mainstream schools in a truly inclusive system (as there would be no special schools – mainstream only having meaning in relation to special) . . . . Inclusive education is based on a philosophy of the positive valuation and celebration of difference. An inclusive school is barrier-free and is accessible to all in terms of the buildings and grounds, curricula, support systems and methods of communication. Inclusion, as conceived here, then, is clearly a far more challenging concept than that of integration, and provides a basis for examples of radical change (Thomas *et al.*, 1998).

[. . .]

However, definitions of inclusion do vary and involve different moral, political, social and educational aims and assumptions (Clark *et al.*, 1997). Although many countries are concerned to desegregate their provision in some way, such change may be based on a variety of rationales and mechanisms (Loxley and Thomas, 1997; Armstrong and Barton, 1999). Furthermore, more traditional notions of integration, following on from the Warnock definitions of locational, social and functional integration (DES, 1978), continue to inform policy and, perhaps most significantly, there have been few real changes in the level of segregation in the UK (Swann, 1988; CSIE, 1992).

This chapter examines changes in policy through a critical evaluation of the changing provision and practice implemented in the name of inclusion within Romantown LEA. We draw on a qualitative research project which has explored the views and experiences of the people most directly involved in a reorganization of special educational needs provision, particularly in the closure of an all-age school for pupils with physical disabilities, which we shall call Adamston, and the opening of 'resource centres' in three mainstream schools.

The main method of data collection has been through semistructured interviews . . . . The main topics covered were participants' views and their experiences of the reorganization; the education provided at Adamston; and the changes through which mainstream schools in Romantown could provide effective education for pupils with physical disabilities. All the tapes were fully transcribed. Group projects were undertaken with pupils, and involved their taking photographs of Adamston and the people at the school before it closed.

By its nature, a policy of inclusion is also inclusive in terms of 'interest groups'. However, restricted resources have limited the sampling in this project, and the viewpoint of a number of interested groups of participants has not been researched, including non-disabled children, parents of non-disabled children and disabled adults. In terms of interest groups, the participants in this research were those most directly involved in the closure of Adamston and the placement of pupils in the reorganized provision – policy-makers, teachers, other professionals, parents and pupils.

We develop the critical analysis by, first, examining the policy statements from the local authority in relation to national policy and the developing notion of 'social inclusion', particularly in terms of principles for the realization of inclusion. This section is based mainly on official documentation and on interviews of local authority policy-makers. Second, we explore the realization of principles in changing practice, looking particularly from the viewpoint of practitioners in the special school and mainstream schools. Third, we summarize some of the experiences of parents of young disabled pupils and of the pupils themselves of changes implemented in the name of inclusion. To conclude, we draw out the main strand of our analysis: that the term 'inclusion' in education policy can be 'integration' by another name and can mask, distort and rationalize segregation in practice and provision. Finally, we come full circle to look at a more problematic and critical notion of inclusion which is precluded by the rhetoric of shared humanistic emotional concerns for 'the needs of the children'.

From the viewpoint of policy-makers: from principles to policy

The starting point for a policy analysis of the reorganization in Romantown is necessarily the views and interest of the LEA policy-makers . . . . (T)he Romantown reorganization was initiated and controlled by LEA policy-makers, starting from the dissemination in 1995 of a document setting out the principles and policy, which would remain unchanged throughout the 'consultation process'.

Under the reorganization, all the special schools in the city would close. Following this, six new schools would be opened: one primary 2–11 and one secondary 11–19 offering places for children with 'profound and multiple learning difficulties (PMLD), severe learning difficulties and associated physical difficulties' (quotations taken from LEA documents); one school for children aged 3–19 with 'PMLD and/or challenging behaviours including severe communication disorders/autism'; and three schools for children with 'emotional and behavioural difficulties'. A number of additionally resourced units (ARUs), including three for children with physical difficulties (one secondary, two primary), were also to be established within mainstream schools.

[. . .]

In the earlier documents relating to the reorganization, the term 'integration' was used rather than 'inclusion'. Inclusion seems to have been used first in the LEA response to the DfEE (1997) green paper.

[. . .]

Inclusion was the preferred term in subsequent documents and in the interviews, and it is clear that the LEA regard the reorganization as a move towards inclusion. In the following analysis of the Romantown policy we draw on a framework for critical analysis developed in Loxley and Thomas's (1997) attempt at a meta-analysis of international literature concerning special needs policy, and its interpretation and implementation.

A major theme for the Romantown policy-makers was what Loxley and Thomas (1997) call *systemic dualism,* that is, the continuation or discontinuation of dual systems of special and mainstream education. The main rationale for the reorganization of special needs provision in Romantown, as emphasized in public statements and documents disseminated by the LEA, was to enable a 'significant reduction in the level of segregation'. According to their own LEA review, Romantown had one of the highest levels of segregation in the country with over 2 percent of pupils attending special schools. The maintenance and, indeed, enhancement of the special sector was also a recurring theme.

[...]

Though the number of special schools in Romantown was to be significantly reduced, from 10 to 4, special schools, remained a significant part of the provision in the reorganized system.

[...]

Resources is a second major theme in the documents and in the interviews with policy-makers. Indeed resourcing issues are given such a high priority that it could be argued that 'policy decisions are shaped by an over-riding concern with resource implications' (Loxley and Thomas, 1997, p. 279).

[...]

Another key theme in Romantown policy is *consumer centredness*, that is a focus upon the needs of individual pupils, and the provision of services to meet their needs. Consumer centredness is clearly apparent in the statement of principles provided in the policy documents as a basis for the planning of provision: 'Statements (i.e. statements of special educational needs) should accurately reflect the needs of individual children and resources should be used efficiently and flexibly to meet those needs.' Indeed, the policy-makers consistently argued that the reorganized system allowed for an extended and improved continuum of provision. There would be a variety of provision for pupils with physical disabilities, according to their particular needs; namely, in individual local schools, the additionally resourced provision in three mainstream schools or special schools for pupils with learning difficulties. Thus, for any child with a physical disability, placements could be individualized. Which takes us to the final theme we would pinpoint: *democratization*, that is the involvement of parents or students in the decision-making processes. Again the policy-makers we interviewed emphasized the increased choice available to parents through extending and improving the continuum of provision.

As Loxley and Thomas (1997, p. 280) state, 'even in the policy documents one can see the tensions between intention and implementation'. To begin to draw out these tensions we turn next to an examination of the views and experiences of professionals in turning policy into practice.

From the viewpoint of professionals: from principles to practice

Adamston professionals

We concentrate first on the analysis of interviews with staff at Adamston and with other professionals involved, for example Chair of governors; parent governor;

head teachers (during the 18-month period leading up to its closure the school had three head teachers); teachers; physiotherapist; speech therapist; nurse; psychologist; and social workers. Though there were some significant differences of opinions expressed by participants, there were recurring themes which were seemingly representative of shared views.... (A)ll the Adamston professionals were, in principle, positive about the philosophy of inclusion of Adamston pupils into mainstream schools. Emphasis was particularly given to the social benefits for young disabled people, including broader integration into the community and access to opportunities. There was also mention of the benefits for pupils already in mainstream education. The decision to close the school had already been taken, and it is in this context that the analysis is made. The following quotations are illustrative:

> I feel a lot of the principles of the reorganization are very good ones. I mean I personally feel the ideology behind it is really good because at the end of the day why should children have to be segregated just because they have physical or medical needs.
>
> I started off feeling very, very enthusiastic. I felt this was a thoroughly good thing and at least the first year of talking with parents in the reviews, I was fired up, I was willing to say trust the authority, this is going to be really something good, it's going to be a great opportunity.

In general, inclusion was seen as requiring far-reaching changes within mainstream schools, with schools adapting to physically disabled pupils, rather than physically disabled pupils fitting in to existing mainstream provision. Such changes would include the physical environment: 'I feel is it sounds so untechnical and so basic but it's something I'm not sure people realize is sheer physical space and access for the kids.'

A multi-professional approach:

> I think it is very much a sort of more integrated, multi-professional approach to the work, teachers will not be able to go into the classrooms and shut the door and think, right this is my responsibility, these thirty youngsters....

The curriculum:

> There doesn't seem to have been much thought given to anything beyond the National Curriculum, whereas we had quite an extensive programme of social independence training which we feel is a vital part of the skills that these youngsters need because they don't generalize their learning.

A whole school approach:

> I don't think inclusion and integration is about whether you can get a wheelchair in the door, it's about including a child in their community and the benefits of that and it's an inspirational thing, it's a faith . . . .

And flexibility:

> It'll depend totally on the good will of the receiving schools and they've got to be ready to change, they've got to be sensitive. You see it's like any other situation that you come to, you have an idea but you've got to be prepared to change the idea if it's not working. You can't be too dogmatic.

Mainstream professionals

A different view of inclusion emerged from the analysis based on interviews with head teachers and SEN staff in mainstream schools that had resource centres for pupils with physical disabilities. From the viewpoint of staff in mainstream schools, the inclusion of disabled pupils would mean positive change for many of those involved, including non-disabled and disabled pupils and the mainstream schools as a whole.

> The existing mainstream youngsters, I could see it would have an impact on them which could be to their advantage. And then there was all the benefits to the physically disabled children . . . wider access to provision which perhaps they hadn't experienced in small special schools. And opportunity to integrate with mainstream youngsters.

The benefits for mainstream schools were also recognized:

> On a practical basis the numbers in the school were quite low and we're still under-subscribed, and there's clearly going to be some finance associated with this . . . and so that is an opportunity to benefit the school.

In general, inclusion was taken to mean the incorporation of pupils from Adamston into the existing curriculum, pedagogy, organization and management of the school, with minimal change within the school. The main changes within mainstream schools to facilitate the reorganization were conceived in terms of architecture, and in terms of the provision of medical and physiotherapy support . . . . This was further emphasized in views expressed about the process selection:

> One thing we have absolutely insisted on is that we will not accept children here unless we are involved in the transfer proceedings . . . . And we have not yet been invited to any of the reviews and I know they have been happening,

but until the authority have assured us that there is going to be a panel these children go before and we are invited to the panel, but I've seen no sign that this is happening yet.

Thus though both those at Adamston and in mainstream schools could be said to be positive about a philosophy of inclusion, there were clear differences in what was meant by the notion of inclusion. In general terms, from the viewpoint of those at Adamston, inclusion involves the replication of the provision and practice at Adamston in mainstream contexts. The prevailing view in Adamston was that the principles of inclusion were not being met by the reorganization:

> I don't know where the philosophy has gone, the philosophy has disappeared somewhere along the line and it has been replaced by practicalities. The same people who were saying segregation is the best thing for your children, are now saying integration is the best thing for your children. How can they embrace it? It's just a policy as far as they are concerned and they are implementing a policy, there is no real feeling behind it, it's not a belief, it is just work to them, it is just a policy and because it's not what they really believe I don't think they are doing it properly.

For the most part, inclusion from the viewpoint of mainstream schools is a process of fitting disabled pupils into existing provision and, thus, a process of selecting pupils who will present the least demands.

From the viewpoint of parents and pupils: from practice to exclusion

We turn now to the experiences of the parents and pupils at Adamston . . . . Perhaps not surprisingly, a major theme for the parents was the strength of their emotional response. Unlike the professionals and policy-makers involved, the reorganization heralded significant personal changes for the young people at Adamston and for their families. The parent described the following responses:

Upset

We were very upset because we knew straight away it [the new special school for children with learning difficulties] was going to be for the severely handicapped and . . . I've known that he probably couldn't go to mainstream.

Disappointment

We had always anticipated he would stay here until he was 11 and obviously we are very disappointed that [Adamston] is closing.

Worry

I keep thinking, is he going to settle well wherever he goes and will I get him in the place, you know, I mean the chance is I might not get him where I want him and it's really worrying.

Shock

My first reaction was it was just a total nightmare. I thought they were very insensitive. They just sort of sprang it on everyone very quickly, just came out of nowhere and I don't think we've really had much choice.

Anger and frustration

Anger, frustration, because they weren't looking at the children as people. They were looking at them as a commodity, like we will just move this one here and this number here and they're not. They're all individual.

Stress

And you don't really know where ... he's going to go or what's going to, happen and for parents I think it is very very stressful and upsetting.

[...]

The parents' highly emotional responses and feelings of fear and trepidation as they faced the impending school closure can be seen, on one hand, as a normal response to change. Such an interpretation, however, could pre-empt a critical analysis of the processes of change and, perhaps more importantly, recognition of the positive contributions parents might make to change. We found that almost all the parents were positive about the philosophy of children with special educational needs attending their local mainstream school, as illustrated by the following quotations. 'Ideally I want my child to go to school with our next door neighbour. Integration with so called normal children, whatever a normal child is, he doesn't get it here ...'.

The parents were asked if they could clearly identify what they believed would be necessary in a mainstream school to enable their child to make progress. Many parents expressed the view that it was vitally important for mainstream schools to offer support beyond the academic curriculum and physical needs. They described support systems that would take into account, not purely their child's educational opportunities, but an environment that would enable their child to feel secure, confident and happy: an environment where their child's special needs were universally recognized and acknowledged. What the parents sought, then, could be thought of as the type of inclusion their child had experienced at Adamston.

The vast majority of parents interviewed, however, while making positive statements about the philosophy of inclusion, voiced serious reservations about the practice within the Romantown reorganization. In a number of important ways, the experiences that many parents and pupils talked of could be characterized as experiences of exclusion.

First and foremost was the exclusion from Adamston. All pupils, parents and family members we talked to were positive about the educational opportunities and wider support their child had received while at Adamston School. Adamston can be seen as a small community which, from the viewpoint of its members, was being eliminated. Many parents described how they had initially wanted/fought for their child to be in a mainstream school, and the struggle they had undergone with their own feelings around being told/realizing that their child could not manage in that situation. These parents had already coped with big changes in their aspirations and plans for their children's education, but had found a school in which they and their child felt included.

[...]

The sense of exclusion as a loss of a community came through most strongly in the project we conducted with the pupils. This project involved the production of a book of memories of the school. The pupils were each given a disposable camera to take photographs for inclusion in the book and each photograph was accompanied by a caption explaining the picture. The project involved pupils in discussions about the school and their experiences there. Their experiences were predominantly positive and related almost wholly to the quality of the experiences themselves, rather than to any educational standards or aims .... The school had a small residential unit (referred to as 'resi'), which provided secondary pupils with the opportunity for overnight stays. This, it seemed, was consistently highly valued:

Pupil: Resi is going to be a really big one for me. It's absolutely excellent. It's probably one of the best things about the school.
Researcher: What do you like about resi?
Pupil: You don't have to be at home being bored. All your friends are there ... your own room.

Some expressions of the loss of the community were poignant. One pupil told us, 'The thing is the school is closing. And the thing is when you leave a school you can come back to see it, but we can't come back and see it ...'.

Exclusion also characterizes the experiences of parents and pupils in relation to the policy-making and planning of the reorganization in Romantown. While parents were involved, ostensibly at least, both in the consultation exercise on the process of reorganization and in the placement decisions about their child, the idea that pupils could or should be involved did not arise for the pupils themselves or anyone else involved. All parents were invited to attend annual reviews, but this invitation did not extend to pupils. Only once did a pupil appear at her own annual review. She burst into the room asking, 'What are you saying about me?'. The meeting immediately stopped and she was gently ejected. The decision at the meeting was that this 14-year old should attend a mainstream school.

[...]

The processes and procedures of placement were experienced by parents as exclusion from the decision-making process, as explained in the following quotations:

> They say it's up to parents but it's not, your hands are literally tied. We can't do nothing, even if we say right we don't want [Jim] to go to that school or wherever, it's not going to make any difference.
> If you've got a good school and a good education system choice is immaterial. The choice thing has become ridiculous and we would gladly lose a large amount of choice to have better support and more limited choice within a better system.
> That's what parents want. They don't want choice. We want good education. Choice is irrelevant.

While pupils were completely excluded from the consultation process, parents were invited to state their views. Nevertheless, the parents consistently and repeatedly maintained that they had been excluded from decision-making processes. They generally felt that they should have been brought into the consultation period much earlier to enable a more in-depth, two-way transmission of information.

[...]

Conclusion: from segregation to inclusion

In this section we look at the tensions in the Romantown policy as a foundation for furthering inclusion, and from this basis discuss an understanding of what could be done in the name of inclusion. A possibly surprising starting point in our analysis was the acceptance of the general principle that disabled pupils should be educated alongside their non-disabled peers. It seems to be an expression of the dominant humanistic ideology in special education. Oliver (1996, p. 85) contends: 'the educational literature on integration sees the whole issue as non-problematic; integration has become received educational wisdom . . . . The concept of integration has become like the idea of motherhood – who can possibly be against it?' From this research we would contend that this also applies to the views of participants – the concept of inclusion has become as non-problematic as the statement in our title, 'We all, at the end of the day, have the needs of the children at heart'.

We return first, then, to the themes within the Romantown policy. There is a fundamental tension between systemic dualism and a policy of inclusion. Indeed it could be argued that the notion of a 'continuum of provision', as conceived in the

Romantown reorganization, compounds exclusion. Inclusion in some mainstream schools furthers exclusion from others.

[...]

The process in the name of inclusion becomes one of selection for inclusion, and thus becomes an exclusive process. Inclusion, through a process of placement decisions for individuals, excludes. It is perhaps significant that in the official documents the first reference to the reorganization as being designed to 'improve the levels of achievement for pupils with special educational needs' is accompanied by the first reference to pupils with special educational needs 'with high ability'. Inclusion in mainstream schools is sought and justified in terms of criteria of success defined for and by mainstream schools.

As described earlier, the redistribution of resources was seen by the LEA representatives as key to their strategy of furthering inclusion. It was strongly contended that the reorganization did not involve the cutting of resources to the education of pupils with special educational needs. The other participants, however, repeatedly expressed the belief that this was a cost cutting exercise. As Vlachou (1997, p. 28) suggests, 'an integration debate which focuses solely on resources and cost-effectiveness contains the danger of integration being viewed as a cheap alternative to special education'.

[...]

The notion of consumer centredness also diverts attention. It is tied to a model of change which is individually driven, does not address the role of the schools in generating special needs and does not necessarily result in the reshaping of the school and system level provision. As Roaf and Bines (1989) argue, emphasis on needs detracts from a proper consideration of the rights of those who are being educated. In Romantown a continuum of provision is being developed which is envisaged as being exclusive in meeting particular individual needs. This is being undertaken in the name of inclusion.

Similarly it can be argued that a continuum of provision creates the illusion of choice and democratization . . . . When the parents we interviewed told us they had 'no choice', they highlighted this illusion within the Romantown reorganization. Here the continuum of education did not, in practice, mean choice as became evident at each child's annual review. When both the parents and the professionals involved considered placement in mainstream schools unviable, the only alternative for most was a special school for pupils with learning difficulties.

The relationship between democratization, particularly in the guise of parental choice, and inclusion seems to us to be problematic. As Whittaker and Kenworthy (1995, p. 4) argue, 'the effective inclusion of learners cannot and should not be a choice'. Choice is only one view of democratization, and it is limited. A more comprehensive notion of democratization, and one which is reflected in the views of many parents and professionals in this study, is that of participation in decision-making processes. In principle, such participation would include those directly involved, for example parents, professionals and pupils, within the processes of reviewing provision and planning for inclusion, rather than simply responding to plans laid out by others and ostensibly choosing between options determined by others. The starting point for democratization is the recognition that those directly involved have legitimate perspectives that can inform and shape moves towards inclusion.

Ultimately we would argue that the policy in Romantown is directed towards furthering integration rather than inclusion. Integration, in the name of inclusion, was defined in terms of numbers of pupils in different types of provision, and the establishment of 'additionally resourced units' in three mainstream schools. The starting point for inclusion, rather than integration, is a clear, agreed and shared set of principles. Inclusion is not about moving children to different schools, but is about the process of changing what has been seen as 'mainstream' education.

We end, then, by suggesting three key messages from the experiences of the participants in the research in Romantown. First, moves towards inclusion need to be founded upon the experiences of exclusion of young disabled people and their parents.... Second, an inclusive system is explicitly designed to cater for all. It involves the establishment of educational institutions and systems within which all children – regardless of ability, impairment, gender, language, ethnic or cultural origin – can be equally valued, treated with respect, provided with equal opportunities and, in a word, included. By definition, inclusive cannot be selective. Third, inclusion must be negotiated in decision-making partnerships. Inclusion begins with inclusion in decision-making. Those who have been excluded need to be included in determining the policies and practices of inclusion.

A change of name is not necessarily a change of policy. Inclusion, in contrast to integration, requires radical change with the rights of disabled people at heart, rather than 'the needs of children'. As Barton (1998, p. 84) states:

> [I]nclusivity...places the welfare of all citizens at the centre of consideration. It seeks to engage with the question of belonging and solidarity, and simultaneously, recognises the politics of difference.

References

Armstrong, F. and Barton, L. (1999) ' "Is There Anyone There Concerned With Human Rights?" Cross-cultural Connections, Disability and the Struggle for Change in England', in F. Armstrong and L. Barton (eds) *Disability, Human Rights and Education: Cross-cultural Perspectives*. Buckingham: Open University Press.

Barton, L. (1998) 'Markets, Managerialism and Inclusive Education', in P. Clough (ed.) *Managing Inclusive Education*. London: Paul Chapman.

Clark, C., Dyson, A., Millward, A.J. and Skidmore, D. (1997) *New Directions in Special Needs*. London: Cassell.

CSIE (1992) *Segregation and Inclusion: English LEA Statistics from 1988 to 1992*. Bristol: Centre for Studies on Inclusive Education.

DES (1978) *Special Educational Needs (The Warnock Report)*. London: HMSO.

DfEE (1997) *Excellence for All Children*. London: DfEE.

Loxley, A. and Thomas, G. (1997) 'From Inclusive Policy to the Exclusive Real World: An International Review', *Disability and Society* 12(2): 273–291.

Oliver, M. (1996) *Understanding Disability: From Theory to Practice*. Houndmills: Macmillan.

Roaf, C. and Bines, H. (1989) 'Needs, Rights and Opportunities in Special Education', in C. Roaf and H. Bines (eds) *Needs, Rights and Opportunities: Developing Approaches to Special Education*. London: Falmer.

Swann, W. (1988) 'Trends in Special School Placement to 1986: Measuring, Assessing and Explaining Segregation', *Oxford Review of Education* 14(2): 139–161.

Thomas, G., Walker, D. and Webb, J. (1998) *The Making of the Inclusive School*. London: Routledge.

Vlachou, A.D. (1997) *Struggles for Inclusive Education*. Buckingham: Open University Press.

Whittaker, J. and Kenworthy, J. (1995) *The Struggle for Inclusive Education – A Struggle Against Educational Apartheid*. Bolton Data for Inclusion, Bolton Institute.

Chapter 7

Parents, professionals and special educational needs policy frameworks in England and Scotland

Sheila Riddell, Alastair Wilson, Michael Adler and Enid Mordaunt

Introduction

A major theme of current social policy debates concerns the ways in which voices of service users are reflected in patterns of service provision. There is a growing emphasis on active citizenship, which calls for more creative engagement in the shaping of local and national policies and services to make them responsive to the needs of diverse service users. A number of recent studies have investigated the extent to which parents may contribute to the democratisation of education. Vincent (2000), for instance, has explored the potential of parent centred organisations (PCOs) in education to act as 'little polities', providing opportunities to challenge existing professionals' hierarchies. Her conclusion is that while most PCOs aim to challenge professional dominance and address general rather than particular issues, they are often made up of socially advantaged individuals and their impact is relatively modest. The research reported here aimed to explore the different forms of procedural justice in special educational needs (SEN) policies between England and Scotland and to illuminate the positions of parents and professionals. Given the social marginalisation of disabled people and their families, we wished to see whether the parents of children with SEN were involved, as active citizens, in the 'democratisation of everyday life' (Pateman, 1989; Phillips, 1993: 80), or whether they continued to occupy the role of client or consumer.

Our analysis of the ways in which parents of children with SEN and professionals negotiate their subject positions is based on the idea that policy is not simply made by elected representatives nor in public fora, but also in the daily interactions and negotiations of service users and professionals.

[. . .]

Research methods

In order to understand the nature of competing policy frameworks in England and Scotland, we first analysed policy texts, conducted interviews with 15 key informants and administered questionnaires to all local authorities. On the basis of our preliminary analysis, we chose four case study authorities, two in England and two in Scotland. These differed in relation to their use of mainstream schools to educate children with SEN and their rate of appeals. In each authority, 16 case studies were conducted with families involved in the process of opening a record/statement of needs. Efforts were made to include children with a range of difficulties and to maintain a balance between 'contested' and 'noncontested' cases. For each case study, interviews were conducted with the parents, the child and the cluster of professionals involved in the particular case, normally including the EP, class teacher, headteacher, medical officer and senior local authority officer with responsibility for SEN. Interviews were tape recorded and transcribed before a thematic analysis was conducted. Finally, a long 'pen portrait' was written for each family. In this chapter, we draw on case study data to illustrate the interactions of parents and professionals in particular case studies. While we are able to present only a small amount of data, we have been careful to ensure that the findings reported in this chapter are supported by our wider analysis.

Contrasting SEN policy frameworks in England and Scotland

During the postwar period, SEN policy in England and Scotland developed along broadly parallel lines. Following the Warnock Report (DES, 1978), educational professionals took over from medical professionals as the dominant group. The promotion of the idea of partnership meant that power continued to rest with professionals, to whose authority parents were expected to defer while taking some responsibility for their children's educational development. During the 1980s, the pursuit of marketisation and managerialism within the public sector characterised policy developments in both England and Scotland (Deakin, 1994), albeit in slightly muted form north of the border where professionalism continued to hold sway (McPherson and Raab, 1988).

Within SEN, the major divergence between England and Scotland occurred as a result of the 1993 Education Act. Promoted by a strong voluntary sector lobby, the legislation put in place a *Code of practice on the identification and assessment of special educational needs* (DfE, 1994) and established the SEN Tribunal to hear appeals. The Act exerted a strong pull towards consumerism and bureaucratisation which weakened professional power while boosting the rights of parents. The new bureaucratised system, however, also dictated the terms on which parents were able to engage. While giving them more power to claim individual rights, this did not necessarily mean an increase in their involvement as active citizens. In Scotland, moves towards bureaucratisation and consumerism took place much more slowly. Little attempt was made to regulate the conduct of educational psychologists and local authority officers during the process of assessment and recording. Whereas England's code of practice prescribed a set of procedures, Scotland's *Manual of Good Practice* (SOEID, 1998) merely suggested actions authorities might wish to consider. It is only since the passage of the Standards in Scotland's Schools etc. (Scotland) Act 2000 that local authorities in Scotland have been subject to inspection. In addition, publication by the Accounts Commission for Scotland of a number of performance indicators, for instance data on the average time taken to open a record of needs, has been strongly criticised. At the time of writing, EPs in Scotland were lobbying for the abolition of recording on the grounds that a child's 'entitlement' to SEN provision should be decided by educational psychologists and the formal involvement of other professionals and parents is unnecessary.

To summarise, the SEN policy frameworks for England and Scotland accord greater rights to parents in England than in Scotland. This is partly as a result of the more active mobilisation of parents' lobby groups such as the Independent Panel for Special Educational Advice (IPSEA) and other voluntary sector organisations. As a result of this, local educational authorities (LEAs) have had to engage more actively in dialogue and negotiation with parents through Parent Partnership schemes, which do not have an equivalent in Scotland. Conversely, in Scotland professional discretion, established as the dominant motif since the Second World War, continues to hold sway.

[...]

In the following sections, using two local authorities (LA1 and LA3), we illustrate how national policies were transformed by grassroots actors, with the effect that quite different national policies became much more similar as they were domesticated in specific local contexts.

Demographic characteristics

LA1 is a small English metropolitan authority in the heart of an old northern coalfield serving a relatively homogeneous and largely disadvantaged community. There are few people from minority ethnic backgrounds and a low proportion of people moving into or out of the area. Unemployment in the area is high (12.8 per cent compared with 7.4 per cent nationally). Education has traditionally had a low profile among the aspirations of the community, signalled by the low proportion of students remaining in education after the age of 16 (53 per cent as opposed to 70 per cent nationally). The 1991 Census showed that higher education qualifications were held by only 7.5 per cent of the population, compared with a national figure of 13.5 per cent. According to Ofsted, standards in schools were low compared with national averages and those of similar LEAs. In this report, the authority was criticised for having done little to raise the profile of education and levels of pupils' achievements and was seen as having complicated and inefficient internal management arrangements.

LA3 is a Scottish city which has experienced a long period of industrial decline. Forty-two per cent of the city's population live in an area of deprivation. In 54 per cent of city schools more than half the children are entitled to free school meals. The city has an unemployment rate of 11.6 per cent, the highest of any council area in Scotland and 29 per cent above the UK level. Forty-one per cent of children in the city are in families dependent on Income Support, The city has a high and increasing number of single parent households and a relatively high minority ethnic population.

SEN provision

In LA1, 3.8 per cent of the school population had a Statement of Needs. Most statemented children (83.5 per cent) were educated in mainstream schools and the authority had only three special schools, four units attached to mainstream and one stand-alone unit. This high use of mainstream schools was not as a result of a major policy change, but rather because special schools had never been built in this area. Some mainstream schools had been adapted to accommodate pupils with physical disabilities while the units attached offer specialised teaching to children with hearing impairments, specific learning difficulties, autism and behaviour problems. LA1 had very low rates of appeals. According to the SEN Tribunal Annual Report, two appeals were registered with the SEN Tribunal in 1998/99 and five in 1997/98. During this period there was one complaint of maladministration to the Commission for Local Administration.

LA3 had a relatively high proportion of children with a record of needs (2.8 per cent of the school population), indicative of the high levels of social deprivation in the area. Due to a major building programme in the 1950s and 1960s, LA3 had a large amount of special provision for children with SEN (31 special schools and three special units attached to mainstream) and as a result had a low proportion of children with a record (18.5 per cent) in mainstream schooling. This was a reversal of the position in LA1.

SEN policies and procedures

In terms of its SEN policy, LA1 was characterised as a benign bureaucracy....

In line with English national policy, many features of SEN policy and procedure in LA1 were geared towards assisting parents to play an active role in the assessment and statementing of their children and to seek legal redress where appropriate. However, many parents experienced structural disadvantage and were therefore unable to exploit fully the options available. For example, with the initial letter, parents were given a DfEE booklet explaining the process of drawing up a statement. However, many parents interviewed did not find this booklet accessible. For a time, a senior officer had hand-delivered all initial notices of the authority's intention to begin the process of statutory assessment. However, this practice was discontinued because of changes in personnel. It was felt that while it had been very worthwhile for some parents in terms of demystifying the process, for others it was 'a waste of time because you go and you can tell they're not listening to you' (senior officer, LA1). Instead of providing parents with more help, this officer concluded that there was no point in trying to secure greater involvement because parents lacked understanding and motivation, thus locating the fault with them rather than with the system of communication.

[...]

While procedures in LA1 sometimes mitigated parental involvement, this was even more evident in LA3. Practice in this authority was often in direct contravention of advice in the Scottish Executive's *Manual of Good Practice*. For instance, the Scottish Executive advises that parents should be invited to attend all statutory assessments, but case study parents were only routinely invited to attend the medical assessment. Whereas LAs were advised to give parents copies of all assessment reports, these were only distributed when specifically requested. This meant that parents often turned up at the case conference without having seen any assessment reports which professionals had had time to digest. Parents in LA3 were given two tightly printed sheets of A4 paper at the start of the statutory assessment process explaining procedures. This document minimised the legal significance of the record....

No mention was made of the authority's obligation to provide resources to meet the needs specified in the record.... Furthermore, the Named Person was described as 'someone to whom you can talk and can help you' instead of a technical adviser and advocate as suggested in Scottish Executive guidance. Only one parent in our LA3 case studies used a Named Person as an advocate. Parents were told that the letters 'may seem very formal and may take a long time'. No attempt had been made by the authority to write the letters in an accessible manner while conveying the necessary legal advice. Finally, no mention was made of the recommended time for the opening of a record (i.e. six months). In 1998/99, LA3 took on average 43 weeks to open a record (average time in Scotland is 34 weeks).

In LA3 it was evident that the desire to control spending on SEN was of major concern. The senior officer explained that she instructed educational psychologists to write the record in general terms without committing the authority to any specific expenditure:

> I do have a certain expectation in terms of content. For example, special needs auxiliary, we now have as a standard phrase in the record 'Access to special needs auxiliary as determined by the Individualised Educatuional Plan', or, if it's transport, 'Transport has to be kept under review'.
>
> (senior officer)

Communication between professionals and parents

LA1 officers sometimes marginalised parents in the statementing process. For example, parents were routinely given copies of all assessment reports with the draft statement, but did not receive them at the same time as the professionals and therefore had a shorter period of time to consult and consider the need for further action (e.g. requesting a second medical opinion). In addition, as required by law, parents were given a list of all the possible schools which their child might attend. However, the LA almost always recommended that the child should be placed in the local mainstream school, thus closing down rather than opening up discussion of alternatives. EPs were invited to comment on the relatively low levels of appeal. It was suggested by a senior official that 'there is quite a lot of effort goes into conciliation'. In addition, the passivity of the local community was seen as a problem, rather than the failure of the local authority to support and encourage the use of legal redress procedures. On the face of it, parents in LA1 were given all the information they needed to appeal. They were informed of their right to appeal, and after the delivery of the draft statement were offered two meetings with a senior official in addition to access to a Parent Partnership Officer. If a resolution was not reached after these meetings, parents were told that they could begin appeals proceedings. However, it was evident that few parents found the appeal route particularly attractive. Unlike more socially advantaged authorities, in LA1 there were few support groups or voluntary organisations, and parents lacked the backup necessary to launch a successful appeal. Parents did have access to a Parent Partnership Officer, but the worker in this post concentrated on explaining what the local authority was doing, rather than suggesting alternatives. Very few parents appointed a Named Person to act as independent advocate.

Psychologists in Scottish LA3 found themselves pulled in different directions by the conflicting expectations that they could act both as honest brokers, giving parents the best possible advice about their children's needs, and as agents of the authority, chairing the meetings and drafting the record in terms of the resources available to the authority. It was acknowledged by psychologists that they were told not to quantify resources on the document. As a result, while a lot of resources were devoted to assessing the child's needs, the record was often bland and meaningless. In contrast, while noting that the SEN budget was constantly overspent, the senior officer insisted that resourcing in this area was 'needs-led'.

Not surprisingly, parents were somewhat confused about the purpose of the record and their role within the process:

> I thought they wanted, like, my input on it, but it wisnae, it was just if I agreed with what they wrote, then you didn't have to write anything, just sign it. But if I didnae agree, then write whit I didnae agree on. I didnae know – cause it was all mumbo jumbo . . . . I thought it [the record of needs] was nonsense an' awe for the whole time it took and I was like, 'Whit the hell is this?' It's rubbish, pure absolute rubbish that's in it. I don't know if it's awe there, or if that's even the kind of copy I got. I never really opened it.

Views like this were typically understood by EPs as evidence that the process was too bureaucratic and difficult for parents to understand. However, this parent's perception that the record had no clear purpose was borne out by the conflicting statements by the EPs and senior officer.

Relationship between education officers and psychologists

In LA1, EPs described themselves as operating as independent agents. They provided important advice to the LEA officers, but did not make the final decision on whether to open a statement nor did they draft the statement itself. Despite this independence, a large number of appeals would undoubtedly have added to the EPs' workload and therefore it was not in their interests to encourage parents to appeal, but rather to accept a place in their neighbourhood mainstream school. This was in line with existing local authority provision; thus, conflict between officer and EPs was avoided.

In LA3, there was a greater degree of conflict between professionals and managers. While EPs complained about the 'raging ambiguity of our position', the senior officer felt that since EPs were employed by the authority it was quite reasonable that they should comply with the authority's guidelines on SEN provision. Medical officers, who had controlled the process of assessment prior to the Warnock legislation, were told that they should simply assess the child's health and not make any recommendations on educational provision.

Overall, LAs 1 and 3 were similar with regard to their high levels of poverty and social disadvantage. Whereas English national policy gave considerable power to parents in assessment and statementing procedures, parents in LA1 were largely disengaged from the process and did not make use of their legal rights of appeal. While formal systems existed to empower parents, EPs and officers were, to some extent complicit in parental passivity.

Scottish SEN policy provided fewer opportunities for parental engagement in the process, and in LA3 professionals downplayed opportunities for involvement even further. The process of opening a record tended to be seen as a formality, with no commitment on the authority's part to provide any resources. Tensions between EPs and education officers were apparent, the former resenting their co-option into a bureaucratic system over which they had no control.

We now present three case studies which illustrate the ways in which parents interacted with the policy frameworks in the English and Scottish authorities.

Rose – (LAI): parent as (tentative) consumer

Rose was aged six and a half at the time of the research and was attending a mainstream infant school. She lived with her father, mother and two older sisters in a terraced house. The family was in the process of selling the house and moving out of town to a nearby village.

From an early stage in her development, Rose's mother felt that her daughter was not developing normally and was frustrated when first the health visitor and then the school appeared unwilling to take her concerns seriously. She instigated the process of assessment, lobbied for the acceleration of the school-based stages and obtained independent assessments to challenge the LA's view of Rose's needs.

Keeping careful notes on her personal computer, Rose's mother had written to and telephoned the LA, taken her daughter to the Dyslexia Unit in another town for assessment, asked for help from the school nurse, approached the IPSEA, sought additional medical assessments including a brain scan and engaged an active Named Person. Throughout the process, Rose's mother was frustrated by the LA's inefficiency. One of her letters, requesting the commencement of a statutory assessment, was 'mysteriously lost', giving the LA additional time to draft the statement.

On her statement, Rose's special needs are described as 'deficits in attention, motor control and perceptions' (DAMP), an unusual diagnosis perhaps reflecting the wide range of professionals drawn into the assessment at the parents' insistence. Rose's mother made it clear that she perceived herself to be fighting for her child's rights and challenging the complacency of the LEA:

> I have felt involved because I've made myself involved . . . . You do it for your child; at the end of the day I'll do anything for my children. And it motivates me to fight for her because she was so unhappy at that point at school.
>
> (Mother)

The written contribution to the assessment made by Rose's mother reminded the LA of its legal duties and chided them for their impersonal approach:

> As Rose's parents, it is our responsibility to see Rose gets the education, by law, she is entitled to. She is our daughter and we love her very much. We feel very strongly about her receiving help quickly. She can get stressed and I am afraid of this affecting her physically making her ill. I will not allow this.
>
> I would just like to add how very disappointed I am at your very poor response to my letters. The two letters I have received from you have been standard letters. I even asked for comments from you on my last letter and yet still no response. I understand that you are very busy but this is no excuse for common courtesy.
>
> (Parental contribution to statutory assessment)

Ultimately, this case was not taken to appeal, although at various stages it was evident that this might have happened. In her statement, Rose was allocated 17.5 hours of support per week individually or in a small group to be delivered by a Curriculum Support Assistant under the direction of the class teacher. Rose's mother had initially requested additional support from a trained teacher, but eventually accepted this compromise. Clearly positioning herself as service consumer and rejecting the position of client, Rose's mother was simply concerned to get the best possible provision for her child. While drawing on the expertise of voluntary organisations, Rose's mother did not wish herself to become involved in discussion or action beyond her immediate concerns.

Jane (LAI): the disengaged parent

The second case study in the English authority illustrates the limits of a consumer or partnership approach. Jane was six years of age at the time of the research. She lived at home with her parents and two older siblings. One of Jane's older siblings had been excluded from school because, according to her mother, she had a pierced eyebrow. The family lived in poor quality local authority housing.

Jane had epilepsy and the statement noted that she had poor language development and difficulty in relating to her peers. Her parents were concerned about her slow progress at school. Her mother commented:

> I just want her to get as much help as she can 'cos she's behind. And like I say, it's not fair her being so behind in the class.

The parents' contribution to the assessment, written by the headteacher on their behalf, noted:

> We just can't understand why she is not making any progress in school, when she seems to be trying.

According to the school, the assessment had proceeded normally and they were satisfied with the outcome of '12.5 hours of support per week from a Curriculum Support Assistant who will work with her individually or in small group situations'. However, it was clear that the parents had been unable to engage in the process. There was concern that Jane had not been presented at a medical assessment and the Educational Welfare Officer had intervened to tell the parents that they were obliged to do this and legal action would be taken if they did not comply. LEA officers were clear that the statement and all reports had been sent to the parents, and the draft statement had been signed by Jane's mother, but she insisted that she had never seen any of these papers. Jane's parents said that if dissatisfied with their daughter's education, they would 'take things further', but were not clear about what course of action this might involve. Jane's mother said she found it easier to communicate with her general practitioner than the school.

Clearly, these parents were regarded as passive recipients of welfare services by the professionals who worked with them. The parents' response was to opt out of the process entirely, denying any knowledge of assessments and correspondence and refusing to take their child for a medical assessment until compelled to do so. Professionals were perceived as punitive rather than benign agents of the state. In order for them to be more actively involved as service consumers or as active citizens, far greater support from the LA would be necessary to overcome the effects of poverty and exclusion. Professionals, however, felt that they had taken all reasonable steps to engage with this family and, while they were concerned about the family's lack of engagement, did not know what else they could do, particularly given the multiple pressures on their time. This case exemplifies the danger of making individual professionals responsible for counteracting the effects of deeprooted social and economic exclusion.

[...]

Ben – LA3: the transgressive parent

Most parents in LA3 adopted the position of passive recipient of services, even if this was at first resisted. However, there were examples of parents who vigorously contested the authority's control. Because parents were expected to accept the views of the educational psychologist and senior education officer, there was considerable consternation when these were challenged and no conciliation system was in place to defuse the situation.

Ben was six years old at the time of the research and had two brothers. The family lived in a deprived area of the city in local authority accommodation. All three children had special needs. Before starting nursery, Ben was diagnosed as autistic with language and communication, social and behavioural difficulties.

Ben's mother was an assertive single parent who wished to get the best for her children and felt she was being manipulated into acquiescence by the authority. She was aware that all her children had special needs, and felt that they should be educated in the same school to maintain the strong bond between them. The authority felt that the children had different needs and therefore should be educated in different locations.

The process of assessment and recording began just before Ben was due to start school. At first, Ben's mother felt confused by the procedures, although she did not like the authority's approach:

> They had told me right up until this year that a record of needs was their choice. The education department were doing me a favour more or less opening a record of needs.
>
> (Ben's mother)

For example, she turned up at a meeting which she believed was to review Ben's progress only to discover that it was to discuss the draft record of needs. She discovered that while the professionals in attendance had all been given copies of the assessment reports, she did not have these documents. After this meeting, she decided to seek independent advice:

> ...so that was when I said to ICSEA [Independent Centre for Special Education Advice; the Scottish equivalent of IPSEA] 'Can I send you this draft copy, can you have a look at it and tell me what's missing?', and she said 'Everything'.

Ben's mother was told by ICSEA that she was entitled to see all assessment reports and at this point she began a telephone and letter writing campaign aimed at forcing the authority to share all information about her child with her. Many requests were necessary to get all assessment reports from the authority. Subsequently, she queried the terms of the record. For example, in Part 5 (measures proposed by the authority to meet the child's SEN), under the 'Other Services' heading, the record stated:

- Community medical officer and links with hospital service.
- Access to physiotherapy and occupational therapy according to changing needs.
- Speech and language therapist as part of a multi-disciplinary team.

According to Ben's mother, she was forced to ask the ICSEA representative to explain what the record meant:

> And I said to her . . . what is this [record] supposed to have, because the psychologist hisnae told me and I thought that's what she was there for, to take us through this and what each part meant and everything. But it disnae even say on this that he needs speech and language therapy and how many times a week he is going to get it. Em, his physiotherapy, I mean they just say that it will be deemed appropriate, but as far as I'm concerned that is not right. He was supposed to get occupational therapy when he started school in August, and he's never been assessed in school yet. So . . . if they say he needs occupational therapy and it's been deemed appropriate, . . . they should agree that he either needs it or he doesn't need it and when he was going to get it and how much he would get.

She also pointed to the lack of clarity in the summary of impairments section, suggesting that it was not enough simply to describe a child as 'autistic', without specifying how this manifested itself. At one point Ben's mother had taken her children out of school in protest and the case had featured in the local press.

The response of the education authority was first to question the purpose of the record:

> I think there's pressure from people who assume the document brings all sorts of additional resources when in fact it doesn't. It is not a resource document.
> (Educational Psychologist)

In addition, doubt was cast on the motives of Ben's mother:

> I would not underestimate the power of the media in that she has got into that sort of groove if you like matched perhaps with an aspect of her own personality that has become rigid and rather tunnel visioned. She is having to go down a route and I don't think she is thinking clearly about the rights – the

needs of her children . . . . She is an articulate lady and she is taking other people along with her and I think the need she is expressing is filling a need in herself.

(Educational Psychologist)

It was evident that the case was causing considerable strain to the Senior Education Officer who said that she had never had her judgement questioned in this way before. Ben's mother was aware that the authority was concerned that she would make a formal appeal on both the school placement and the terms of the record. The nature of the authority's reaction, particularly when compared with the routine nature of appeals in many English authorities, indicates that appeals are regarded far more seriously in Scotland perhaps because they are so rare. Most authorities do not have conciliation procedures and therefore as soon as a parent embarks on an appeal it is likely that it will be taken to the LA appeals committee and subsequently to Scottish ministers. If a Scottish parent adopts the position of consumer, then many LAs in Scotland treat this as an aberration. Lacking conciliation procedures, education officers feel extremely vulnerable and uncertain about how to respond.

Conclusion

This chapter has illustrated the tensions between different policy frameworks in local authorities in England and Scotland. In England, traditional forms of bureaucracy and professionalism have been challenged by legality and consumerism. In Scotland, professionalism is still the dominant motif, although in LA3 EPs appeared to be operating as 'bureau–professionals' (Exworthy and Halford, 1999) rather than independent advisers of parents and children. Despite the fact that parents were actively deterred from adopting the position of consumer, there appear to be fears at authority level that the system is becoming too 'adversarial', prompting moves by the Association of Principal Educational Psychologists to abolish the process of recording.

Policy formation and implementation are clearly dynamic processes. Politicians attempt to implement policy objectives which accord with their broader goals, and these are transformed as they are implemented at local levels. Within each of our case study local authorities, elements of professionalism, bureaucracy and consumerism could be observed. While efforts have been made to empower consumers, particularly in England, our case studies illustrate the factors which prevent parents from exercising control. Professionals may resist attempts to regulate their actions and parents may be unable to adopt the role of critical consumer because of structural constraints. Viewed as a broad topography, English and Scottish SEN frameworks appear to be diverging even further following devolution. However, a closer look indicates that each has a mixture of elements, and parents and professionals sometimes challenge the framework within which they are operating.

It is also evident that, within any system, there is likely to be considerable variation in the experiences of individual families . . . .

Overall, our study illustrates the importance of charting the emergence of contrasting national policies following devolution, but also shows the importance of examining fine grained experience at local level.

References

Deakin, N. (1994) *The Politics of Welfare: Continuities and Change*, London: Harvester Wheatsheaf.

DES (Department for Education and Science) (1978) *Special Educational Needs* (Warnock Report), London: HMSO.

DfE (Department for Education) (1994) *Code of Practice on the Identification and Assessment of Special Educational Needs*, London: DfE.

Exworthy, M. and Halford, S. (1999) (eds) *Professionals and the New Managerialism in the Public Sector*, Buckingham: Open University Press.

McPherson, A. and Raab, C.D. (1988) *Governing Education*, Edinburgh: Edinburgh University Press.

Pateman, C. (1989) *The Disorder of Women*, Cambridge: Polity Press.

Phillips, A. (1993) *Democracy and Difference*, Cambridge: Polity Press.

SOEID (Scottish Office Education and Industry Department) (1998) *A Manual of Good Practice in Special Educational Needs*, Edinburgh: HMSO.

Vincent, C. (2000) *Including Parents? Education, Citizenship and Parental Agency*, London: Open University Press.

Chapter 8

Comparison of a traditional and an inclusive secondary school culture

Suzanne Carrington and John Elkins

Introduction

A number of writers have analysed schools' responses to student diversity from organizational and sociological perspectives (e.g. Bines, 1986; Skrtic, 1991; Carroll, 1992; Dyson, 1992; McIntyre, 1993). These writers have begun to demonstrate how the organization of schools underpins the models of service delivery to students . . . . (I)t seems likely that teachers' collective understandings about students with different learning needs (Idol *et al.*, 1994; Bender *et al.*, 1995) and inclusive schooling (Forlin *et al.*, 1996; Scruggs and Mastropieri, 1996) are likely to impact on teaching practices in a school organization.

[. . .]

Australian attempts to educate students with disabilities in regular schools can be traced back more than 30 years. Policy recommendations to increase funding for integration were made by Andrews *et al.* (1979) and taken up by the Commonwealth Schools Commission. A valiant attempt to move Victorian state schools towards inclusion was made with the release of a report on Integration in Victorian Education (1984), though it did not have much effect on the number of special schools. Rather, it created a class of 'integration students' and 'integration staff' somewhat out of keeping with the spirit of the report.

In Australia, it was the introduction of anti-discrimination legislation that has enabled parents and disability advocacy groups to challenge the exclusion of students from regular schools (both public and private).

[. . .]

Secondary schools: traditional school culture

A more traditional culture in a secondary school frequently emphasizes content rather than student needs, and, as a result, accommodations for individual needs of students are frequently not top priorities for teachers and administrators (Tralli *et al.*, 1996). Consequently, in a more traditional secondary school organization, all students will not match society's expectations of success in school. This is because the organizational characteristics of the more traditional secondary school do not cater to different learning needs. Rather, the focus is on the transmission of a set curriculum content that is organized in routine ways by teachers who usually work in isolation (Clark *et al.*, 1999). In a traditional model, class teachers may identify students who have different learning needs from the majority, and refer them to a specialist teacher. The responsibility for school success for such students is then transferred away from the class teacher. This movement of responsibility for students from regular education to special education has prevented regular educators from problem solving and developing more innovative teaching methods to meet students' needs.

The maintenance of a traditional school organization that is content focused creates a barrier to recognition of problems and experimentation with alternative ways of organizing schools that are necessary in meeting the needs of diverse learners.

[. . .]

Secondary schools: inclusive school culture

It has been suggested that teachers who work in successful inclusive schools have an explicit value base that provides a platform for inclusive practices (Salisbury *et al.*, 1993; York-Barr *et al.*, 1996). Inclusive school cultures value diversity. In Barton's (1997, p. 235) words, 'difference is now to be viewed as a challenge, a means of generating change and an encouragement for people to question unfounded generalisations, prejudice and discrimination'. It should allow students with extraordinary gifts and talents to move at their natural learning rate; students who are average and slower than average to learn to the best of their ability, and students with specific learning needs to receive creative and effective supports to maximize their success. Above all, inclusion is about a philosophy of acceptance where all people are valued and treated with respect.

[. . .]

Models of support for learners with diverse learning needs

The contributing characteristics of a school culture, such as teachers' beliefs and attitudes about roles and responsibilities of teaching, influence the ways students are taught and correspondingly the model of supporting students with diverse learning needs (Carrington, 2000). There is no one accepted model for organizing support for students with different learning needs in secondary schools, however, some models could be described as more inclusive and some as more traditional. In reflecting on practices and models for supporting learners in schools, Ainscow (1996) noted that there were different patterns of relations between staff and students.

The more traditional model has been a withdrawal system or pullout programme where students are extracted from class for supplementary instruction by special education teachers. Some schools have part-time special classes for students with significant learning or adjustment problems and some schools have full-time special education classes. Programmes using volunteer helpers, teacher aides and peer tutors are also ways of supporting students with special learning needs. Some schools use ability grouping in some subjects, particularly maths. Some schools provide specialist teaching support for students and teachers in the regular classroom. Frequently, it is a combination of these types of programmes that provide support in learning for students.

[. . .]

Secondary schools: inclusive model of support

In-class support for students with different learning needs has become more common (Lavers *et al.*, 1986) and can be described as more inclusive. Research has highlighted the need for the child with different learning needs to be included in the regular classroom with support from a specialist teacher (Englert *et al.*, 1992; Dyson, 1994; Idol *et al.*, 1994). The student is provided with access to a broader pedagogy and this inclusive model has obvious benefits not only for the students with special needs, but also for the whole school.

[. . .]

However, in-class support may not automatically result in benefits for teachers and students. This is because an inclusive model needs to focus not only on support of individual children in regular classrooms but also needs to include an examination and redevelopment of teaching and learning styles across the curriculum. Students can be supported in a regular classroom that continues to offer unchanged pedagogy and curriculum. This type of support can in fact contribute to the learning difficulty. Therefore, in some cases, it seems that in-class support may actually exclude students more from accessing the curriculum.

[. . .]

In an inclusive model, the support role of the specialist teacher must extend beyond support provided to students in an individual lesson. Joint planning and collaboration are necessary so that teachers have opportunities to bring their knowledge and skills together and the support teacher can make valuable input to the subject departments with rippling effects to other staff (Beveridge, 1993). The needs of the teachers must be considered alongside the needs of the students (Larcombe, 1987). This is crucial to prevent the possibility of the regular classroom teacher accepting support in his or her classroom to avoid the necessity of changing his or her teaching practice. In this situation, the special education teacher continues to 'deal with' the special learning problems of a student and is responsible for them (Bines, 1986). An inclusive school system would enable *diverse* individuals to participate in *common* educational experiences (Dyson, 1994).

Description of this study

The case study data reported here were collected within the context of a larger research project. The aim of this project was to compare the school culture and model of learning support of two secondary schools in Brisbane. One school could be described as more traditional and the other school as more inclusive. The school principals, special education staff and a sample of four regular teaching staff at each school were participants in the study. Qualitative data were collected over a year (6 months in each school).

[. . .]

School settings

The secondary schools selected provided two different service delivery models for supporting students with special learning needs. The first school provided mainly in-class support for students and collaborative planning support for teachers and will be called Yarra Secondary School (pseudonyms have been used for the schools). This school is a co-educational institution situated in Brisbane. The community consists of a diversity of socio-economic, ethnic and cultural backgrounds, and the school prospectus reports that about 12 per cent of students come from non-English-speaking countries. The school offers a wide range of subject offerings and vocational-oriented subjects are also included in the school's curriculum. The school has a flexible senior schooling programme, which includes independent learning and individualized instruction. Student numbers are about 500 and there are 40 teachers in the school. The community is very supportive of the school with parents involved on all committees.

At the time of the study, the school had a number of students in the school who required special assistance in learning. Many of these students had difficulties with the regular secondary school curriculum. For some students, English was a second language. As one teacher said '[these] students 10 or 15 years ago would have left school and would be out doing physical work and they would have been good at it'. The principal believed the number of students experiencing learning difficulties was increasing. The school also had what the special education teacher described as a 'small group of special needs students'. This group of students included two students who had been diagnosed with Asperger's syndrome and three students who had been ascertained[1] as having an intellectual disability. By contrast, the principal also described a group of students who were very capable and motivated in the school.

Moffat Secondary School, the second school, withdrew students from class for tutorial assistance and offered a number of special classes with a modified curriculum. Some students in the lower grades of the secondary school were offered in-class support which involved a regular class teacher sitting with them in classes. Moffat Secondary School serves a community that consists of a broad cross-section of society and includes a wide range of socio-economic, ethnic and cultural backgrounds. Student enrolment is 1,250 and there are 80 staff members. The school also provides a wide range of subjects similar to those at Yarra and offers an increasing number of vocational subjects in Years 11 and 12. Students are encouraged to be well motivated with a positive attitude towards education. The school takes pride in high academic standards and high standards of behaviour.

At the time of this study, there was a range of students who needed assistance at Moffat. Many had problems with learning due to learning difficulties or difficulties associated with learning in the English language. There were three students with intellectual impairment, one with visual impairment and two who had been diagnosed with Asperger's syndrome.

[. . .]

Findings and discussion

The schools were compared across selected categories that emerged in the interview data to demonstrate the differences in school culture and organization of models of support. The following categories will be discussed: (1) model of support and the role of the special educator; (2) student-focused culture or content-focused culture; and (3) beliefs and attitudes relating to inclusive schooling and teacher responsibility for catering to diverse learning needs.

[. . .]

Model of support and the role of the special educator

The model of support for students with different learning needs at Yarra included a broad range of alternatives for students and teachers. These included special funded programmes, teacher aide support in class, streamed classes, non-streamed classes with class teacher support, in-class support from a special education teacher, small tutor groups, some students missing enrolment in one subject so that they could access extra support in literacy and many students enrolling in non-board vocational subjects. It was interesting to note that there was no 'Resource Room' or 'Learning Support Centre' at Yarra. Students and staff worked across the school campus usually in the mainstream classrooms.

The special educator's role within this school included a broad range of activities with a major focus on professional development and training for staff across the school.

[. . .]

The special education teacher at Yarra described her aim to achieve major changes in teaching and assessment practices in the school, which would enable teachers to meet the diverse learning needs of the students more effectively. To achieve these goals, she worked with the heads of curriculum departments. Some of these programmes focused on the learning needs of students who were high achievers. However, she believed that raising the awareness of different learning needs would help teachers address the learning needs of students in general.

The special education teacher described her goal of assisting teachers to develop the skills of planning for a diverse class rather than simply modifying teaching in the classroom.

[...]

At Moffat, the range of support for different learning needs also included teacher aide support in class, non-streamed classes with extra teacher support, in-class support from the special education teacher, small tutor groups or individual assistance from the special education teacher, modified English classes (streamed) and some students missing a timetabled subject so that they could access extra support in literacy. Students were also able to enrol in non-board subjects similar to those offered at Yarra.

However, the special education teachers at Moffat worked differently in comparison with the model of support at Yarra. For example, at Moffat, one special education teacher worked from a 'Resource Room', which was used to conduct assessments of students' literacy skills. The room was also used for individual and small group instruction for students who had been referred by their teachers. This special education teacher provided streamed classes for students with learning difficulties in English.

[...]

The streaming of the English classes was supported by the head of the English department who said, 'We do the English syllabus but in a modified manner . . . all the other classes benefit because they don't have the bottom weighting them down.' Labelling and grouping students according to ability does not fit with an inclusive approach and therefore could be described as more traditional.

The second special education teacher at Moffat was based in a regular staffroom and worked mainly with the lower school. She coordinated the ascertainment process for students and the allocated government support from teacher aides. She was also responsible for the organization of an additional programme of support in the lower school. This programme involved regular class teachers, who did not have full teaching timetables, working in classes where students needed extra assistance.

This programme of support within the regular classroom seemed inclusive but after observing the in-class support and discussing the process with staff it became clear that it could not be described as inclusive practice. For example, on one occasion the researcher observed a science class where a regular class teacher was timetabled to support three students. These students were sitting at the back of the class and working on a task with the supporting teacher. The regular class teacher did not include the students and the support teacher in the regular science lesson that was taught for the remainder of the class.

[. . .]

The lack of responsibility for individual learners' needs and commitment to modification of the curriculum is evident in a quote from the special education teacher, 'If I come up with a suggestion for a class teacher, as long as I do all the little bits and pieces that might be annoyances if I can present them [the teachers] with something and say I've taken care of this, I have no problems whatsoever, as long as I don't put any impositions on their time or anything like that.' This implies that the class teachers wished to carry on with their regular teaching with as little disruption as possible and were not really taking responsibility for all learners in their classes. This is a characteristic of the traditional model (Wilson, 1984).

One of the special education teachers at Moffat summarized her role by saying, 'A lot of my work is administrative with timetabling, running seminars, keeping track of the students who have got learning difficulties, making sure that things are going right for them, writing IEPs, modifying exams, modifying content, and providing and helping teachers do modified worksheets.' These special education administration duties could also be described as traditional in nature.

Student-focused culture or content-focused culture

Interview data indicated that Yarra was more student focused in culture in comparison with Moffat, which was more content focused. These issues were evident in teacher's views about the students and in discussions about the school curriculum. For example, at Moffat, teachers spoke of the rigid structure of the curriculum, the high value placed on academic excellence in the school and the expectation that 80 per cent of students would achieve a passing grade . . . . Data from Yarra . . . which indicate a developing focus of students' needs. For example, one teacher spoke of the change that had occurred in the school. 'I think the staff attitude is changing over the last few years towards more acceptance of these kids . . . previously we would still [be] deluding ourselves to trying to push the academic nature of the school.'

[. . .]

With regard to the curriculum restraints mentioned in the data from Moffat, the focus on curriculum was different at Yarra. Teachers recognized that there were problems with the curriculum, but teachers were working in different ways to modify it to meet students' learning needs. An example is included here from one teacher:

Yes there are curriculum constraints, you are expected to get through a certain amount of economics or social science or English or whatever it is, but to tell you the truth, I don't really. As far as curriculum things go, I like to change things as we come along and particularly you can't really do it when you've got the 12s [the senior year], but I think that every other year you can. You can follow the students' interest areas far more, so if they really like a particular aspect of weather for example, then you can go off and you can look at that in depth.

Beliefs and attitudes relating to inclusive schooling and teacher responsibility for catering for diverse learning needs

Staff at both schools expressed different types of views on teaching students with different learning abilities. Yarra staff seemed to accept that the current school population included students with a broad range of abilities from a broad range of backgrounds. The teachers knew that they needed to adapt the teaching and curriculum to meet the learners' needs. Some staff were not particularly happy about this because it meant changing teaching strategies and presentation of content but they accepted this change as necessary . . . . The positive attitude was also explained by the special education teacher at Yarra who stated that 'teachers are generally really supportive and inclusive and agree these students have the right to be here' . . . . (O)ne teacher said, 'Multiculturalism: we are supportive of each other, we are tolerant of each other. You have these children from all these different cultures.' Indeed one teacher remarked that the staff could learn much from the students, 'you have a staff who are supposed to be leading and managing this group of children who do not exhibit one tenth of what these children do on inclusivity'.

The inclusive views at Yarra are in contrast to the views expressed by the Moffat staff. One teacher from Moffat revealed, 'We don't accept "learning disability kids," we tell the parents that we cannot cater for the kids with learning problems here . . .'.

The principal reinforced the focus on high academic achievement and appropriate behaviour:

> Basically our mission is to ensure all students reach their full potential and then we say . . . that we value academic achievement, behaviour, discipline, presentation and they're the three things I suppose that we push all the time if you ask the teacher or you ask a student they'll come up with those three things. In terms of academic focus, we get kids to set goals and study plans and we check homework and all that type of thing.

The principal expressed support for inclusion in his interview. However, the traditional focus on academic achievement and delivery of a set curriculum meant that students' learning needs were not met in practice in the regular classroom.

[. . .]

This study suggests that students may be accepted into a class but may not have their learning needs met effectively if the teacher does not believe that she or he is responsible for teaching all students in their classroom.

Summary

Differences in data from each school, across the described categories, have been presented. In particular, there were notable contrasts in the service delivery models of support for learners. Collective beliefs and values relating to teachers' roles and responsibilities, affected school organization of teaching and support for students in each school.

At Yarra, there was evidence to suggest that the special education teacher was restructuring her role and weakening the boundaries between special needs provision and mainstream teaching. She was frequently involved in joint curriculum projects with regular classroom teachers. Organizational conditions were in place to allow discussion and sharing between teachers. This enabled opportunities for teachers to question existing practice, review performance, encourage experimentation and work across boundaries.

[. . .]

In contrast, the more traditional system at Moffat perpetuated the conceptualization of difference and maintained the status quo in teaching methods and school structure. Students with different learning needs provide an opportunity for a school organization to learn about the limitations in current practice and to create new knowledge and skills that are needed to include all students (Dyson, 1994). However, if schools maintain the traditional practices of teaching and models of support, there may be little opportunity for innovation and change.

[. . .]

The process of working towards inclusive school development will involve opportunities for teachers, students, and the community to collaborate, solve problems and develop greater respect for each other. The values and beliefs embedded in more inclusive practices create a new set of possibilities, expectations and commitments. This change will demand a series of deconstructions and reconstructions of beliefs and knowledge, rather than transformations of traditional beliefs, knowledge and practices (Skrtic, 1991). Above all, the school community will need to develop a shared vision or philosophy that will enable them to move out of the boundaries of traditional school organization and practice.

Note

1 A process in Queensland called 'ascertainment' is used to recommend the level of specialist educational support needed by students who have disabilities.

References

Ainscow, M. (1996) Inclusion: how do we measure up? Paper presented at the Forum on Inclusive Education, Bardon, Brisbane, 26 April.

Andrews, R.J., Elkins, J., Berry, P.B. and Burge, J.A. (1979) *A Survey of Special Education in Australia: Provisions, Needs and Priorities in the Education of Students with Handicaps and Learning Difficulties* (St Lucia, Qld: Fred and Eleanor Schonell Educational Research Centre).

Barton, L. (1997) Inclusive education: romantic, subversive or realistic? *International Journal of Inclusive Education*, **1**, 231–242.

Bender, W.N., Vail, C.O. and Scott, K. (1995) Teachers' attitudes toward increased mainstreaming: Implementing effective instruction for students with learning disabilities. *Journal of Learning Disabilities*, **28**, 87–94.

Beveridge, S. (1993) *Special Educational Needs in Schools* (London: Routledge).

Bines, H. (1986) *Redefining Remedial Education* (Beckenham: Croom Helm).

Carrington, S. (2000) Accommodating the needs of diverse learners: the impact of teachers' beliefs on classroom practice. Unpublished doctoral thesis, University of Queensland.

Carroll, T.G. (1992) The role of anthropologists in restructuring schools. In G.A. Hess (ed.), *Empowering Teachers and Parents: School Restructuring Through the Eyes of Anthropologists* (Westport: Bergin & Garvey).

Clark, C., Dyson, A., Milward, A. and Robson, S. (1999) Theories of inclusion, theories of schools: deconstructing and reconstructing the 'inclusive school'. *British Educational Research Journal*, **25**, 157–177.

Dyson, A. (1992) Innovatory mainstream practice: what's happening in schools' provision for special needs? *Support for Learning*, **7**, 51–57.

Dyson, A. (1994) Towards a collaborative, learning model for responding to student diversity. *Support for Learning*, **9**, 53–60.

Englert, C.S., Tarrant, K.L. and Mariage, T.V. (1992) Defining and redefining instructional practice in special education; perspectives on good teaching. *Teacher Education and Special Education*, **15**, 62–86.

Forlin, C., Douglas, G. and Hattie, J. (1996) Inclusive practices: how accepting are teachers? *International Journal of Disability*, **43**, 119–133.

Idol, L., Nevin, A. and Paolucci-Whitcomb, P. (1994) *Collaborative Consultation* (Austin: Pro-Ed).

Integration in Victorian Education (1984) *Report of the Ministerial Review of Education Services for the Disabled* (Melbourne: Government Printer).

Larcombe, T. (1987) *Learning Difficulties in the Secondary School* (Oxford: Oxford University Press).

Lavers, P., Pickup, M. and Thomson, M. (1986) Factors to consider in implementing an in-class support system. *Support for Learning*, **1**, 32–35.

McIntyre, D. (1993) Special needs and standard provision. In A. Dyson and C. Gains (eds), *Rethinking Special Needs in Mainstream Schools: Towards the Year* 2000 (London: David Fulton).

Salisbury, C.L., Palombaro, M.M. and Hollowood, T.M. (1993) On the nature and change of an inclusive elementary school. *Journal of the Association for Persons with Severe Handicaps*, **18**, 75–84.

Scruggs, T.E. and Mastropieri, M.A. (1996) Teacher perceptions of mainstreaming/inclusion, 1958–1995: a research synthesis. *Exceptional Children*, **63**, 59–74.

Skrtic, T.M. (1991) *Behind Special Education: A Critical Analysis of Professional Culture and School Orgnization* (Denver, co: Love).

Tralli, R., Colombo, B., Deshler, D.D. and Schumaker, J.B. (1996) The strategies intervention model a model for supported inclusion at the secondary level. *Remedial and Special Education*, **17**, 204–216.

Wilson, A.K. (1984) 'Integration' means putting resources not pupils, into regular classrooms. *B. C. Journal of Special Education*, **8**, 231–245.

York-Barr, J., Schultz, T., Doyle, M., Kronberg, R. and Crossett, S. (1996) Inclusive schooling in St. Cloud. *Remedial and Special Education*, **17**, 92–105.

Chapter 9

Exclusions from school

Different voices

Jean Kane

School exclusions in Scotland

Procedures

In Scotland, two categories of exclusion, temporary exclusion and 'removed from
the register' (of the current school), are recognized in the regulations governing
school exclusions (Schools General (Scotland) Regulations, 1975). The period of
exclusion for particular kinds of misbehaviour is not prescribed but Local Authorities usually place a ceiling of twenty school days on the term of the exclusion, with
pupils being asked to leave the school for a period of between two days and four
weeks depending upon the nature of the incident. Schools would usually develop
their own 'tariff' system where offences judged to be less serious, or first misde-
meanours, would be punished with periods of up to three days. The tariff would
usually rise on each subsequent occasion if the pupil were judged to have again
breached the disciplinary code. The lack of regulation of the period of exclusions
leads to inequities with the same or similar 'offence' attracting widely differing pun-
ishments depending upon the school, the pupil, the teachers involved and other
factors. While this situation leads to unfairness, it is also seen (by professionals) as
having a positive side, as it allows schools to respond flexibly and in ways which
take account of factors such as the personal circumstances of the pupil, as well as
the seriousness of the disciplinary incident. SEED guidelines endorse the use of
professional judgement:

> Education authorities and schools, when deciding whether exclusion is nec-
> essary must have regard to the particular facts and circumstances surrounding
> individual incidents and/or pupils.
>
> (SEED, 2002, 2: 10)

The second type of exclusion practised in Scotland – 'removed from the register'
of the school – is utilized where the offence is regarded as serious, or where a particular pupil has had a number of previous temporary exclusions for earlier breaches
of the code. In such cases and within the four-week period of the exclusion, the

headteacher of the school would be invited to attend a meeting with representatives of the education authority, the pupil, his/her parents and their representatives so that the school placement offered to the pupil might be considered in a welfare as well as a disciplinary light. In spite of the intention to make the interests of the pupil central to the decision about placement, the process sometimes breaks down at this point, for example, when the alternative placement offered to the pupil and his family is unacceptable to them for reasons of distance from the family home. Pupils can therefore be out of the school system for much longer than the period of the original exclusion.

Extent of exclusions in Scotland

Since 1998, when the Scottish Office Education and Industry Department issued Guidance on Issues Concerning Exclusion from School: Circular 2/98 (SOEID, 1998), Local Authorities have been obliged to collect and report exclusions data on an annual basis. In July 2000, the results of the first annual survey of school exclusions were published (SEED, 2000) and the results of subsequent surveys have been published annually since then (SEED, 2001, 2002, 2003). During session 1999/2000 there were 38,769 exclusions from Local Authority schools. Overall in Scotland, this represents an average 51 exclusions per 1,000 pupils but some education authorities excluded with far greater frequency, with the highest rate for the 1999/2000 session recorded as 109 exclusions per 1,000 pupils.

Reasons for exclusion

Young people and children are excluded for widely different reasons – sometimes even for non-attendance (Cooper *et al.*, 2000). Statistics on school exclusions produced by SEED (SEED, 2001) offer information on the circumstances prompting the exclusion. To take one session as an example, in the 1999/2000 school session, there were 42,340 exclusions from Scottish schools, 397 of which were exclusion leading to removal from the register of the school concerned. Of the total number of exclusions, 23.9 per cent ($n = 10,058$) were recorded as being the result of 'general or persistent disobedience', 16.1 per cent ($n = 6,794$) were for verbal abuse of members of staff and 13 per cent ($n = 5,466$) were for the physical abuse of fellow pupils. These three categories are the most frequent reasons for exclusion but the statistics show a range of other categories of behaviour leading to exclusion such as 'aggressive or threatening behaviour' (10.2 per cent or $n = 4,291$); 'insolent or offensive behaviour' (8.8 per cent or $n = 3,733$) and physical abuse of members of staff (2.7 per cent or $n = 1,146$).

Appeals against exclusion

There is no right of appeal at the point of exclusion but the excluded pupil and his family can institute an appeal to the education authority during the period of the exclusion. Few families take up that option. In the session 1999/2000, only 0.3 per cent of exclusions were appealed against (SEED, 2001).

Effects of school exclusion

The cumulative effect on individuals of exclusions is difficult to gauge from official statistics. For example, although SEED statistics (SEED, 2001) show that 9 per cent of those excluded in 1999/2000 were excluded five times or more during that session, the duration of these exclusions is not shown. It is not possible, therefore, to quantify the total number of school days lost to individual pupils in that session. This is unfortunate when the repeated and lengthening exclusion of some individuals is likely to indicate a higher level of social exclusion than that prevailing amongst the 61 per cent of excluded pupils in Scotland who were excluded just once during that same session (SEED, 2001).

A number of commentators (Munn *et al.*, 2000; McDonald and Thomas, 2003) have written of the personal impact of school exclusion not just on pupils but on their families. In these studies, parents are reported as experiencing a strong sense of powerlessness and hurt as a result of their child's exclusion from school.

The research project

Key informant interviews

These interviews were with a series of 'experts', each of whom, by virtue of her/his personal or professional experience, would be able to

- illuminate issues of policy and practice for the researcher;
- allow the identification of strengths and difficulties in current policy;
- assist in directing the fieldwork in schools towards problematic issues.

The interviews were not intended to be a representative sample. Rather, they were organized to allow the research to be informed by a broad range of personal and professional perspectives on exclusions.

Interviews were conducted with seventeen key informants drawn from four areas of the education system: SEED, education authorities, schools and the research community. In schools, interviews were conducted with those with key responsibilities for exclusions and also with young people who had themselves been excluded. Access to the young people was arranged through the agency of the school and the interview in this case was conducted with four young people as a group. All were boys although the request to the school had not stipulated this gender representation. The young people were

Ross
Michael
Robert
Joe.

Methods

All of the interviews were taped and transcribed, with the exception of the interview with SEED officers where permission to tape the proceedings was not granted. The principle of informed consent was observed by providing key informants with a briefing paper about the research and forwarding the appropriate interview schedule in advance of final permission for the interview being given. Payment was made to the young people who participated in their own time (as distinct from professionals who participated as part of their paid employment).

The interview schedules were developed from schedules used in a previous project carried out by the author and colleagues in the case study education authority (Head *et al.*, 2003). The broad themes covered were

> Purposes of exclusions
> Policy on exclusions
> Operation of exclusions procedures
> Effectiveness of exclusions
> Future developments in policy and practice.

The schedules were semi-structured to allow subsequent analysis to compare the perspectives offered, whilst also leaving scope for interviewees to contribute to the process the full breadth of their understandings and expertise. The broad themes of the interview schedules were used as the framework for collating and analysing the transcripts and notes.

Analysis of data

Across the group of key informants seven purposes of exclusion were identified. Some of these purposes were endorsed by all respondents, others were more contentious. The ordering of these purposes below is a rough rank order, intended to reflect the weight of endorsement across the range of key informants. The purposes identified were

> (i) as a signal to the excluded pupil and his/her parents that his/her behaviour was unacceptable
> (ii) as a deterrent to bad behaviour
> (iii) as a means of protecting the continuity of learning and teaching in the classroom/school
> (iv) as respite for other pupils and teachers
> (v) as respite for the excluded pupil
> (vi) as a punishment for wrongdoing
> (vii) as providing a gateway to special provision.

These purposes are discussed in turn with an indication of the key informants' views.

Exclusion as a signal to the pupil and his/her parents

This purpose was cited frequently by professionals in schools and education authorities. Exclusion could be constructive in that it prompted all those concerned to take time to review what had happened and to try to change the young person's behaviour. Senior managers in schools said that an exclusion might be used to attract parental attention where previous attempts at contact had failed: 'They are all going to be grown-ups and they have got to be effective grown-ups. None of this should be about hurting or damaging. It should be about changing' (Assistant Headteacher). Sometimes an exclusion was needed to find out if there were other, deeper reasons for the pupils' behaviour. Then more appropriate support systems could be put in place. By this account, from a school outwith the LA sector, exclusions were not the end point in a hierarchy of sanctions but the means of providing a broad forum for planning the future support of the pupil.

The contention that an exclusion can be used to trigger a more positive and purposeful partnership with the parents concerned is not borne out by studies elsewhere. McDonald and Thomas (2003, p. 116) found that parents' negative experiences of school were intensified when the parents concerned were those of pupils who were excluded. These parents felt that they had no voice in the processes leading to exclusion and neither did their children: 'In not being given a voice the students and parents could not influence the dominant discourse of the school and therefore could not effect any change to the power relations within the schooling system.' Hanafin and Lynch (2002), writing about the involvement in education of working-class parents in Ireland, found that although there was a continuum of parental involvement in schooling (in terms of frequency of contact), parents at both ends of that continuum were unhappy with the quality of their involvement in spite of their clear desire to participate:

> Belying theories of cultural deficit, parents throughout this study have shown themselves interested, informed and concerned regarding their children's education. Failure to participate in the schooling process cannot be attributed to lack of interest among these parents. Responsibility lies with the structures and practices of the school system as it operates, at least in the working-class areas of our community.
>
> (ibid., p. 46)

However, the research discussed here revealed that parental involvement varied considerably between Local Authorities and between schools in the same LA area. Schools in areas of high social exclusion reported great difficulty in involving parents in preventative measures and in securing their support once the decision to exclude had been taken. These difficulties, however, related not just to the school factors noted by Hanafin and Lynch (2002) but to wider economic and cultural circumstances such as access to means of communication:

> A lot of parents either do not have a phone or the number keeps changing or they have not bought a card for their mobile phone. Because our parents are

so poor, I am talking about a lot just now, they have just a mobile phone in the house – there is no land line. It seems to them to be cheaper because you do not have a big bill coming in at the end.

(Assistant Headteacher)

By contrast, representatives of schools serving areas of very low social exclusion reported the wide range of media at their disposal when contacting parents in an emergency – home phone number, work phone number, mobile number, fax number and e-mail address and most of these were available for two parents. This differential access to communications, limits schools' chances of off-setting an exclusion by drawing parents in at an early stage when difficulties arise. In a very tangible sense, there were clearly some parents who were more difficult to 'hook-in'.

Exclusion as a deterrent to bad behaviour

SEED representatives indicated that this was one of two broad purposes to exclusion but emphasized that exclusion for this purpose was always a last resort. It was felt by a number of school respondents that exclusions could operate as a deterrent along with a range of other, lesser, sanctions but that they operated best as a deterrent for those pupils who were rarely, if ever, excluded. This point is borne out by exclusion statistics (SEED, 2001) which show that the majority (61 per cent) of pupils in Scotland who were excluded during the 1999/2000 session were excluded just once (SEED, 2001). However, 9 per cent of those excluded in the same session were excluded five times or more during that session. For these young people, who were repeatedly excluded, the deterrent effect clearly was minimal and, from evidence emerging here, was recognized to be so by the schools concerned. For these young people, exclusions were not a deterrent but a punishment.

The phrase that was used [at an education authority meeting to discuss an exclusion] I had really major concerns with – zero tolerance. We use zero tolerance for violence in this school. I really have doubts about the concept of zero tolerance.

(Principal Teacher of Learning Support)

This raises issues about consistency of policy approaches which aim to tackle school exclusions within a whole framework for tackling social exclusion whilst, at the same time, punishing certain kinds of adolescent behaviour.

Exclusion as a means of protecting learning and teaching in the classroom/school

This was the second broad purpose cited by SEED representatives and this view was supported strongly by school-based key informants. It is separated out here as a purpose distinct from respite, for it was cited in the context of policy on raising attainment where schools saw disruption to learning and teaching as a hindrance to meeting attainment targets. Exclusions could safeguard the progress of other pupils through the curriculum and the young people who were interviewed recognized and sympathized with the view that their exclusion could provide this safeguard:

> But see all of us man, people must get fed up of us because we are bamming up the teacher and they can't get on with their work, know what I mean like? J--- B----, he is dead smart, know what I mean? He likes getting into his work because he likes to get it done, know what I mean? We are all bamming up the teacher, so the teacher's not got time to say like, this is what we are doing, because we are all giving it to him stinking and that is how we get excluded.
>
> (S3 pupil)

With regard to this purpose, exclusions were seen by the pupils interviewed as fair, a way of reconciling conflicting interests in the classroom:

> But if you look at it from the teachers' point of view, you know what I mean, they're fair, because think about sitting in that classroom teaching thirty pupils, man, and they are all sitting bamming you up, know what I mean?

SEED representatives indicated that schools seemed to be experiencing difficulty reconciling policies on inclusion with raising attainment. From the pupils interviewed there were indications that secondary schools in their community were gaining reputations for being good at either inclusion or levels of attainment, but not for both. Two of the boys interviewed had been at denominational primary schools, as well as special SEBD primary schools. At transfer to secondary, they had opted for their current non-denominational secondary school because it was seen as less 'strict':

> Aye, once I was going to St M's but my ma said to come here because it is better for my behaviour. My big sister goes to St M's. She gets a punnie and all that for forgetting a ruler.

The school chosen had also been selected in preference to a nearby non-denominational secondary school: 'I wanted to come here because it has got more help. See, like, if I had gone to R Secondary I would have been made to get out in my first four minutes.' The school chosen by the boys and their families was a New Community School. If families are indeed choosing schools based on their perceptions that different schools offer different kinds of education, schools will function under very different expectations from their communities, and even from the same community. This raises issues about the fairness of judging all schools by the same sets of criteria.

Exclusion as respite for teachers and other pupils

This purpose links to the last one but, from some respondents, the respite provided was not just about protecting learning and teaching but was also a means of removing from the classroom community significant personal and social pressure on others. At the extreme, exclusions could ensure that adults and young people in the classroom no longer had to tolerate on a daily basis the threat and the experience of abusive and aggressive behaviour. Exclusions as serving this purpose were supported strongly by professionals in schools and by education authority staff:

> It is shocking that I have to do it. But if he tells a member of staff to fuck off in front of other children . . . staff are human beings with rights as well. I mean it is totally detrimental to the good order of the school.
>
> (AHT)

Exclusions as respite for the excluded pupil

The LA respondents recognized that exclusions could also provide respite from a difficult situation for the young person himself/herself. The young people interviewed strongly endorsed this view of exclusions and some claimed that they engineered situations in order to gain official leave from school:

Pupil: At times, I've just been cheeky to teachers. One time I battered a wee guy that was taking a liberty . . . it was wee Leslie, man, because he was annoying me. Just to get myself put out of school really.

I: Were you trying to get put out of school?

Pupil: Aye, because I just don't like it. I had just . . . I was off school for about six months or something and I had just come back like that. It was getting up in the morning, you know, you are like that, 'Aw, naw, man, do ah need to go to school?'. And it just puts you in a bad mood and when you come you are just in a bad mood already so you just start annoying teachers and that and you start giving them lip.

This attitude towards exclusion was also expressed by a second boy:

> I started . . . because I didn't want to go to school. Just kept giving lip, and lip, and lip, and I ended up just getting out with a suspension: this was about three days after I just came back to school. So I came back, I just got suspended.
>
> (S2 pupil)

It is possible that there was some bravado in these claims. The boys did not portray themselves as ever having lost control or having reacted in anger to teachers or other pupils. Rather, they represented themselves as always in control and always able to manoeuvre situations to their own advantage. The PT Learning Support interviewed disputed the idea that some children go out to engineer their own exclusion:

> There is a myth that some children, just to get a break from school will try to get excluded. It is not my impression here that pupils go out to set up a situation that may lead to their exclusion. They may lack self-control, or a situation may escalate but it is very rare that a child will provoke exclusion.
>
> (PTLS)

This view was endorsed by an AHT from another LA: 'Like people saying that some children laugh at exclusion, I have yet to hear, to see, a child that is happy to be excluded. I genuinely mean that' (AHT). On the other hand, the boys interviewed had also truanted or excluded themselves from school and so there was evidence of their need for time out of schooling and of their preparedness to achieve this by whatever means they could.

Exclusion as a punishment for wrongdoing

The responses of the pupils were in some ways contradictory in that, as well as being viewed as respite, exclusion was also seen as a form of punishment which blocked off access to an important social forum – school: 'My highest suspension has been ten days and I didn't like it because I was sitting in and I was bored and everybody else was at school.' This view was endorsed by a second pupil, lending weight to the notion that exclusions do act as a deterrent to bad behaviour: 'I have been suspended twice for five days each time. I got snibbed because I got suspended and it was pure boring because nobody was about.'

The deterrent effect seemed to rely on parental cooperation in that young people who were confined to their homes during exclusion were more likely to experience the exclusion as a punishment. There seemed to be differences in the level of parental support schools could expect in the event of an exclusion. One AHT (in LA3) could usually rely on parents reinforcing that the behaviour was unaccepatable: 'It means you have to see their parents and, touch wood, you very seldom find parents complaining about an exclusion' (AHT). Not all schools represented in the key informant interviews experienced the same level of parental support, with a consequent diminution in the impact of the exclusion as a punishment.

Exclusions as a gateway to special provision

An interesting point of difference between secondary-school interviewees and education officer from the same LA was on whether or not exclusions served as a gateway to special provision. Some school respondents saw exclusions as a way of ensuring consideration of placements in the special sector. LA representatives and SEED maintained that there were two quite separate processes governing exclusions and decisions about placement outside mainstream. The PT Learning Support interviewed claimed that exclusions were used as a fast track to secure LA consideration of alternative placement in the special sector or alternative support arrangements. He illustrated this point with reference to an S4 pupil:

> We have considerable doubts as to whether he will get to the end of fourth year in a mainstream school, but the only we can trigger any consideration, any other facility was because of twenty-day exclusion... the only way you can actually say we are really concerned is to use this sledge-hammer approach.

In contrast, the LA representative from this LA emphasized that the Case Conference system was not to be used as a gateway to special provision: 'If a young person's social and emotional and behavioural difficulties are such that specialist provision is required, then those children should not be coming through an exclusion route' (Senior Education Officer). Two of the young people interviewed had themselves spent part of their primary school careers in special SEBD schools subsequent to a number of exclusions from mainstream primary. Some of the blurring of the lines of response to young people with behavioural difficulties might be clarified by new legislation in Scotland (Scottish Executive, 2003) which establishes behavioural difficulties as indicative of additional support needs.

Conclusion

There was significant overlap in perceptions of the purposes of exclusions, for example, in the agreement between professionals and young people that certain kinds of behaviour were unfair to those trying to pursue the curriculum. But there were also interesting differences of view, for example, in the extent to which exclusions could be used as a platform for building constructive responses to some young people.

Whether or not there was agreement about the purposes, though, there was evidence from young people living in an area of high social exclusion that repeated school exclusion challenged for them their sense of belonging to the school community. Even in their understanding that their behaviour interfered with learning and teaching, they identified themselves as being out of harmony with the school's values and norms.

Can schools as they currently function promote social inclusion through the building of social capital? Perhaps the notion of reciprocity between the school and its community will allow for the pursuit of shared norms and values. However, this implies such a significant shift in the way in which schools are organized that it is hard to see how it will happen. It is more likely that social inclusion will be pursued in its 'weak' version with the incorporation of those on the margins through responses which combine welfare with punishment.

References

Cooper, P., Hart, S., Lovey, J. and McLaughlin, C. (2000) *Positive Alternatives to Exclusion from School*, Routledge Falmer, London.

Hanafin, J. and Lynch, A. (2002) *British Journal of Sociology of Education*, **23**, 35–49.

Head, G., Kane, J. and Cogan, N. (2003) *Emotional and Behavioural Difficulties*, **8**, 33–42.

McDonald, T. and Thomas, G. (2003) *Emotional and Behavioural Difficulties*, **8**, 108–119.

Munn, P., Lloyd, G. and Cullen, M.A. (2000) *Alternatives to Exclusion from School*, Paul Chapman, London.

Scottish Executive (2003).

SEED (2000) Scottish Executive, Edinburgh.

SEED (2001) Scottish Executive, Edinburgh.

SEED (2002) Scottish Executive, Edinburgh.

SEED (2003) Scottish Executive, Edinburgh.

SOEID (1998) Scottish Office, Edinburgh.

Chapter 10

Inclusion, exclusion and children's rights

A case study of a student with Asperger syndrome

Audrey Osler and Chay Osler

Introduction

In this chapter, we examine questions of inclusion, exclusion and children's rights from the perspective of a student with Asperger syndrome and from the perspective of his family. Chay Osler is the student and Audrey Osler is his aunt. Chay's hope is that this chapter may influence teachers and lead to improvements in the schooling of other young people with Asperger syndrome.

Statutory guidance explicitly states that a decision to exclude a student should be taken only

> in response to serious breaches of a school's discipline policy; and . . . if allowing the pupil to remain in school would seriously harm the education or welfare of the pupil or of others in the school.
>
> (DfEE, 1999a, p. 31)

Parents (but not students under the age of 18) have the right to appeal against a permanent exclusion if they believe it is unjustified. The serious adverse effects of an exclusion on academic attainment and examination performance were recognized when the appeal system was first proposed in 1986 . . . . Parents have the right to challenge an exclusion if the student is 'at a critical stage of preparation for school-leaving examinations' (*Hansard,* House of Commons, Standing Committee B, 1 July 1986, quoted in Harris and Eden, 2000). Consequently, a parent may appeal against a permanent exclusion of a Year 11 student on the grounds that it will have an adverse effect on GCSE examination performance. Since 1994 schools have not been permitted to exclude for an indefinite period.

We examine the experiences of a student with Asperger syndrome who was excluded twice from a mainstream secondary school during Year 11, while preparing for GCSE examinations. The exclusions were both for an indefinite period and were triggered as a result of the school's inability to respond adequately to recurring epileptic seizures. The exclusions lasted for a total of 19 working days and resulted in him missing mock GCSE examinations and assessed coursework. There was no question of any infringement of the school's behaviour policy.

The school was aware that the student had been diagnosed as epileptic when he was admitted. At the time of his first exclusion in November 2000 he was under the care of a consultant paediatrician, but prescribed medication was not controlling his condition and he was experiencing regular seizures at school; it was rare for a seizure to occur at home. They were usually mild and took the form of a faint. He was generally able to continue with normal activities within an hour or so. Nevertheless, the school had ruled that he could not participate in residential activities unless accompanied by his mother.

During Year 9 the student was also diagnosed as having Asperger syndrome. At the beginning of Year 10 he received a statement of special educational needs (SEN) relating to this condition. This entitled him to 5 hours support per week from a learning support assistant. He displays a number of the features of Asperger syndrome (e.g. Attwood, 1998) such as difficulty in forming friendships with other young people, a disregard for peer pressure, intense absorption in certain subjects (notably, language, literature and wildlife), and a strong commitment to following rules. He often interprets visual art and literature in an original way. These differences leave him vulnerable to bullying.

[...]

A medical problem?

Following Chay's seizure during a mock GCSE examination, the deputy head-teacher rang his mother and told her not to send him to school until he was 'sorted out'. The implication was that he should not attend school unless he could guarantee that he would not experience a seizure during the school day. In taking this action, the deputy showed a lack of understanding of the nature of epilepsy, since one cannot predict whether a seizure will occur on any particular day. Official guidance makes it clear that 'Only the headteacher may exclude a pupil' and that a telephone call informing the parent should be 'followed by a letter within one school day' (DfEE, 1999a, p. 31). This indefinite but unofficial exclusion was never confirmed in writing. Table 10.1 outlines the course of events from this first exclusion in November 2000 until February 2001 when Chay was reinstated following a second exclusion.

[...]

The family met with the headteacher in early January. Given the difficulties encountered, we requested that an LEA representative attend, but this request was declined. The headteacher was accompanied by the school's SENCO. Also present was a community nurse who had trained school staff in dealing with epilepsy. At his own request, Chay attended the beginning of the meeting and made a short statement outlining his distress at having been excluded, the difficulties he had encountered relating to bullying and learning, and his concern that staff were simply labelling him as epileptic (see Box 10.1).

Table 10.1 Timetable of events from first exclusion in November 2000 to February 2001

Date	Events
30 November 2000	*Chay is excluded* for an indefinite period.
18 December 2000	Family fax letter to headteacher requesting urgent meeting to discuss Chay's absence. Deputy headteacher declines to meet Chay's mother or to arrange meeting with headteacher.
20 December 2000	Family ring LEA. A senior officer confirms that Chay should be in school unless a doctor declares him unfit.
3 January 2001	LEA officer rings headteacher requesting meeting between headteacher and family.
4 January 2001	Chay's mother is invited to a meeting with the headteacher.
5 January 2001	Family attends meeting with headteacher, SENCO and epilepsy nurse. *Chay reinstated from 8 January.*
8 January 2001	Chay returns to school. No seizures.
10 January 2001	Chay experiences first seizure since 1 January, at school.
11 January 2001	Chays mother attends parents' evening.
18 January 2001	Chay's mother meets SENCO to discuss learning targets.
19 January 2001	Chay requests mentor.
22 January 2001	Family phone LEA officer to express concern that actions agreed on 5 January not implemented.
25 January 2001	Family informed that Annual Review of Statement set for 2 February.
26 January 2001	Chay reports physical bullying, leading to seizure at school. Head faxes LEA saying school is unable to meet Chays medical needs.
29 January 2001	Family fax LEA requesting agenda and supporting documents for Annual Review.
30 January 2001	AEO visits school. Headteacher phones Chay's mother asking her to keep Chay at home until further notice. *Chay excluded for the second time.*
31 January 2001	Headteacher confirms the exclusion by letter. LEA officer declines to direct school to reinstate Chay. Family contact DfEE. DfEE officer agrees to ring LEA.
1 February 2001	DfEE officer reports she is confident that LEA has done all it can. Chay's mother and Audrey (co-author of this chapter) receive Annual Review documents.
2 February 2001	Family attends Annual Review meeting. No educational psychologist present despite mother's request. Headteacher reports a nurse has been recruited. He expresses concern that family has undermined school's reputation. Family request that learning support be increased. *Chay reinstated from 5 February.*
15 February 2001	LEA increases learning support to 11 hours per week.

Box 10.1 Chay's viewpoint

Negligence?

I feel offended that the school has not asked me for my opinion on what I need. For this reason I have written this chapter setting out my viewpoint. I've tried to do this politely, but I realise that it might be difficult for some teachers to accept, because my perspective is so different from theirs, and at this stage I feel very frustrated.

I want to learn but that right has been denied.

I feel that at the last meeting (at the beginning of January while I was still excluded from school) I was not listened to. I am shocked and dismayed that I have had to wait for three weeks following that meeting for anyone to so much as mention a mentor, even though that was agreed and promised at that stage. I tried to raise the subject and even went to see Mrs Y, the deputy head, about it, because she had previously been responsible for organising mentors for Year Nine. She apparently knew nothing about it. I think it was a shame she was not at the meeting as she had spoken to both my mother and my aunt on the phone at the time of my exclusion and during it.

Obviously, my having epilepsy is no fault of the school but I have for too long been under the impression that the school thought that it was mine. Having seizures occurs when I am under stress and also, at the moment, while I am on the wrong medication. Seizures rarely happen at home. I would like the school to reflect whether they are in any way responsible for the seizures. Being weaned off tablets can be a slow and painful experience. It cannot and must not be rushed and I should like more understanding on the part of the staff, both teachers and first-aiders.

Excluding me from school because of the seizures was, of course, very wrong. I should like something, other than a long-awaited mentor to make up for it. I should like decent realistic and sensible advice from my teachers as well as my future mentor when s/he is selected on how I might deal with bullies, other than 'Ignore them!' or 'These are the best years of their life and they are spoiling them. Just remember that'.

I'd like to make similar comment with regard to Asperger's Syndrome: I would like all my teachers to understand what this means and how it may affect my learning. I hope they will begin to consider this so that other students with this condition might be better understood. I hope my family will highlight this at the meeting which reviews my statement and I feet confident that Dr C will also do this.

Academically, I should like tots of support to enable me to achieve something in each subject which will be of value for my future. I would like a special needs assistant in some of my weaker subjects or all subjects if necessary. I feel this is particularly important as I missed the whole of December and my mock GCSEs as a result of the school's exclusion. It would be bad enough to be sent home on the grounds of bad behaviour but to be sent home and asked to stay away until my seizures were 'sorted out' is exceptionally distressing.

The special needs department deserves to feel part of the school and not just a little island which is overlooked by all except wretches like myself, escaped from a shipwreck. In maths there is a single special needs assistant to help a teacher in a class where the other students hardly ever want to learn. She has really got her work cut out because I understand that all in the class, save two, also have special needs statements.

I want to feel as if I am, at least to some small degree, good at something. I get encouragement at home and in the special needs department. Where is everybody else? I have been given the Foundation English GCSE exam paper, when even I know I can do better. I love English. I used to be praised for the stories I wrote in Middle School yet I have not written a single story in [this school] since Year Nine. If I can write a novel outside school, as I am doing, I should not be underestimated within school. Could a 'normal student working on Foundation English translate Beowulf? –

Da Comme of more undre mist-hleothelm
Grendel gongon; Goddes yrre boaer.

And what about reading? I have read Chaucer, Tolkien, Philip Pullman, Charles Dickens, Edgar Allan Poe . . . I can quote from any one of these and yet at the moment I am feeling, in a word, quite 'thick'. Yet bullies would have everyone believe that I am. I have no way of demonstrating that I am not. How do you think that makes me feel? Does anyone care? I have set targets here from the school. I believe that its now their turn to challenge me and enable me to get established in my future career, whatever that may be.

In short, I want to learn. If you were to ask 'What do you want done first?' I could not answer. If the seizures were to stop the school would have no excuse to neglect me and I would be less stressed. On the other hand, they will not stop until the school can support me and enable me to be less stressed. I can see that I have written a tot and I am sure I could make this longer. But really all this is a desperate cry for help. Now!

At the January meeting, support for Chay was agreed and he returned to school. However, the support was not in place. He was again excluded and was out of school until February.

Rethinking special educational needs

Management

The *Code of Practice on the Identification and Assessment of Special Educational Needs* (DfE, 1994) outlines the responsibilities of the headteacher in mainstream schools:

> the head teacher has responsibility for the day-to-day management of all aspects of the school's work, including provision for children with special educational needs. He or she will keep the governing body fully informed. At the same time, the head teacher will work closely with the school's SEN coordinator or team.
>
> (para. 2.7)

One of the problems encountered in attempting to resolve the first unofficial exclusion was that the senior management team appeared to have delegated responsibility for the management as well as the provision for students with special educational needs to the head of learning support (SENCO). The SENCO was not a member of the senior management team and did not have the authority or overview to address some of the problems we were raising about inclusion and school ethos. Some teachers assumed that the progress of a child with SEN was not their responsibility but that of the learning support assistant, and this appears to have gone unchecked by anyone in a senior position.

The SEN department was obliged to address problems at an individual level and was unable to make wider institutional responses. Simple individualized technical solutions to problems were found, for example, arranging for an individual student to spend time in the library if bullied, rather than more complex institutional solutions which involved a change in the wider student body or in the whole school ethos. As Chay noted: 'The special needs department deserves to feel part of the school and not just a little island which is overlooked by all except wretches like myself'.

Realizing academic potential

Another problem related to the way in which a number of the teachers appeared to conceptualize SEN. These teachers appeared unable to imagine a student with SEN who might have the potential to achieve academically. At a parents' meeting to discuss sixth-form options, teachers explained that Chay was no problem and that he was 'a lovely boy'. As his mother noted: 'They didn't seem to expect much of him.' She again asked for learning targets but these were not forthcoming.

On his return to school following the first exclusion Chay was given extra learning support for 2 days 'to help him settle in'. Nevertheless, few teachers appeared to recognize that they shared responsibility for Chay's academic progress. He approached teachers to make appointments for the parents' evening. He wished to study English in the sixth form but his English teacher had no available appointments. His mother phoned this teacher to arrange an appointment at an alternative time but she failed to return the calls.

Following the first exclusion no work was sent home. On 18 January, 9 school days after Chay was reinstated, the SENCO arranged a meeting with his mother and set targets 'to catch up' in each subject. These were not the specific learning targets his family had asked for and which the school had agreed to provide.

At the annual review meeting an LEA officer with a SEN brief raised the question of Chay's post-16 options. He spoke of his ambitions to go on to higher education. Yet the SENCO persisted in talking about further education rather than higher education. In doing so she reinforced the assumption that a student with SEN is not expected to achieve academic success. Nevertheless, the other (non-teaching) professionals present listened to Chay and supported him in expressing his viewpoint. The meeting had some positive outcomes. In particular, we requested additional in-class learning support and this has been forthcoming. It was agreed that it might well be in Chay's best interests to retake Year 11 at another school, given the disruption experienced through exclusion.

One concern raised by the family was whether Chay was in a position to access the learning support to which he was entitled. For example, in English it appears that the learning support assistant tended to offer support to a student who had problems with basic literacy, rather than support Chay in checking his understanding of tasks. As Chay expressed it: 'He seems to need her support more than I do.'

Accountability

After the second exclusion the AEO told the family he had warned the headteacher that we might go to the Department for Education and Employment (DfEE) or the press. On 31 January the family approached the DfEE, speaking to an officer in the School Inclusion Division and to a member of the SEN team which has responsibility for the LEA in question. We expressed our concern over the two 'unofficial' exclusions and their timing. We argued that Chay should be in school while the LEA was arranging the necessary support.

An officer in the DfEE's School Inclusion Division shared our concern about the timing of the exclusion. He told us: 'I have been cautioned by lawyers never to say that something is unlawful, but this does sound as though it is!' A member of the DfEE SEN team promised to speak to an LEA officer. The next day she reported that she was confident that the LEA was doing all it could in the circumstances.

The LEA appears to have limited or ineffective powers of intervention. As one LEA officer dealing with our case observed:

> If parents attend the Ofsted pre-inspection meeting and complain about the school's provision for special educational needs but there is no mention of SEN problems in the inspection report then there is little we can do. All we can

do is respond to the cases of individual pupils. Schools with good inspection reports can afford to ignore those pupils who they see as a problem.

External measures of accountability, such as school inspections, may not identify the practice of unofficial exclusion, or inadequacies in supporting children with SEN. In Chay's case, the first 6 days' absence were recorded as due to sickness, after which the register had been left unmarked until his reinstatement. It would appear that if a school is able to maintain a favourable position in examination league tables and secure a sound Ofsted report, it may prove difficult to address any weakness in its SEN provision.

Our research into the Ofsted school inspection framework confirms that equality and SEN issues are dealt with inconsistently. Whether they feature in reports depends to a large extent on the level of awareness of the reporting inspector; they may be lost in the processes of reporting (Osler and Morrison, 2000). If staff (and inspectors) assume that 'special educational needs' equates not only with low attainment but also with low ability then the needs of those who have the potential to achieve academic success may easily be overlooked. A child with Asperger syndrome may have no way of demonstrating that s/he is academically able.

Impact of exclusion

It has long been recognized that official statistics on exclusion do not include: 'the hidden numbers of children who have not been formally excluded but who are out of school because they have clearly been rejected by their schools' (Advisory Centre for Education, 1993). Researchers have identified the practice whereby parents are encouraged to find another school before a school formally excludes a child (Mayet, 1993; Gillborn, 1995). Stirling (1994) cites cases of informal exclusions disguised as medical problems and schools persuading parents to keep children at home 'while the school approaches the LEA to make special provision'. As Munn (2000) observes:

> Schools are now required to collect statistics on attendance, truancy and exclusion....Unlike public examination results, however, attendance and exclusions data are supplied by schools themselves, with all the scope for massaging the data that such a system brings.

Our own DfEE-funded research suggests that schools are increasingly using 'unofficial' exclusions, either to meet government targets or because headteachers believe that an unofficial exclusion enables a child to avoid the stigma of an exclusion on their school record (Osler et al., 2001).

The timing of the two exclusions caused them to have a disproportionate impact. Chay was first excluded during mock GCSE examinations, at a vital point in his academic career. He was well enough to attend school but no work was sent home, nor was any guidance given on assessed coursework. (Although work was promised the second time, it was only available on the fourth day of absence.) When he returned to school he was keen to sit his exams, but his teachers said this was not important. His predicted grades showed a sharp downturn on the predictions made in the previous year. It is not clear on what basis these predictions were made since he had missed his mock examinations and essential coursework. Clearly, these mock examinations are important both in providing students with examination practice and in enabling predictions which may determine whether or not a student is offered a place in a sixth form or college.

During the five-week period when Chay was excluded he was somewhat isolated and had shown signs of distress and depression. He felt rejected by his school and the exclusions had an impact on his self-esteem.

Neither before nor during the exclusion was there any attempt to discuss the issues with Chay, liaise with his family, or identify additional sources of advice or support. It was not until his reinstatement that his family was given information about a key parents' meeting to discuss post-16 options, information which had been sent to other parents the previous term. It would appear that the needs of students who require additional resources can be overlooked with impunity. A number of commentators have highlighted how schools which are assured of their place in the educational market can afford to neglect those students who are more costly to educate (Searle, 1996; Blair, 2000).

[. . .]

Rights and respect

Children's participation rights, as outlined in the UN Convention on the Rights of the Child, are highlighted in the SEN Code of Practice (2001). We are reminded that under Articles 12, 13 and 23: 'children have a right to obtain and make known information, to express an opinion, and to have that opinion taken into account in any matter or procedure affecting the child' (DfEE, 2001, para. 3.1, p. 13).

The Code of Practice notes that a vital factor in ensuring the participation of both students and their parents is the provision of information allowing them to make informed choices. It is seen as critical that children and young people are able to become 'active participant[s] in any programme of intervention proposed by the school or related services'. Among the responsibilities of schools and other professionals are the requirements to

- consult with students who need learning support to ensure that that support enables them to participate in learning;
- recognize the potential stress of assessment and review arrangements;
- ensure that a student has access to a designated member of staff with whom s/he can discuss difficulties or concerns.

(DfEE, 2001, para. 3.3, p. 14)

Such considerations not only are important from the student's perspective but also may be critical in enabling teachers (and the school as an institution) to understand the needs of a student with Asperger syndrome. In our case study Chay's difficulties have been accentuated because he has not been consulted, and because teachers have failed to recognize the links between seizures, bullying, academic progress and school practices. The school has failed to address adequately the bullying and learning needs which cause stress and trigger the seizures. By medicalizing his 'problem' the staff effectively absolve themselves from professional responsibility for his learning and welfare in school. Chay's personal account (see Box 10.1) clearly identifies needs and proposes some solutions, yet the school failed to take his opinion into account.

A failure to consult adequately with students is revealed in the school policy on bullying, which outlines procedures, including the prompt reporting and investigation of incidents. The policy states

> We value all our students, so bullying by a member of...School community is totally unacceptable. Bullying is any malicious, unprovoked, physical or psychological attack on another person. It could include fighting, pushing, other forms of physical aggression, extortion, name calling and general intimidation.

Although students are told that 'All bullying will be dealt with seriously' and that 'the Headteacher may exclude persistent bullies', the policy does not state that victims will be *informed* of action taken against bullies. The case study illustrates the importance of ensuring that, at an institutional level, provision is made to inform and consult students, including those who report bullying.

There was, throughout the proceedings, little apparent concern for Chay's privacy. The first reinstatement meeting was convened in the staffroom and only reconvened in the head's study at the family's request. Chay first heard of the second exclusion from a fellow student, who had been informed by their form teacher that from then on Chay would be working at home. The evidence suggests not only that the school authorities failed to recognize the educational benefits of consulting a student as part of the decision-making process, but also that they had very little respect for his rights.

Conclusion

The case study highlights how a popular school in a relatively affluent area, with a good reputation and a sound set of GCSE results, can confidently demonstrate academic success and receive a favourable inspection report while failing to address adequately the government's inclusion agenda. All schools now need to recognize that failure to anticipate the needs of students with disabilities or SEN may well lead to unlawful discrimination. The anticipatory duties of schools, as envisaged by the SEN and Disability Act 2001, have far-reaching implications for school ethos and culture. Inclusive schools will need to act in the best interests of all students recognizing that in meeting students' individual needs the institution itself may need to change. The case study reveals some of the real barriers that currently exist in enabling parents to be genuine partners in their children's education. Even where a family had privileged professional knowledge and access to information, these barriers were daunting and, at times, insurmountable. Finally, the case study suggests that the realization of children's rights in schools will require further cultural change both within certain institutions and among teachers generally. This implies further investment and a programme of training and support.

Postscript

A month after Chay was reinstated at school the original diagnosis of epilepsy was revised. His doctors now believe that the seizures were not epileptic in origin but entirely stress related. He is no longer on medication. At the time when the chapter was written (December 2001) Chay was out of school awaiting the results of a statutory re-assessment of his special education needs.

References

Advisory Centre for Education (1993) *Children out of School: A Guide for Parents and Schools on Non-Attendance at School*. London: ACE.

Attwood, T. (1998) *Asperger's Syndrome: A Guide for Parents and Professionals*. London: Jessica Kingsley.

Blair, M. (2000) '"Race", School Exclusions and Human Rights', in A. Osler (ed.) *Citizenship and Democracy in Schools: Equality, Identity, Diversity*. Stoke on Trent: Trentham.

DfE (1994) *Code of Practice on the Identification and Assessment of Special Educational Needs*. Department for Education, London: Central Office of Information.

DfEE (1999a) *Social Inclusion: Pupil Support*. Circular 10/99. London: Department for Education and Employment.

DfEE (1999b) *Social Inclusion: The LEA Role in Pupil Support*. Circular 11/99. London: Department for Education and Employment.

DfEE (2001) *Code of Practice on the Identification and Assessment of Special Educational Needs*. London: Department for Education and Employment.

Gillborn, D. (1995) *Racism and Antiracism in Real Schools*. Buckingham: Open University Press.

Harris, N. and Eden, K. (2000) *Challenges to School Exclusion*. London: RoutledgeFalmer.

Mayet, G. (1993) 'Exclusions and Schools', *Multicultural Education Review* 15: 7–9.

Munn, P. (2000) 'Can Schools Make Scotland a More Inclusive Society?', *Scottish Affairs*, 33, Autumn.

Osler, A. and Morrison, M. (2000) *Inspecting Schools for Race Equality: OFSTED's Strengths and Weaknesses*. Stoke on Trent: Trentham for the Commission for Racial Equality.

Osler, A., Watling, R. and Busher, H. (2001) *Reasons for Exclusion from School*. London: Department for Education and Employment.

Searle, C. (1996) 'The Signal of Failure: School Exclusions and the Market System of Education', in E. Blyth and J. Milner (eds) *Exclusion from School: Inter-Professional Issues for Policy and Practice*. London: Routledge.

Stirling, M. (1994) 'The End of the Lind', *Special Children* 76: 27–29.

Part III

Alternative systems and policies

Special needs education as the way to equity

An alternative approach?

Alan Dyson

I want to examine whether special needs education has led, or is likely to lead, to an education system which is more equitable in its outcomes than would otherwise be the case.

In doing this, I realise that both terms of my inquiry are highly problematic. For the present purpose, therefore, I wish to avoid the potential arguments about when education becomes 'special' and start from the premise that we can identify a more or less distinct set of structures in our education system – schools, resource-bases, teaching groups, teachers, training programmes and so on – which, together with their associated practices, constitute 'special needs education'. Likewise, I want to operate with a deliberately vague notion of educational equity as being to do with offering comparable educational experiences to and generating the highest possible level of educational outcomes for all learners. I make an assumption that, in order to do this, some weighting of effort and resource towards those most at risk of experiencing difficulties in the education system will be necessary.

For all the many problems with these definitions, they do at least indicate the extent to which special needs education is an equity-oriented system. I take the Warnock Report's famous argument (DES, 1978, 1.4) – that the goals of education are the same for all but that the help needed by some children to reach them might be different – to be essentially an argument for educational equity. It is premised, in other words, on the assumption that broadly common experiences and outcomes are to be pursued by supplementing the standard provision of mainstream schools with a special needs system able to target higher levels of intervention and resource to those students who are most 'in need'. The question arises, therefore, as to how effective the special needs system has been in pursuit of this aim.

Special needs as the way to equity

There are certainly some ways in which special needs education has achieved its laudable purposes. For instance, it has successfully channelled substantial additional resources to 'needy' students . . . .

Moreover, these resources are not only financial. Special needs education has accumulated a substantial infrastructure of buildings, equipment and materials.

Even more important, we have in this country a veritable army of SEN specialists . . . .

Through many years of effort we have developed procedures for identifying the most needy children, for analysing the precise nature of their needs, for targeting resources to meet those needs and for offering legal and other forms of guarantee that those resources will be protected. For all of these reasons, the special needs education system has claims to being regarded as an effective means of delivering at least some important elements of equity. It offers some of the most vulnerable students in our schools some important guarantees of additional resourcing and specialist attention . . . .

The problems of special needs education

Despite these substantial achievements, I wish to argue that there are some fundamental problems in the special needs system as a deliverer of equity. The first is that its resources, however substantial they may seem, are spread too thinly. For instance, our research on pupils with moderate learning difficulties showed that those with the least serious difficulties in mainstream schools received additional provision costing just over £1,000 per pupil per annum (Crowther *et al.*, 1998), Broadly speaking, this buys support from an LSA for half a day per week or additional time from a teacher for less than an hour per week.

This is not to say that such limited forms of additional provision may not have some value. However, it seems unlikely that they effect a major transformation of the contexts within which students are expected to learn. This is particularly the case since, despite years of effort at reform, special needs provision in mainstream schools continues to be made to a significant extent either outside the ordinary classroom or in a somewhat semi-detached manner within it (Croll and Moses, 2000, pp. 81–87). The implication is one that has long been understood by critics of special needs education: if the 'standard' provision within which children are educated is not adequate to meet their learning needs, the relatively limited top-up provision delivered by special needs education is unlikely to make much difference.

This would seem to be confirmed by the difficulty there is in finding evidence that the typical ways in which special needs resources are deployed have any significant impact on children's learning . . . .

There is one final problem with seeing special needs education as the way to equity: how children's difficulties get described and what provision (if any) is made for them depends on the extent to which different stakeholders – parents, teachers, LEA officers and so on – can get their views and interests to prevail (see, amongst many others, Tomlinson, 1985; Riddell *et al.*, 1994; Armstrong, 1995; Gross, 1996). Under these circumstances, special needs education appears less a rational and equitable response to children's difficulties than an ill-defined battleground in which different interest groups engage in contests governed by only the vaguest of rules.

The root of the problem

I see the special needs system, viewed as a means of delivering equity, as flawed not only in its surface practices but also in its fundamental structure and conceptualisation.

Ironically, the two main difficulties arise from features which are often taken to be its greatest achievements. The first is the individualisation which is at its heart – that is, the determination to see children's 'needs' as intelligible only on an individual rather than categorical basis, and to respond to those needs through individualised interventions. This individualisation has a series of perverse consequences. It leads us to locate the source of those difficulties in the characteristics of learners and to avoid analysing the features of schooling which might be dysfunctional. This is, of course, likely to generate the sorts of ineffective (because misdirected) interventions we have noted earlier. Moreover, since it implies that some learners cannot participate effectively in mainstream education, it is also likely, as critics have long pointed out (Golby and Gulliver, 1979; Skrtic, 1991), to produce all the apparatus of segregation and discrimination which has characterised the special needs system.

Individualisation, however, has other perverse consequences. For instance, it makes it extremely difficult to accumulate any trustworthy evidence in the special needs field, since each case is seen as being different from the next (Crowther et al., 1998). The constant reinvention of the wheel which this entails contributes to a wider inefficiency in which large amounts of energy and resource have to be directed towards individual assessment and planning on the grounds that no two children's difficulties are alike.

If inefficiency alone does not quite count as inequity, then another consequence of individualisation surely does. In an individualised model of assessment and provision, there is simply no way of comparing like with like in order to ensure similar provision for similar cases . . . .

These problems are compounded by a second fundamental difficulty. That is the concept of 'special need' itself. The notion of 'specialness' is not tied down, either within the Warnock Report or in subsequent practice, to any clearly operationalised definition of where the boundary between special and ordinary might lie. Again, it is a matter for professional judgement within the context of a particular set of circumstances. Likewise, the concept of 'need' is only loosely anchored to any notion of aims or purposes. In other words, all the intention is focused on what a particular child needs rather than on why – to what end or educational purpose – s/he needs it.

This is not simply a conceptual issue. The free-floating nature of these fundamental notions means that 'special needs' are held somehow to emerge from the individual assessment process and the means of 'meeting' those needs to become self-evident once the needs themselves are specified. However, there is nothing in that process which rules out any child from having a 'need' for some form of 'help' – or, indeed, which guarantees that any child will actually receive 'help'. The apparent precision of educational, medical and psychological descriptions of children's difficulties may well disguise this inherent vagueness, and custom-and-practice in particular schools and LEAs may create an illusion of stability. However, the system itself offers no certainties and, above all, no guarantees of equitable out-comes. Since the concept of need is so ill-defined, moreover, and there are rewards available (in the form of additional resources) for taking up a child's needs, the system is inherently inflationary. The 'strategic behaviour' (Meijer, 1999) through which stakeholders seek to maximise their advantage in such a situation will, of course, produce some winners. However, so long as resources are finite, for every winner there will inevitably be a loser, and it seems highly unlikely that the outcome will have much to do with an equitable distribution of resources.

The radical alternative approach to equity

Typically, critics of special needs education proceed from an analysis of the kind I have set out earlier to arguments that the concept of special needs is non-necessary and that therefore its structures and practices should be dismantled (Clark *et al.*, 1998) . . . .

Such arguments have much to commend them. However, they do rather depend on the assumption that schools and teachers will be able to develop the skills, practices and, above all, attitudes and values to operate in this new and flexible way. Moreover, they assume that they will be able to do this for the full range of individual differences and without any categorical supports – a process which is arguably even more individually based and non-cumulative than the special needs system which it replaces. Finally, they assume that the powerful special needs lobby groups can be persuaded to accept the dismantling of existing structures without displaying their customary resistance. I have no doubt that these conditions can be met in certain circumstances. However, I do have doubts as to whether they form a basis for a system which reliably guarantees equitable provision for its more vulnerable children. Some other approach, operable by 'good enough' schools and teachers is, it seems to me, now needed.

A third way?

I believe the analysis I have set out thus far makes it possible at least to identify some of the principal features of such an approach.

An alternative approach should be founded on some clear articulation of educational purpose

Even the radical proposals currently on offer have little to say about educational goals and purposes beyond a broad commitment to 'learning' and 'participation' (see, for instance Booth *et al.*, 2000). It seems to me essential to specify what is to be learned and participated in and why. Without this it is impossible to be clear which children are at risk of not achieving these goals or what form of intervention is necessary to ensure that they do so. Moreover, it seems to me that any notion of educational goals needs to be fully operationalised in terms, for instance, of curricular and social experiences and of educational outcomes. Such specification does not need to be as narrowly conceived as the current obsession with 'standards', understood as test and examination results; nor, indeed does it necessarily have to be undertaken centrally (though the difficulties of squaring equity with local variation are clear). However, we do urgently need a public debate on what education is for and on the level of variation in educational outcomes (broadly defined) which we regard as acceptable or otherwise.

An alternative approach should move away from the dominant individualisation of current approaches and current radical proposals

At the same time, it should not succumb to the crude categorisations that have characterised special needs education. If any new approach is to avoid the inefficiencies, the absence of cumulative knowledge and the lack of cross-case comparisons which beset both special needs education and its proposed alternatives, it has to operate on the basis that many children who currently experience difficulty in our schools share important characteristics and are educated in settings which themselves have similarities. It ought, therefore, to be possible to specify what sorts of interventions are likely to be effective in overcoming the difficulties they experience and to ensure some comparability across interventions in different cases. It ought also to be possible to specify those interventions for (and with) teachers so that they are not required to invent them individually for themselves or (more likely) to rely on custom and practice. Moreover, establishing the notion that large numbers of children experience similar difficulties makes it more likely, I would argue, that systemic rather than individual interventions will come to seem appropriate to practitioners and policy-makers.

An alternative approach should offer guarantees to children

However flawed special needs education might be in other respects, it has at least offered some limited guarantees to otherwise vulnerable children in terms of a measure of concern for their individual progress and protection for the resources which are thought necessary to support that progress. Any alternative approach would need to offer at least equivalent guarantees. In some cases, as I argue later, these might still have to be offered on an individual basis. However, in the vast majority of cases, the move towards a less individualised system means that they can be offered on a 'group' or even institutional basis by guaranteeing the quality of a school's provision overall rather than case-by-case – in other words, on precisely the same basis as such guarantees are offered to all other children.

An alternative approach should be embedded in mainstream classrooms

This is not simply another call for a more inclusive system, but follows from the equity arguments set out earlier. If children are unable to learn effectively in the context of 'standard' provision, then the marginal enhancements of that provision which special needs education delivers are unlikely to make much difference. Indeed, maintaining a form of standard provision in which some children do not thrive is itself inherently inequitable. What might make a difference, therefore, is an approach which takes standard provision as problematic and seeks to reform it in ways which make it more effective for all children – and hence more equitable. Not surprisingly, such empirical evidence as there is – and it is regrettably limited, especially in the UK – tends to support this position (see, for instance, Wang *et al.*, 1997; Crowther *et al.*, 1998).

Where to from here?

I believe it is possible to move from these general features towards describing some specific steps that could now (or in the near future) be taken to move us nearer to the approach I have set out earlier. First, we need a sustained effort to know more about children's difficulties in and with the education system, to systematise what we know, and to make it more readily available to policy-makers and practitioners. If at the same time the focus of professional development can shift away from implementing the procedures of the special needs system towards the sensitive and flexible implementation of proven strategies, so much the better.

Second, we probably need to abandon the special needs apparatus for the large majority of children who currently fall within its ambit. This means, however, that we need to consider what, if anything, we put in its place. I am inclined to the view that equitable provisions for children who might otherwise experience difficulties in school require some form of 'affirmative action' in terms of attention, approach and resourcing. Such action requires some sort of a conceptual 'hook' on which to hang – a hook, moreover, which can translate into specific funding mechanisms and practices.

Notions such as 'risk' and 'resilience' have for some years been powerful in the USA, Australia and, to some extent in western Europe (Franklin, 1994; OECD, 1995; Wang *et al.*, 1997; Howard *et al.*, 1999), but play little part in educational discourse in the UK. Despite the dangers of any label, it seems to me that they offer the sort of 'hook' that is now needed, without retreating to the individualistic approach of special needs education. As an additional advantage, they provide a means of 'reconnecting' educational difficulty to wider issues in social and economic disadvantage (Dyson, 1997) in a way which the concept of 'special educational needs', with its individual approach, was never likely to do effectively – and indeed was explicitly barred from doing (Warnock, 1999). Likewise, the notion of developing 'resilience-building' schools and classrooms has the further advantage that such developments cannot be separated from mainstream provision. On the contrary, the programmes that would be fostered would be programmes of school and classroom reform rather than programmes of individual intervention.

However, equity may demand (I am not entirely convinced on this point) the retention of a residual special needs system offering guarantees to a small minority of children. Such a system would not need to be as complex or extensive as the current one since it would be explicitly administrative rather than educational in intent. In other words, it would not be based on an assumption that some children were sharply demarcated from all other children by virtue of their 'special' needs or the 'special' provision they required. The demarcation would simply be in terms of the viability of resourcing and monitoring provision through the systems which apply to the majority of children. In particular, this residual system would come into play in the case of very low incidence characteristics where resources could not be delivered through recurrent formula funding, even under some form of school clustering arrangement. Retaining such a system potentially means also retaining some of the inequities of the current special needs system – hence my hesitation – but it may be the only way of offering guarantees to some children and, incidentally, of keeping their parents and advocates on board during any change process.

Finally, picking up on the monitoring theme, any new system would need to hold schools accountable for the provision they made and the effectiveness of that provision. For the vast majority of children this would not need to be done through an individual system of planning and monitoring such as the statement or IEP but through institutional-level strategies. These would include targeted funding and programme evaluation on the one hand and institutional performance monitoring on the other. In other words, precisely the same combination of inspection and outcomes-analysis that is used to monitor provision for the majority of children would apply here too.

If we look at some recent developments, there is evidence of the early beginnings of moves in the direction I have outlined here. The Government's notion of 'social inclusion' to some extent overlaps with and supercedes the notion of special needs (Blunkett, 1999, 2000). It brings with it a raft of programmes – EAZs, Excellence in Cities, Sure Start, Schools Plus, Connexions, the Children's Fund – which carry all the hallmarks of affirmative action but are not predicated upon a highly individual approach. Moreover, it is now beginning to permeate the school inspection process in a way which shows how institutional-level monitoring in this field might work (Ofsted, 2000). At the same time, the Government is showing some willingness to reshape (if not reform) the special needs system by exerting downward pressure on statements and reducing the numbers of children falling within its ambit (DfEE, 1997, 1998, 2000).

I do not wish to exaggerate the extent to which the Government has got these policies right, nor to underestimate the deleterious effects of some of its other policies on vulnerable children (Bines, 1999), nor to be over-optimistic about the extent to which it is yet prepared to move beyond the special needs system as we currently have it. Nonetheless, it is not difficult to see how we might progress from where we are now towards a substantially reformed system. Whether the political will for such progress exists, or whether the internal pressures in the current system will be powerful enough to force change remains to be seen.

References

Armstrong, D. (1995) *Power and Partnership in Education: Parents, Children and Special Educational Needs.* London: Routledge.

Bines, H. (1999) Inclusive standards? Current developments in policy for special educational needs in England and Wales. *Oxford Review of Education,* 26, 1, 21–31.

Blunkett, D. (1999) *Social Exclusion and the Politics of Opportunity: A Mid-term Progress Check.* A speech by the Rt Hon David Blunkett MP. London: DfEE.

Blunkett, D. (2000) *Raising Aspirations for the 21st Century.* Speech to the North of England Education Conference, Wigan, 6 January. London: DfEE.

Booth, T., Ainscow, M., Black-Hawkins, K., Vaughan, M. and Shaw, L. (2000) *Index for Inclusion: Developing Learning and Participation in Schools.* Bristol: Centre for Studies on Inclusive Education.

Clark, C., Dyson, A. and Millward, A. (1998) Theorising special education: time to move on? In Clark, C., Dyson, A. and Millward, A. (eds) *Theorising Special Education.* London: Routledge.

Croll, P. and Moses, D. (2000) *Special Needs in the Primary School: One in five?* London: Cassell.

Crowther, D., Dyson, A. and Millward, A. (1998) *Costs and Outcomes for Pupils with Moderate Learning Difficulties in Special and Mainstream Schools.* RR89, London: DfEE.

DES (1978) *Special Educational Needs: Report of the committee of Enquiry into the Education of Handicapped Children and Young People.* The Warnock Report. London: HMSO.

DfEE (1997) *Excellence for All Children: Meeting Special Educational Needs.* London: The Stationery Office.

DfEE (1998) *Meeting Special Educational Needs: A Programme of Action.* London: DfEE.

DfEE (2000) *SEN Code of Practice on the Identification and Assessment of Pupils with Special Educational Needs & SEN Thresholds: Good Practice Guidance on Identification and Provision for Pupils with Special Educational Needs* (drafts for consultation). London: DfEE.

Dyson, A. (1997) Social and educational disadvantage: reconnecting special needs education. *British Journal of Special Education,* 24, 4, 152–157.

Franklin, B.M. (1994) *From 'Backwardness' to 'At-Risk': Childhood Learning Difficulties and the Contradictions of School Reform.* Albany, NY: State University of New York Press.

Golby, M. and Gulliver, R.J. (1979) Whose remedies, whose ills? A critical review of remedial education. *Remedial Education,* 11, 2, 137–147.

Gross, J. (1996) The weight of the evidence: parental advocacy and resource allocation to children with statements of special educational need. *Support for Learning,* 11, 1, 3–8.

Howard, S., Dryden, J. and Johnson, B. (1999) Childhood resilience: a review and critique of the literature. *Oxford Review of Education,* 25, 3, 307–323.

Meijer, C.J.W. (ed). (1999) *Financing of Special Needs Education: A Seventeen-country Study of the Relationship between Financing of Special Needs Education and Inclusion.* Middlefart, Denmark: European Agency for Development in Special Needs Education.

OECD (1995) *Our Children at Risk.* Paris, OECD.

Ofsted (2000) *Evaluating Educational Inclusion*. London: Ofsted.

Riddell, S., Brown, S. and Duffield, J. (1994) Parental power and special education needs: the case of specific learning difficulties. *British Educational Research Journal*, 20, 3, 327–344.

Skrtic, T.M. (1991) *Behind Special Education: A Critical Analysis of Professional Culture and School Organization*. Denver, CO: Love.

Tomlinson, S. (1985) The expansion of special education. *Oxford Review of Education*, 11, 2, 157–165.

Wang, M.C., Haertel, G.D. and Walberg, H.J. (1997) Fostering educational resilience in inner-city schools. *Children and Youth*, 7, 119–140.

Warnock, M. (1999) If only we had known then . . . . *Times Educational Supplement*. London, 31st December, 33.

Chapter 12

Early interventions

Preventing school exclusions in the primary setting

Meg Maguire, Sheila Macrae and Linda Milbourne

Exclusion from primary school

Recent studies in the UK have highlighted a significant increase in the numbers of children being excluded from school (Donovan, 1998; Social Exclusion Unit, 1998; Osler and Hill, 1999; Parsons, 1999). From the late 1980s to the late 1990s, exclusions increased from nearly 3,000 in 1990 to nearly 13,000 in 1998.

While only 1,500 of the children recorded as permanently excluded from school in 1997/98 were in primary school (DfEE, 1999a), exclusion at this stage is especially worrying. Education disrupted at this stage can be difficult to compensate for in later schooling (Hayden, 1996).

Exclusion is the relatively new name for a child being (temporarily) suspended or (permanently) expelled from school. As Wright *et al.* (2000, p. 1) explain, the decision to exclude a child is initially taken by the headteacher of a school and confirmed by the school governors and the Local Education Authority (LEA). Exclusion policy was clarified in the 1986 Education Act (HMSO, 1986), which proposed three types of official exclusion: fixed term (fewer than five days), indefinite and permanent. The Education (No. 2) Act of 1993 (HMSO, 1993) abolished indefinite exclusions and allowed up to three fixed-term periods of 5 days exclusion a term (15 days a term, 45 days in a school year). However, it did place a duty on LEAs to provide alternative education for excluded children. The Standards and Framework Act of 1998 (HMSO, 1998) now permits up to 45 days of fixed term exclusions in one term, although it also stipulates that these 45 days, or nine school weeks, should be a maximum for the school year.

Some studies suggest that school exclusions are more numerous than the official statistics record (Stirling, 1996; Hayden, 1997; Parsons, 1999). Stirling (1996) provides evidence of 'informal' or 'unofficial' exclusions used by schools to conceal the real situation. Bourne *et al.* (1994) and Cohen *et al.* (1994) report the practice of 'internal' exclusions where children remain on the premises but are prevented from joining their peers for routine school activities. The outcome is the same; these children are excluded from the curriculum and everyday classroom activities as well as social relationships with their peers.

If children are formally excluded from school, this can have implications which extend far beyond their schooling to the capacity to participate fully in society later in life (Wright *et al.*, 2000, p. 96). The UK government has recognised that early interventions, especially through education, are crucial in preventing later marginalisation from society (DSS, 1999). Thus, it is critical to tackle the issues which can lead to formal and informal exclusions from school, particularly at the foundation stage of primary education. Children have a right to education, a point which is frequently overlooked in the exclusion debate (Harris *et al.*, 2000; Spring, 2000).

Who is excluded from school?

Significant differences have been found in the rates of exclusion between local education authority areas and even between schools in similar areas, with similar intakes and similar challenges (DfEE, 1998; Wright *et al.*, 2000). Certain groups, boys, children of African-Caribbean origin, 'looked after' children, and those with special education needs (SEN) are disproportionately excluded. The work of Bourne *et al.* (1994), Gillborn and Gipps (1996) and Osler and Hill (1999) further illustrates the disproportionately high number of minority ethnic exclusions across different areas of the UK, particularly in England.

In effect, successive Education Acts have sanctioned the use of exclusion as a means of 'punishment' for, and as a measure for dealing with, individual children (their families and carers), who do not or cannot conform to the norms of behaviour established within particular educational or school environments. Yet, certain groups of children, who start their schooling in contexts of social disadvantage, appear to be excluded in disproportionate numbers. Few families manage to appeal against exclusion decisions and relatively few of these appeals are successful (Parsons, 1999), despite the media attention given to those that are. The sanction is in marked contradiction to the principles underpinning the UK Children Act 1989 (HMSO, 1989), which stresses the protection of the child as paramount.

Both Parsons *et al.* (1994) and Hayden's (1997) studies identify difficult and aggressive behaviour, particularly towards peers, as the main reason given for exclusion among primary children. The obvious conclusion to be drawn from this is that helping children to understand and change this behaviour and develop positive relationships with their peers will reduce exclusion.

At this point it is useful to consider an assumption which characterises much of the work on exclusion from school. Implicit, and sometimes explicit, in much of the literature, is the view that if the child can change or be changed the difficult behaviour can be stopped or even 'cured'. Simultaneously, some children cannot be changed because they are highly disturbed and cannot help 'acting out' their anxieties. In both cases, there is a 'problem' within the child. The implication is that interventions must focus on the 'deficit' child. However, the reality is that some schools manage challenging behaviours better than others and thus, the school environment or culture may provoke or exacerbate negative behaviours (Wright *et al.*, 2000). This aspect of exclusion is often less explored (but see Munn *et al.*, 2000; Scottish H. M. Inspectorate of Education, 2001).

Exclusion: the wider policy context

The UK Government has been concerned to reduce permanent exclusion rates. Thus, there has been a marked shift in policy (Social Exclusion Unit, 1998; DfEE, 1999b) towards inclusiveness and the provision of full-time educational alternatives. Schools have been compelled to work towards reducing their numbers of fixed term and permanent exclusions through in-school tactics.

But schools are not just attempting to manage behaviour and support 'at risk' children. They are caught up in a deluge of policy initiatives and requirements to focus on performance, standards and attainment which may well work to displace some of their more traditional concerns with social and emotional welfare needs (Rustique-Forrester, 2000; Weare, 2000).

One concern of this study is that excluding children from primary schools may simply be a process of dealing with an individual school's problem which may do little to tackle the fundamental issues which have led to the exclusion. If schools are able to provide support, it could be that in-school action could work to prevent exclusion and promote inclusion.

It has been suggested that helping children to explore and work with their feelings, to understand others' needs as well as their own while learning to limit and redirect negative feelings, has a critical part to play in promoting mental, emotional and social health. Indeed, 'teachers could take heart from realising that work in social and affective health can support their efforts to teach the academic curriculum' (Weare, 2000, p. 5). Schools that appreciate this dimension of emotional intelligence (Goleman, 1996) may well be in a stronger position to support the 'difficult' child and may well provide a positive framework which works to prevent formal and informal exclusion. However, this approach to emotional support-work may displace consideration of the broader social and material dimensions which characterise the lives of many 'at risk' children (Parsons, 1999).

Challenging exclusion study

This chapter 'draws' on an exploratory study in which we have examined the ways in which Government policies, aimed at reducing exclusion rates in primary schools, have been interpreted and implemented using a partnership approach in one English urban locale (Macrae *et al.*, 2003). Our research, funded by the Economic and Social Research Council (ESRC), has three main aims: to explore the interpretation of national policies to reduce exclusion at a local level; to describe and document multi-disciplinary team approaches to young children 'at risk' of exclusion and to explore and explain the particular partnership model being deployed. Specifically, the focus of our study has been with one initiative set up to work collaboratively to reduce exclusions in one set of high excluding inner-city primary schools.

The particular initiative with which this study is concerned – Including Primary School Children (IPSC) – ran from April 1999 to April 2002 and worked in a range of primary schools across one London LEA. The multi-agency IPSC team from this initiative comprised two staff from the statutory sector (a clinical psychologist and an educational psychologist) and a social worker from the voluntary sector – a member of the Family Services Unit. These three worked with children identified as being at risk of exclusion. The primary schools in which they worked were identified as being high excluders from school exclusion figures held by the LEA.

Our research (Macrae *et al.*, 2003) has involved attending IPSC meetings, interviewing the three key workers, their line managers and other senior managers within the HAZ in order to explore their views about multi-agency partnerships. We have interviewed key personnel in schools where the IPSC team has worked in order to explore the impact of the project. We have also observed individual/group intervention work and have interviewed parents, headteachers and other staff involved in the IPSC project in order to explore the ways in which national policy is enacted at a local level. Additionally, we have collected documents and publications which relate to the work of the HAZ, in general, and the project, in particular.

In what follows, we draw on data collected from semi-structured interviews with a small number of headteachers and SENCOs (special educational needs co-ordinators) in the first set of IPSC schools. (Pseudonyms have been used for all people, places and schools.) We outline the range of strategies which were initiated by the IPSC workers and then we examine in-school outcomes in more detail in order to consider the potential of these particular early interventions in preventing school exclusion.

Strategies to challenge exclusion

Despite some initial resistance from several schools, most headteachers welcomed the help and support offered by the IPSC team, once the aims of the initiative had been explained. For some headteachers, the offer of additional support for which they would not be charged, was an offer they could not refuse. For other headteachers, becoming involved with the project would indicate to the LEA that they were serious about reducing their exclusions.

The approach taken in each school depended upon the needs of the children, the staff concerned and the skills of the individual IPSC team workers. The three key workers believed it was important to take an 'individual' approach towards each school; what worked well in one case might not have been appropriate in another. The strategies they deployed were drawn from their professional repertoires and reflected these backgrounds; the clinical psychologist tended to work with individuals, the educational psychologist tended to work with classes and teachers, and the social worker tended to work with families.

> Well first and foremost the important thing was to look at reducing exclusion in the schools, and to do that via developing behaviour management strategies within schools, either working directly with children, with their teachers or with their parents, a combination of those things, really.
>
> (IPSC team member)

One specific strategy used by the IPSC team when working with children at risk of exclusion has been 'Circle of Friends' (Pearpoint *et al.*, 1992; Newton *et al.*, 1996). This technique, which originated in Canada, has proved successful when trying to change the behaviour of children with emotional and social difficulties. Briefly, after obtaining informed consent from the family and targeted child, the person running the Circle works with the targeted child's class to discuss ways in which everyone can help this child, elicits empathy in the group for the targeted child and then the group considers strategies through which that child can be supported. A smaller group of children volunteer to be the actual Circle which will work with the focus child. This 'is simply one tool to help a community to support and accept one of its own vulnerable but challenging members' (Newton *et al.*, 1996, p. 47).

Staff in one particular school had heard of 'Circle of Friends' but did not feel confident enough to use it. One IPSC team member ran an in-service training session (in the school at the end of the day) on its use, with very positive results.

> ...and we tried that [Circle of Friends] out with some of the children who were on the special needs register. So I met the parents and we talked about it with them, and to some of the children who really did have social problems which were affecting their emotional behaviour...and because all of us were trained to do it, you know, I'll do Circle of Friends with a group. So if I'm not teaching that class I'll take them, and then if it's different circumstances and it's a child in my class, then I could get another teacher to do it, because they'd had the same training.
>
> (SENCO, Ashvale Primary School)

It was felt in one school that, where a child was at risk of exclusion, any intervention work should be done with the whole class because so many behavioural and attainment problems were associated with poor peer relationships and 'interacting elements' (Docking, 1996). The IPSC team member then suggested ways in which teachers could work with children to promote good class relationships.

Other work has included anger management strategies either with individual children or with small groups, the introduction of play therapy for younger children and anti-bullying techniques as part of school in-service education. Specific interventions have been made, drawing on published materials which encourage role-play, drama based activities and therapeutic work with puppets. These approaches have focused on helping children to explore and come to understand some of their difficulties and extend their strategies to cope with these situations. Children have been encouraged to 'think aloud' about their reactions to situations that could cause them conflict and get them 'into trouble' and work through possible ways of handling these situations in ways which are positive and affirming.

Important work has also been done with parents but, as with the headteachers, some initial resistance has had, understandably, to be overcome. Essentially, this resistance was to do with the fact that it was the school that defined the situation, saying that a certain child was 'difficult' or had a 'problem'. The school then contacted the family, suggesting that IPSC could help.

According to one teacher, several working-class parents in her school were reluctant to engage with the IPSC team for fear that their children would be labelled 'difficult' and that this label would appear on the child's school records, which could have possible repercussions when choosing a secondary school. The teacher added that this reaction was in contrast to more middle-class parents who actively sought to have their children labelled, for example, dyslexic in order to secure extra help. (It should be noted that these descriptions by the teacher of the social class of the parents as well as the dichotomised reactions reported here, were her perceptions only.)

In general terms, schools (and some parents) that might have been apprehensive to start with, have seen value in being involved with the IPSC team. At the very least, the project has brought with it additional expertise, sometimes accelerated access to specialist provision, such as Child Guidance, as well as potentially introducing new strategies for staff through which to manage challenging behaviour and promote inclusion in school.

Outcomes in three schools

In what now follows, we draw on interviews with three senior teachers who were responsible for accepting the IPSC team into their schools. The data that are reported in this section were collected after IPSC had concluded its work in their schools. According to the reports from two of these informants, the work carried out by the IPSC team has left their schools in a stronger position to support vulnerable children and those potentially 'at risk' of exclusion. In the third school, a great deal of work had gone into supporting parents whose children had been 'at risk' of exclusion, and while the IPSC team member had worked with these parents the children had done well in school. When the support was withdrawn, the children were again 'at risk' of exclusion. However, what we are interested in is the way in which these individual schools responded to the project.

Anne is the Headteacher of St Congan's, a denominational school which had been identified as a high excluding school. She described her intake of children as 'quite mixed, really'. The school draws from a mixed housing area and attracts children from middle and working-class backgrounds. Anne was concerned about aggressive playground behaviour which led to exclusion. She argued that the class-rooms were more structured and thus there was less scope for aggression and acting out:

> Bad behaviour, difficult behaviour that often took place in the playground and it was like, you know, the sort of behaviour like bullying, aggression to others and other children getting hit and the ladies on playground duty, and they're very good, they reported the same children day after day.
>
> (Anne, Headteacher, St Congan's Primary School)

At St Congan's, the approach taken was individual focused. That is, the difficult child was identified and targeted for support:

> We do have children who find it really difficult to concentrate, children who've got behaviour problems etc., and it makes a huge difference if they've got somebody working with them one to one, it makes a difference to all the others in class as well.
>
> (Anne, Headteacher, St Congan's Primary School)

However, while there are some immediate gains in this approach, there are costs involved as well. Working to support one individual child who is 'at risk' of exclusion may indirectly signal to other children, parents and teachers, that this child is needy/to blame, etc. Targeting one child directly, may work to maintain negative stereotyping and a culture of individual 'blaming'. Working with one child who has overt emotional and behavioural difficulties may also mean that the competences that underpin social and emotional well-being are not shared with the other children – who will all have different sorts of needs in this affective domain (Weare, 2000). At the same time, this one child may be excluded from other mainstream activities and the curriculum while receiving individual support. Anne saw one problem as being related to issues of equality of treatment (Kelly, 1997).

> The whole bit about inclusion is that it isn't always equal opportunities for all the other children in the class, you know, when resources are constantly being diverted ...
>
> (Anne, Headteacher, St Congan's Primary School)

And while all the hard work with a small number of targeted children may be useful, Anne was not really convinced: 'It's sad and we work so hard but at the end of the day, we've contained them but have we done anything for them? I sometimes wonder'.

In this case, it seems as if the school has not really become actively involved in preventing exclusion but has relied on outside intervention to take on this challenge (Miller, 1996). Children at high risk of exclusion, because of aggressive behaviour and bullying, have been dealt with individually which may have resulted in the school not taking responsibility for an in-school ethos and culture which indirectly may have sustained some of the unwanted conduct (Docking, 1996).

Clara was the SENCO at Garthdee School, a school which serves a challenging community. The majority of the children are members of minority ethnic communities, many are refugees. The number of children who receive free school meals is high, even for the area, and the school is recognised as serving a disenfranchised and deprived constituency. The school has been identified as a 'high excluder' and as Clara explains:

> It would be, well in relation to teachers, it tends to be more, it's just kind of insolence and defiance, maybe tantrums, and I guess like self, lack of self control, you know, like having big tantrums, walking out of class, that sort of thing.

As a result of working with the project, the school has moved from a position where they were using exclusion almost as a form of self-preservation to a situation where they are conscious of the role they can exert to include and support the children. However, while there is a commitment towards inclusion, there are still some issues for the staff: 'I would say the teachers don't necessarily feel that they should be teaching those children, so inclusion, yes for the majority, but not all, as yet' (Clara). In some challenging schools such as Garthdee, there can be dilemmas about the rights of individual children set against and alongside the rights of other children and indeed, the rights of classroom teachers. Like Anne, Clara recognises that managing inclusion is not a straightforward or always manageable process:

> It seems to me that the children that we have at risk of exclusion, and then sort of, they'll have a little settled period and then they're at risk of exclusion again.
>
> (Clara, SENCO, Garthdee Primary School)

This irregular pattern can obviously result in teachers becoming disheartened. However, Garthdee has worked hard, particularly with a core of 'troubled' children. As Clara explains,

> We probably have identified I'd say about 30 or 40 children who have EBD [emotional and behavioural difficulties] problems as well, and then more recently, and as a result of the IPSC involvement, we've kind of looked within that category at pupils at risk of exclusion and the kind of support we have is to have, well very tight home school liaison, parental reviews on a two weekly basis for those children. This is for the risk of exclusion ones, we have dedicated time with some LSAs [Learning Support Assistants] for nominated children.
>
> (Clara, SENCO, Garthdee Primary School)

The IPSC project has given some very practical support to the school. Clara was emphatic that without the project, some hard-to-reach parents would not have been persuaded to come and talk about their children. She added, 'they've helped me get support for children through other agencies'. Tactics like Circle of Friends and counselling had made an enormous impact: 'I think to give the child some kind of positive forum to explore stuff is really vital'. Importantly, Clara appreciated the constraints imposed on her school by changes in the National Curriculum as well as other initiatives in primary schooling (Weare, 2000; Wright *et al.*, 2000).

Clara was able to identify ways in which her school had moved on in relation to preventing exclusion and trying to extend the school's capacity to become more inclusive. However, this was not going to happen overnight, and informal tactics of exclusion (Stirling, 1996; Parsons, 1999) were still deployed.

Overall though, the school and the staff have extended their capability to support 'difficult' children and are clearly more 'pro-active' and 'innovative' in supporting their children. In particular, Clara felt they had been able to build on the family liaison work started by IPSC, to the extent that they were trying to locate funding for a part-time post to sustain this. Thus, in this case, a 'mix' between an individualised approach, set within awareness of the social context, has proved to be positive in working to reduce exclusion.

> For example, one of those children, he was excluded formally for three days recently, and we spoke to his mum about how we could, you know, rein-tegrate him, given that he was causing a lot of trouble at dinner times, and she came and supervised him for a week, and it was a fantastic idea because he was completely embarrassed at the thought of having his mum, you know, Mr Toughie!
>
> (Clara, SENCO, Garthdee Primary School)

This quotation illustrates the ways in which not only specialist but also flexible and pragmatic strategies can provide valuable outcomes, as in the case of a parent helping teachers to review approaches to challenging behaviour. Sometimes it may be about validating common-sense approaches as the following example show.

> Just sort of thinking of sort of different ways of dealing with their anger, so we've got one boy where we let him, if he knows he's going to blow, he can come up to my room and just kind of sit there, and then eventually he calms himself down and goes back down. He's actually been able to manage himself much better as a result of doing that.
>
> (Clara, SENCO, Garthdee Primary School)

Trish was the Acting Headteacher and SENCO at Ashvale Primary School when IPSC started their intervention. Ashvale was also identified as a 'high excluder' although this designation was mainly due to one extremely challenging boy who had been excluded on 45 different occasions in one year. While the school served a predominantly middle-class intake, Trish made the point that

> just because you come from a nice middle-class background doesn't mean that you don't have problems.

Ashvale School was working hard to promote a whole school culture and ethos which supported all the children socially and emotionally as well as educationally. This culture, it was stressed, was intended to embrace all the children, not just those more obviously 'at risk' of exclusion. Trish worked with the school's IPSC key worker to extend the range of support being offered to the children in the school. All the staff, teaching and non-teaching, were involved. They asked for in-service training which enabled them to use Circle of Friends for themselves. The school extended its work through its School Council and set up a 'worry box' so that children could communicate (anonymously) their concerns to adults in the school. The school also initiated a process whereby the children could self-refer for counselling.

> They referred themselves because they were having problems with friendships, and how do they cope with groups of friends that didn't want to be with them any more and somebody new had come into class – things like that.
> (Trish, Acting Headteacher and SENCO, Ashvale Primary School)

In its approach towards formal exclusions and the desire to reduce these, Ashvale reached out to develop and extend its provision. The school saw a need for a coherent and wide range of tactics to empower children and to make space in which to promote their social and emotional well-being. In many ways, reducing exclusion was a by-product of their work and not the central concern – the IPSC project had been a useful starting point.

> The issue for the child that was excluded was to do with bullying. So, you know, if perhaps if the intervention [an anti-bullying initiative] had been there earlier, that [the exclusion] may not have happened.
> (Trish, Acting Headteacher and SENCO, Ashvale Primary School)

The intervention made by the IPSC worker chimed with many of the ideas which Trish had been trying to put into place. In her position as Acting Headteacher she was able to give a lead, but the culture and organisation of the school was sympathetic to the approach being suggested in the IPSC project. Bedding in characterises what occurred in Ashvale School.

> Lots of the things that we did that we actually enforce on the children, we didn't actually ask their opinion and what they felt they needed . . . it was about

ensuring that the children did have a voice and that they had somebody [the IPSC worker] that was neutral in the school.

(Trish, Acting Headteacher and SENCO, Ashvale Primary School)

Trish stressed the central importance of looking at the problem in the community of the classroom. In many ways, this echoes what Miller (1996, p. 209) claimed: 'mechanisms must exist so that lessons learned during an individual intervention can be generalized within the school'.

You've always got some children that have real problems of anger management and, on the whole, the sort of thing we needed was something that we could do that was all inclusive. You know, the whole class, to do with the whole class, something that became the fabric of the school.

In primary school you've got that opportunity to really get to know them and to be sympathetic to needs and things like that. You know, you're aware of the home issues, whereas in secondary school you lose part of that. And I think if you can teach children from early on to be able to talk about things and to understand one another, then I think that has to carry through to secondary school.

(Trish, Acting Headteacher and SENCO, Ashvale Primary School)

Discussion

What we have argued in this chapter is that children who are 'at risk' of being excluded from primary schools and those children who experience temporary or permanent exclusion from school, potentially run the risk of being socially excluded throughout their lives. Children who 'act out' in primary schools are frequently vulnerable and sometimes have a very fragile hold on making progress in the mainstream school system. They are therefore more likely to be excluded.

However, the one thing which schools and support agencies can do is help children understand and manage conflict more effectively, and thus maintain themselves at school.

Little (1996, p. 304) has argued that

the idea of prevention has much appeal to any profession. Why spend so much time and effort dealing with difficult problems – often ineffectively – when the problem could be stopped from happening in the first place.

The HAZ was keen to help prevent social exclusion in later life and funded the IPSC intervention project. The intention was preventative but it was also concerned with early intervention and some forms of 'treatment' (Little, 1996).

One of the real and continuing issues has to be with the extent to which the interventions have made any lasting differences. In some of the cases reported in this chapter, the schools perceived a real and immediate change for the better. This might have been because an 'outsider' came and talked with the teachers and gave them a space in which to voice their concerns. In other schools, the interventions clearly extended the range of the teachers concerned with the project and their in-school work to support 'at risk' children.

What we are suggesting in this chapter is that schools need to work to support 'at risk' children in school. While we have focused on young children 'at risk' of formal exclusion from their (English) schools, the tactics described in this chapter have currency for all teachers working in challenging environments with 'at risk' children, wherever these might be located. There is a real need to educate all children and teachers in, about and for, social and affective development in order to create and sustain the positive atmosphere and inclusive culture described in the Elton report (Elton, 1989). There is a fundamental need to see schools as places that support emotional growth and emotional literacy (Sharp, 2001).

Tactics such as worry boxes, School Councils where children are empowered, as opposed to merely being spectators of adult-defined concerns, and therapeutic interventions like counselling and Circle of Friends can make a difference in schools. Improving links with families also appears to have made some difference. While these approaches may well reduce exclusion rates from school, what we are suggesting is that these holistic, educative tactics work to support the emotional needs of all children. In policy terms, this may require a re-consideration of the current focus on academic standards and a re-orientation towards broader social and emotional needs. These early interventions would then work as a form of prevention rather than (institutional) 'cure' to promote inclusion and prevent exclusion.

References

Bourne, J., Bridges, L. and Searle, C. (1994) *Outcast England: How Schools Exclude Black Children* (London, Institute of Race Relations).

Cohen, R. and Hughes, J. with Ashworth, L. and Blair, M. (1994) *School's Out: The Family Perspective in School Exclusions* (London, Barnardos).

Department for Education and Employment (DfEE) (1998) *Permanent Exclusions from Schools* (London, HMSO).

Department for Education and Employment (DfEE) (1999a) *Permanent Exclusions from School 1997/8, Government Statistical Service, Statistical First Release 11/99 June 1999* (London, HMSO).

Department for Education and Employment (DfEE) (1999b) *Social Inclusion: Pupil Support Circular 10/99* (London, DfEE).

Department of Social Security (DSS) (1999) *Opportunity for All − Tackling Poverty and Social Exclusion: A Summary of the First Annual Report* (London, DSS).

Docking, J. (1996) *Managing Behaviour in the Primary School* (London, David Fulton).

Donovan, N. (Ed.) (1998) *Second Chances: Exclusion from School and Equality of Opportunity* (London, New Policy Institute).

Elton, L. (1989) *Discipline in Schools: Report of the Committee of Enquiry Chaired by Lord Elton* (London, HMSO).

Gillborn, D. and Gipps, C. (1996) *Recent Research on the Achievement of Ethnic Minority Pupils* (London, HMSO).

Goleman, D. (1996) *Emotional Intelligence* (London, Bloomsbury).

Harris, N.S. and Eden, K. with Blair, A. (2000) *Challenges to School Exclusion: Exclusion, Appeals and the Law* (London, RoutledgeFalmer).

Hayden, C. (1996) Primary school exclusions: the need for integrated solutions, in: E. Blyth and J. Milner (Eds) *Exclusions from School: Inter-professional Issues in Policy and Practice* (London, Routledge).

Hayden, C. (1997) *Children Excluded from Primary School: Debates, Evidence, Responses* (Buckingham, Open University Press).

Her Majesty's Stationery Office (HMSO) (1986) *Education (No. 2) Act 1986* (London, HMSO).

Her Majesty's Stationery Office (HMSO) (1989) *Children Act 1989* (London, HMSO).

Her Majesty's Stationery Office (HMSO) (1993) *Education (No. 2) Act 1993* (London, HMSO).

Her Majesty's Stationery Office (HMSO) (1998) *School Standards and Framework Act* (London, HMSO).

Kelly, D. (1997) Education and difficult children: the teaching dilemma, *Young Minds*, 29, pp. 17–18.

Little, M. (1996) Prevention and early intervention with children in need: definitions, principles and examples of good practice, *Children and Society*, 13, pp. 304–316.

Macrae, S., Maguire, M. and Milbourne, L. (2003) Social Exclusion: Exclusion from School, *International Journal of Inclusive Education*, 7(1), pp. 1–13.

Munn, P., Lloyd, G. and Cullen, M.A. (2000) *Alternatives to Exclusion from School* (London, Paul Chapman).

Miller, A. (1996) *Pupil Behaviour and Teacher Culture* (London, Cassell).

Newton, C., Taylor, G. and Wilson, D. (1996) Circles of friends: an inclusive approach to meeting emotional and behavioural needs, *Educational Psychology in Practice*, 11(4), pp. 41–48.

Osler, A. and Hill, J. (1999) Exclusion from school and racial equality: an examination of government proposals in the light of recent research evidence, *Cambridge Journal of Education*, 29(1), pp. 33–62.

Parsons, C. (1999) *Education, Exclusions and Citizenship* (London, Routledge).

Parsons, C., Benn, L., Hailes, J. and Howlett, K. (1994) *Excluding Primary School Children* (London, Family Policy Studies Centre).

Pearpoint, J., Forrest, M. and Snow, J. (1992) *The Inclusion Papers: Strategies to Make Inclusion Work* (Toronto, Inclusion Press).

Rustique-Forrester, E. (2000) Exploring the policy influence of England's national curriculum on school exclusion: a dilemma of entitlement and unintended exclusion, in: C. Cullingford and P. Oliver (Eds) *The National Curriculum and its Effects* (London, Ashgate).

Scottish Her Majesty's Inspectorate of Education (2001) *Alternatives to School Exclusion* (Edinburgh, The Stationery Office).

Sharp, P. (2001) *Nurturing Emotional Literacy: A Practical Guide for Teachers, Parents, and Those in the Caring Professions* (London, David Fulton).

Social Exclusion Unit (SEU) (1998) *Truancy and School Exclusion* (London, The Stationery Office)

Spring, J. (2000) *The Universal Right to Education: Justification, Definition, and Guidelines* (London, Lawrence Erlbaum).

Stirling, M. (1996) Government policy and disadvantaged children, in: E. Blyth and J. Milner (Eds) *Exclusions from School: Inter-Professional Issues in Policy and Practice* (London, Routledge).

Weare, K. (2000) *Promoting Mental, Emotional and Social Health: A Whole School Approach* (London, Routledge).

Wright, C., Weekes, D. and McGlaughlin, A. (2000) *'Race', Class and Gender in Exclusion from School* (London, Falmer Press).

Chapter 13

Inclusive education in accelerated and professional development schools

A case-based study of two school reform efforts in the USA

Susan Peters

Introduction

This chapter is a comparative analysis of two of the Professional Development School (PDS) and Accelerated Schools Project (ASP) schools in which I acted as a participant–observer, as exemplars of these two reform efforts. I have selected these two schools as particularly positive examples of their respective reforms in order to illuminate the possibilities that school reform holds with respect to including Special Education Needs (SEN) students.

Both school reform efforts have developed a substantial following and presence in the USA. PDSs were spearheaded in the 1980s by a consortium known as the 'Holmes Group', consisting of 90 leading institutions of higher education concerned with improving pre-service teacher education in tandem with improving K-12 public school education. The ASP began its work at about the same time as PDS and has currently been adopted by over 600 public schools nation-wide, receiving considerable attention in the popular media as well as scholarly journals for its successes in improving academic achievement of large numbers of 'at-risk' students in these schools.

Drawing from my experiences in two of these PDS and ASP schools, I examine the implementation processes of school change and evaluate their effectiveness in terms of specific inclusive education goals and values. In my analysis of these schools' experiences, I use data from several research projects over the course of my ten-year involvement from 1990 to 2000. Both schools were located in urban areas (within the states of California and Michigan). Both enrolled large numbers of at-risk, disadvantaged, minority and SEN students. The Accelerated School I chose for this study is an elementary school that serves grades kindergarten through fifth (i.e. students ages 5–10). The Professional Development school I chose is a middle school that serves grades 6–8 (i.e. students ages 11–14). The majority of students in the PDS were of African-American descent, and in the Accelerated School, the majority of students were of Mexican-American, Hispanic or Latino descent. Both schools exemplify particularly challenging efforts in terms of their urban contexts, and 'minority' populations. I consider both schools and their respective school reform approaches in order to anticipate the challenge that one school represents an 'island of excellence'. I also assert that if successes can be achieved in these two very challenging schools, then a strong potential exists for wider adoption and success.

[...]

Professional development schools: towards equity and quality in education

Professional Development Schools are community-based K–12 public schools in partnership with universities in order to accomplish four generally agreed upon goals and six guiding principles (Clark, 1999, p. 9). In addition, the National Council for Accreditation of Teacher Education (NCATE) has identified five critical attributes of PDSs, along with threshold standards and specific indicators of these attributes (NCATE, 1998). These goals, principles, attributes and standards are summarized in Table 13.1.

Table 13.1 Goals, principles, attributes and standards of professional development schools in the USA

Goal	Principle	Attribute	Standard
1 Provide clinical setting for preservice teachers	• Commitment to new organizational structures	• Organization, roles and structures	• Resources, time and processes promote continuous improvement in teaching, learning, and organizational life
2 Engage in continuous professional development of practising teachers	• Learning community • Teaching and language of adults and students	• Norms and practices support adult and student learning	• Integration of preservice and practising teachers, learning with school instructional programmes
3 Promote and conduct inquiry to advance knowledge	• Reflection and inquiry are central to teaching and learning	• Collaboration	• Research is jointly defined and implemented among school staff and university faculty
4 Provide exemplary education for K–12 students	• Teaching for understanding • High expectations for all students	• Equity • Accountability and quality assurance	• Norms and practices support equity and language by all students • Accountable to public and professional standards for teaching and language and preparation of preservice teachers

Holmes Middle School: a PDS at work

Demographic and cultural context

Located in an urban area near Detroit, Michigan, Holmes Middle School became a PDS in partnership with Michigan State University in 1990, with approximately 500 seventh- and eighth-grade students (ages 11–14). Enrolment jumped 25 per cent during the academic year 1995–96, with the addition of 226 sixth-grade students. As of 2000, the school was serving between 700 and 800 sixth-, seventh- and eighth-grade students.

Holmes began its partnership with MSU in 1990 with a school-wide decision-making team and subject-area inquiry groups. Now the school is organised in eight semi-autonomous learning community groups, each one consisting of five teachers, a community representative and 80 students. Block-scheduling and integrated curriculum studies replaced subject-area and self-contained classes mid-way in the school's development during the ten years of the study. Finally, Holmes began its participation at the low end of student academic achievement in its district (composed of approximately 40 schools within the city limits), and has risen dramatically, achieving temporary accreditation, and becoming the only middle school in the district to take on the responsibility of a prototype 'Explorer II' school reform project in 1998.

Process of change: building an inclusive school culture

Explanations of these changes are complex, but some of the outcomes are clear: effective organization for school-improvement, implementation of school-based decision-making processes, a school culture of inquiry and risk-taking, powerful teaching and learning and improved student academic achievement. These accomplishments raise important questions regarding the processes of change. Specifically, how did Holmes Middle School achieve these outcomes? What were the factors influencing change?

To begin with, the processes and events that took place or 'set the stage' for Holmes' commitment to school-wide change began with 'pockets of excellence'. From 1990 to 1995, MSU faculty involvement included upwards of 15 faculty participating in 22 distinct projects at its peak in 1995. At Holmes, the partnership began with matching specific teacher and faculty areas of interest, mainly focused in content/subject areas: mathematics, literacy, social studies and science. Projects in these subject-matter areas played a significant role in developing a culture of inquiry. As one teacher put it, 'That first year was an opportunity to reflect, think, and envision the needs of an ideal urban middle school'. From the perspective of several of the teachers, these opportunities for reflection (in-services, coursework, summer institutes, content area study groups, site-based management team meetings and various forms of systematic inquiry and action research) fostered a desire to change through exposure to multiple styles of teaching and becoming more knowledgeable about content.

In this work of improving teaching through inquiry and collaboration, the partners chose to focus on two explicit overarching goals that characterized their work from roughly 1990 to 1995. These goals were (1) to create effective learning communities whereby students (*and* teachers) would be motivated, engaged active learners and (2) to learn to teach for understanding whereby experiential, project-based, 'reality-based' curriculum and instruction interacted. As a result, problem-solving, cooperative learning and mixed ability groupings that promoted social justice and democratic values permeated many of the projects they undertook.

From the beginning, a significant amount of energy was focused on reaching out to explicitly address the needs of the most marginalized youth, and those SEN students who were struggling with extreme behaviour and academic issues. Holmes staff were dedicated to diversity and equity issues within the goals of developing learning communities and learning to teach for understanding. This dedication was evidenced by two projects specifically aimed at SEN students: the Integrated Language Arts Partnership and Project Choice.

The Integrated Language Arts Partnership (ILAP) teamed a seventh-grade teacher and a SEN teacher with two faculty members from the university. Previous Language Arts instruction at Holmes had focused on rote learning of grammatical rules, teacher-directed learning and standardized texts with short stories geared toward white middle-class student's background and experiences. In developing the ILAP, these two teachers focused on a more appropriate literacy curriculum for urban middle school children. They based the experiences in ILAP on the two school-wide methods described earlier (creating effective learning communities, and teaching for understanding). Findings after the first year of ILAP implementation revealed students were much more articulate than the previous year about what they learned from literature, how it connected to people and events in their own lives, and how they learned the content. Provided with books by African-American writers, students chose to write about the stories and novels they had read, and read a complete novel for the first time. Samples of student writing collected throughout the year revealed an increasing range of purpose. The quality and quantity of students' written work continued to improve the more the team created a social-justice-based curriculum that emphasized and supported students' choices about the different kinds of writing they could produce. Reflecting on this shift to student-centred teaching based on relevance, democratic values and active learning, the (general education) language arts teacher asserted:

> [Through this project] we learned about collaborative grouping. We saw leadership abilities emerge from some of these kids that normally you wouldn't have found. So we are able to see, because of the cooperative learning, that everybody is good at something.

Holmes PDS faculty involved in the ILAP studied the academic achievement and self-esteem of SEN students who were included in general education classrooms.

Results showed that SEN students were able to function effectively in general education classes while their self-esteem, grades and standardized test scores remained at levels equal to those prior to their inclusion in general education classrooms.

The second project, *Project Choice*, paired peer-helpers with severely multiple-disabled SEN students to enhance effective communication and to bring these students in to the social and academic mainstream of the school. Holmes PDS faculty participating in the Project Choice classroom for severely disabled students examined how electronic communication boards could affect the lives of students, their parents and educators. Pre-intervention data were collected on students' expressive and receptive language, initiation of conversations and student performance on 15 tasks involved in operating the communication boards. Results indicated student gain in expressive vocabulary, frequency of initiations of conversations and mastery of tasks needed to operate these boards.

These projects are examples of 'pockets of excellence' that gradually contributed to an overall *climate of collaboration and inquiry* throughout the school. As one general education teacher put it, before PDS initiatives, classrooms at Holmes were 'closed doors', but through her interaction with MSU faculty, she learned to 'open my door and not feel threatened'. A special education teacher commented that collaboration 'increased expectations of myself, colleagues and students and contributed to a more united feeling within departments and the total school community'. This special education teacher 'became more confident' and gained 'a higher respect' for her colleagues. This gain in confidence was reportedly experienced by a significant number of teachers and is supported by the fact that twelve of Holmes' teachers have assumed substantial leadership positions within the school and/or school district.

Once the work of establishing a viable partnership had developed to a sufficient level that collaborative work could be undertaken, emphasis in the partnership expanded from individual projects to school-wide efforts characterized by curriculum integration, instructional support and innovation and systematic assessment strategies for overall school improvement. Holmes teachers and staff underwent substantial changes in the ways that they made decisions, organized to do their work and monitored their progress. These changes resulted in substantial outcomes and benefits for *all* students as well as teachers and administrators. Block scheduling, with integration of subject-matter teaching replaced individualized classes. Grade level teams became organized into learning communities with semi-autonomous decision-making authority.

Negotiating tensions

This new school climate, and the leadership that it spawned in teachers, was mediated by the need to implement district-level standards and benchmarks and to incorporate these in to state-mandated school improvement plans in 1996. (Schools in the USA are organized in districts comparable with Local Education Authorities in the UK.) At this point, individual 'PDS Projects' as they were called, became folded into the overall goals for school improvement. Members of the school improvement committee linked these projects with these goals and developed content standards into school curricula.

Related to this effort to develop content standards at Holmes, an overriding concern regarding the school improvement plan was to achieve accreditation status. Accreditation in the state of Michigan is linked to improvement in state-wide assessment scores of students (known as the 'MEAP'). The 'open door' climate and norms of collaboration that had been established, supported and complemented a school-wide effort not only to assess students and tailor instruction to address weaknesses, but also to support strengths of students in particular subject areas and learning styles. The school as a whole agreed to focus on literacy, and in particular story-comprehension, adapting a school-wide instructional strategy of graphic organizers, to be used across all content areas and departments (including special education). A teacher in the school was identified as the 'MEAP Coordinator' and she organized curriculum-based pre- and post-test assessments of students at three week intervals. Collation and analysis of data from these teacher-developed assessments were followed by instructional strategies targeted to individual strengths and areas needing improvement. This school-wide organization to improve student achievement met with visible success (20 per cent pass rate in the first year, 40 per cent in the second, 67.5 per cent in the third), which increased morale and established the efficacy of systematic needs-based assessment, evaluation and modified instructional interventions to meet specified goals.

However, pressure to 'teach to the test', as in many schools and school districts in Michigan (and the USA) did not go unquestioned by teachers at Holmes. One teacher at Holmes expressed her beliefs as follows:

> I hate the MEAP test. I hate it because it uses comparisons among school districts and individual schools. . . . I don't think it's fair that kids in our school take the [same] test . . . [as] white students from a high economic class. I maintain that if our kids had a story about an African-American whom they admire, they would be more involved and they would do a better job. . . . I know the MEAP is here and we can't do anything about that. However, . . . there are some things these kids need that aren't part of any standards.

This teacher's beliefs exemplify the critical, reflective stance toward teaching and learning that had developed at Holmes PDS – a stance that is student-centred, committed to the principles of equity and social justice and that openly contests the pervasive positivist governmental school improvement policy agenda in the USA. The collaborative inquiry groups, teacher leadership in decision-making regarding school improvement, along with school-wide organization into broad-based learning communities all demonstrate the five criteria identified as essential to successful inclusive education.

Emerging as an inclusive school

For Holmes, a watershed event in the evolution of professional development school practice was the school-wide decision to become a prototype middle school for the district in 1998. Schools had to apply to the district for this status and commit to school-wide reform that is outcomes-based, standards-driven and organized in learning communities and high performance work teams. As the principal put it, 'At this point, Holmes has become standards driven, but at the same time we are committed to excellence in our teachers and students'.

Prototype schools commit themselves to a collaborative learner-centred approach that is characterized by (1) continual focus on research and development and (2) careful training of teachers and administrators which involves continuous development of new knowledge, skills and talent among leadership and experienced staff as well as novices ('An Emerging Operational Vision' January 1997, 16). Expectations are that 'professional development and professional conferral are now integral to all teachers' work – as is their regular participation in research, development and policy making' (p. 20). In addition, teachers in prototype schools must recognize that roles have changed, as they become part of an educator's collaboration, involving networks of institutional and community partnerships. These characteristics are essentially those of the six goals that had been articulated as the vision of PDS in the beginning of our partnership, and they constitute significant *cultural aspects of change*.

Taking on new roles and making decisions beyond the classroom, teachers came to have a significant impact on the quality and inclusive education of SEN students. During a learning community meeting at Holmes in the Fall of 1999, discussion of these students provides perhaps the most compelling evidence that inclusive education had become a philosophy rather than an add-on programme.

Teacher 1:   We have 150 special education students and 49 of the LD (Learning Disability) students have two or more general education classes.

Teacher 2:   We have a problem with block scheduling [with these students].

Teacher 3:   One hundred and fifteen of these students have been put on teams. Some are really struggling academically.

Teacher 4:   Have the parents been informed? Do the IEPs (Individualized Education Plans) reflect their Inclusive Education?

Teacher 5:   Sometimes the general ed. students have more trouble than the special education students. The LD students in my class are always in the top two-thirds of class in academic achievement.

Teacher 6:   We should see what the kids need, not how it will fit into the Learning Community block scheduling or the district's operational vision.

Teacher 7:   We need to adapt our lessons for pace and level.

This in-depth description of PDS activities and initiatives at Holmes Middle School, provides strong evidence that teachers are engaged in changing, improving and evaluating their own practice. In the process, they developed a school culture that sustained and withstood external pressures from the positivist school effectiveness and school reform agendas imposed by the district. Ultimately, the partnership between university faculty and school teachers at Holmes succeeded in creating an environment in which the teachers at the school could work together collaboratively to improve teaching and learning for *all* students as the core focus of their work.

Accelerated schools in action: the case of Esperante School

In the Preface to *Accelerated Schools in Action*, Edward St John describes the Accelerated Schools Project as a movement that, since its inception in 1986, has focused on 'transforming schools with students at-risk of dropping out into schools with high expectations for all students. The project is intended to transform school cultures that slow down learning through remediation into cultures that accelerate the learning of all students' (Finnan *et al.*, 1996, p. ix). Specifically, as Henry M. Levin, the individual who spearheaded the ASP, explains, accelerated schools are 'dedicated to bringing all students into the academic mainstream by providing highly enriched educational experiences for all children' (Levin, 1996, p. 3).

The ASPs philosophy, formally the exclusive purview of SEN students labelled as gifted and talented, was seen as at least equally of benefit to students at-risk for school failure. An accelerated school holds itself up to a set of values which include equity, community, risk-taking, experimentation, reflection, participation, trust and communication. An accelerated school also strives toward a set of practices based on the goal of creating for all children the dream school all parents would want for their own children. This goal is embodied in four central principles of the ASP: (1) unity of purpose, (2) empowerment with responsibility, (3) building on strengths and (4) powerful learning. These are described here.

- *Unity of purpose*: this principle refers to a common purpose embodied in the educational practices of a school on behalf of all its children. It is a living vision and culture working together toward high expectations for all children, and children internalize these expectations for themselves.
- *Empowerment with responsibility*: this principle promotes the concept that all school staff, parents, and students take responsibility for the major decisions that determine their educational experiences and outcomes. It is characterized by a collaborative effort that embraces the entire school community. At the same time, everyone in the school and community takes responsibility for the consequences of their collaborative decisions through continuous assessment and accountability. This responsibility is accomplished through a system of governance and problem-solving that includes students, staff and parents in the daily life of the school policy and practices.

- *Building on strengths*: this principle includes not only traditional measures of intelligence, but also areas of interest, curiosity, motivation and knowledge that grow out of the culture, personalities and experiences of all children and teachers. It is characterized by reciprocal teaching, cooperative learning, peer and cross-age tutoring and individual and group projects. It includes models of collaborative consultation. All participants are expected to contribute to the success of all children.
- *Powerful learning*: this principle integrates school climate, organization, curriculum and instructional strategies to build on strengths of students for optimal learning outcomes. Powerful learning is characterized by students who are pro-active learners, and skill development through intrinsically challenging activities.

Finally, accelerated schools also differentiate between the 'big wheels' of the school and the 'little wheels'. The big wheels are the school philosophy and overall change process shared by everyone. The little wheels are innovations that grow out of group or individual activities as they face the challenges of implementing innovations in classrooms. An inquiry process is central to the operation of both big wheels and little wheels. Schools form cadres of individuals who focus on specific areas of need that have been identified by the school as a whole.

Esperante Elementary School: accelerated means inclusive too

Demographic and cultural context

Located in a large metropolitan area of a city on the West Coast of the USA, Esperante became an accelerated school in 1993. It contains a large number of at-risk, low socio-economic, minority and SEN students, grades K-5. The majority of students are Spanish-speaking.

During my six months' study of Esperante in 1995, I became convinced that every moment (planned or unplanned) is a learning moment for teachers and students in the school. In the following description, I focus on examples of powerful learning, as this element of accelerated schools is where all of the principles and values of accelerated schools come together to promote inclusive education.

All of the teachers I observed at Esperante displayed a variety of teaching styles geared toward powerful learning. These teaching styles seemed particularly to exemplify all four ASP central principles. The following description focuses on three teachers as exemplars of these principles in action: Mrs Chavez, Mrs Maine and Mr Black.

Mrs Chavez began her teaching career after several years in management. She applied these management skills to classroom practice. In her words: 'I have to be structured. I don't reward for potential. I reward for doing the job'. The physical classroom organization reflected this structure. Students' desks were arranged in a long U-shaped row with clearly demarcated work centres at the periphery of the room. The students in Mrs Chavez' class knew what was expected of them. From the first day of class, she informed them that everyone is responsible for their own behaviour. She expected her students to be 'self-governing'. To accomplish these goals, students took responsibility for correcting their own work, so they could 'see their own mistakes and correct them'.

Mrs Maine used a whole-language approach with her class. Her 'Readers and Writers' workshops required independence and self-initiative on the part of her students. Much of her class time was spent in collaborative work in small groups or in pairs. She encouraged divergent thinking, and 'no single way of doing something'. Students were encouraged to share their writing and to help each other. The room often seemed noisy and chaotic, but when one looked closely, one noticed children enthusiastically talking about and reading their stories to each other or sharing their predictions regarding what is in a 'Mystery Box'. The students' desks in her room were arranged in groups of four to facilitate this sharing, with a large rug at the centre of the room for people to collaborate in different groups. Students who were independent and self-initiators seemed to thrive in this kind of environment. They always found a way to fit in, and no one seemed to notice that they were doing something different, because everyone was doing something different.

Mr Black's style of teaching was epitomized by the microphone at the front of the room. He was an emcee, as he elicited responses in an interactive form of whole-group instruction. The desks in his room were arranged as in an orchestra, with seats radiating out from a centre arena. His style was one of choreographing and orchestrating as he guided students through the discovery process of learning. He would stop from time to time to point out creative variations in responses from students, to encourage questioning and to reward accomplishments.

Behind the unique teaching styles of each of these teachers, several elements of powerful learning in curriculum and instruction are common to all of them. These are flexibility, high expectations, balance of academic and social needs, relevance of curriculum to students' lives, importance of peers as role models and working together to develop a community of learners. These elements are described in depth here.

Flexibility is a crucial condition for SEN students to be successful in the general education classroom. Tom, a SEN student with Down's syndrome, could not be included if Mrs Chavez insisted that he do his basic number facts at the same rate of speed as other students, and without the aid of a calculator. Mrs Maine's activities tended to have multi-ability components, so that Derek, a student with learning difficulties, could use this flexibility to choose his own ability level and extent of participation. William, a student with severe emotional disability, needed flexibility to choose the timing and circumstances under which he could perform classroom activities. In all of these situations, the key question that Mrs Maine believes must be asked is: should the child have to adjust to the curriculum or should the curriculum adjust to the child?

This element of flexibility in powerful learning relates to issues of *academic excellence and high expectations*. All of the teachers I interviewed referred to the fact that they don't treat the SEN students any differently from other students. What they were referring to was differences in expectations. Academic excellence is something all teachers strive to accomplish for all students. Again, Mrs Maine asked a key question: 'If it's not one [single] way, as long as you reach the goals what does it matter how?' She held the belief that there are different ways to demonstrate ability in the classroom. Mr Black's science class involving the study of force by building levers allowed students to work in pairs, to help each other, and to attempt different levels of difficult lever systems. However, all of these levels of difficulty produced the same outcome in terms of academic excellence: students learned the importance of force and how it operates in their environment. Mrs Maine's geometry activity – working with pentaminos – is another example of multiple ways to reach the same academic goal. In order to determine the properties of shapes and how they change, some students wrote stories about 'the shape shifter', some made predictions and estimated how many boxes they could make from different configurations of pentaminos; and some recorded the findings and declared whether or not the pentamino had been made into a box. Finally, *Young Author's Books* for some students contained long stories, and some were a few sentences. However, all of them clearly demonstrated the ability to organize thoughts, sequence actions in a story and provide imaginative story lines.

All of these examples of academic excellence retain high expectations for students. They do not compromise the learning goal or the expectation that students will demonstrate mastery of a concept. However, they are not simple 'paper and pencil' activities. They all require multi-ability components and flexibility of both method and outcome.

All teachers stressed the importance of a *learning community*. They spent considerable time demonstrating the principles of working together and providing opportunities for students to learn from each other. As Mr Black asserted, 'Learning takes team work'. He told the students at the beginning of the year, 'Let's help Nathaniel [a student with Down's syndrome]. Let's work together'. Beyond the sense of community in the classroom as a whole, each SEN student had a Circle of Friends who provided a close-knit, personal sense of community. Derek's peers often intervened to comfort him when things didn't go well, and to encourage him to 'get his work done first'. Tom received assistance from the girl next to him in correcting his math problems. William boosted his self-esteem by being able to demonstrate his athletic skills as a 'slugger' in softball.

This sense of community is very difficult to obtain in self-contained classrooms, where students are separated from their peers for all or part of the day. This sense of community is also beneficial for all students, not just the SEN students. As Mr Black stated: 'The greatest benefit of inclusion has been that all the kids get a sense of compassion. They get a sense of themselves on a continuum of ability to get things done. And they say to themselves, 'If Mr Black loves Nathaniel, you don't have to be smart to be loved'. Finally, these examples of community involve learning socialization skills, but they are not developed in isolation from the academic skills expected of all students.

Process of change: building an inclusive school culture

The examples given before demonstrate the integral components of the powerful learning principle of ASP that are essential to developing proactive learners in a nurturing classroom environment. Overall, teaching styles combine with elements of flexibility, high expectations and balance of academic and social needs, to promote inclusive education for all students. However, for powerful learning to be effective and enduring, it must have support from the school as a whole.

Collaborative teamwork was important to building a positive school culture at Esperante. In reflecting on the changes at Esperante, the Principal asserted that teachers were isolated before the change to the Accelerated Schools Project. As a result of inquiry work in cadres and a school-wide taking-stock process, teachers no longer felt isolated. The ASP, according to the Principal, 'strengthened teachers' ability to share, their expertise, and their ability to ask questions'. This collaborative teamwork created a unity of purpose, which is the first basic principle of accelerated schools. This unity of purpose was evident among teachers, as they met and planned for their weekly rotation schedule. As an example, third-grade teachers rotated students one-half day a week among all four of them, teaching special interest subjects in geometry, math, science, social studies and language arts. Students signed up for a four-week course with one of the four teachers. Each teacher was assigned one-fourth of the students from each class.

Time to plan for students' learning collaboratively included not only adaptation of curriculum but also *adaptation of learning contexts*. To enhance probability of success for SEN students, the full-time inclusive education specialist in the school who was formerly a SEN teacher, discussed students' progress with other teachers as often as possible. However, she asserted: 'We need more collaborative work in classes. When I know what's going on in a class, I can plan. It's easier to support a student'. Across all grades, the general education curriculum was planned in concert with the learning resource teacher who adapted the curriculum by providing individualized folders for students' work that was complementary to the general education curriculum. She also provided direct classroom support by her presence during instruction. In her 'pull-out' hour she taught SEN students strategies for doing their homework, and other operational skills for being ready to learn.

The unity of purpose demonstrated in the teachers' collaboration for classroom instruction and curriculum adaptation was also evident in the work of one of the school's cadres – the integration cadre. One integration cadre member stated: 'Integration *period* is the goal here'. The integration cadre worked on bilingual students' access to curriculum as well as SEN students' issues.

Cadres also provided an opportunity to demonstrate the second principle of accelerated schools – *empowerment with responsibility*. The curriculum cadre at Esperante was responsible for scheduling staff development days and the school as a whole voted on priority topics. Instructional associates and other members of the Esperante school-community participated in these staff development activities. When an in-service on inclusive education was developed in collaboration with staff and parents' input, the vision that these are *our* children was reinforced.

Negotiating tensions

Taking ownership for students is dependent to a large extent on school climate and expectations. Traditional 'pull-out' programmes for SEN students have served to reinforce the impression on the part of general education teachers that these students 'belong to special education' and thus are the responsibility of the resource specialist teacher. The inclusive education specialist reflected that there is a pervasive feeling on the part of general education teachers that these kids are different, and that they don't have the expertise to teach SEN students. However, she asserted: 'A special education credential doesn't suddenly give you a gift of dealing with these kids.'

Her response to the 'pull-out mentality' was to change the paradigm to that of a 'push-in' philosophy. In this way of thinking, SEN students belong in the general education classroom and can be successful there with appropriate supports. Mrs Chavez, the general education third-grade teacher who worked with Tom, agreed. After her first year of experience in a school culture of inclusive education, she stated:

> I really do believe in a push-in program. Pull-out programs should only be used if they are focused and have set outcomes that are short term. Otherwise, any time the student leaves the room [for pull-out] they wonder what's going on while they're gone.

Taking ownership of students has very important consequences for *building on strengths* of students. A pull-out programme tends to remediate weaknesses in the classroom. A push-in programme forces a focus on building on strengths necessary for success in the classroom. In addition, SEN students at Esperante learned many of their skills from peer modelling. Their Circle of Friends provided ongoing support for them in academics as well as areas of socialization. Derek's, Nathaniel's and William's peers recognized their strengths and naturally rewarded success more effectively than teachers could. Because these students were learning together in the general education classroom, students also took ownership through developing normal friendships – opportunities that are lacking in a pull-out programme.

Emerging as an inclusive school

Parent involvement and support was mentioned by all the teachers as crucial to the success of inclusive education in an accelerated school. Evidence of parental involvement at Esperante was pervasive. Mrs Chavez had nearly perfect attendance by parents at the school's annual open house, and the school as a whole did nearly as well. Derek's mother was an active member of the integration cadre. Several parents attended school-as-a-whole meetings. Parents were also instrumental in finding consultants who provided weekly enrichment programmes at Esperante – programmes such as dance and music that had been widely curtailed from school budgets in the district. These consultants freed up teacher time so they could meet by grade level to plan powerful learning activities. The teachers also welcomed parental support in the classroom. One parent I talked with assisted regularly in Mrs Chavez' class with small groups of students.

As Mrs Chavez asserted: 'One of the best parts of accelerated schools is parental involvement'. She felt that parents had built a sense of community that extended beyond school walls. As an example, one of the key issues in deciding to integrate SEN students at Esperante was the decision that parents would take responsibility for teaching these students daily living skills such as tying shoes and telling time. These skills were formerly the purview of SEN or Special Day Class instruction in pull-out classrooms. Parents and teachers met and agreed to take on these responsibilities themselves in order to free up the teachers' time for instruction in support of academic skills in the general education classroom (a priority expressed by parents).

Classroom support is crucial for all general education teachers. One teacher's statement exemplified this need: 'I couldn't do it [include SEN students] without the support of my classroom aide or the SEN teacher!' The interventions that were provided for William in curbing his anger allowed him to stay and function in Mrs Maine's class. She worked in equal partnership with the inclusive education support personnel and believed that aides have to be 'self-initiators'. Specifically, they need to be able to assess situations on the spot and provide timely interventions.

Support staff also provided assistance for *all* students in the general education classroom. Inclusive education support staff often met with a small group for reading instruction at the back table in Mrs Maine's class. These student groupings were spontaneously constructed based on current assessments of any students in the class needing special attention on a short-term basis.

Further, support need not be directly present in the classroom to be helpful. The inclusive education support staff prepared individual folders for students to work on which were placed in a specified location in the classroom. When the support staff was not present, students knew that they were to retrieve these folders and work on their adapted assignments while the other students were completing theirs. All of this support would not have been possible without the ability of the school as a whole to schedule flexible time for teachers. The full-time inclusive education associate, along with a half-time instructional associate rotated every two weeks among the three third-grade classes. Either one might spend time in four different classrooms during one instructional hour. Scheduling and planning time was built in during consultant days on Thursdays, with the addition of an early release day each Wednesday for school-as-a-whole planning and cadre meetings.

These factors identified by teachers as being crucial to their success with SEN students – collaboration, taking ownership, curriculum adaptation, parental involvement and classroom support – demonstrate the five specific criteria for effective inclusive education laid out in the introduction to this study. In addition, collaboration, along with curriculum adaptation and parental involvement, provides a unity of purpose for including students and for powerful learning situations in the classroom. Taking ownership provides empowerment with responsibility, building on the unity of purpose that enforces the vision the principal voices as the mentality that 'all children are *our* children'. Classroom support allows teachers to carry into action the notion of building on strengths.

Conclusion

School reform and inclusive education: bridging the gap and 'doing what comes naturally'

In a recent comprehensive review of school effectiveness research, Lipsky and Gartner (1997, p. 225) assert that school reform and the movement for inclusive education have largely proceeded along separate tracks in the USA, with little attention being paid to SEN students in the former. However, an in-depth examination of the processes of change and building an inclusive school culture that were involved in the two schools' reform efforts in this study – Accelerated Schools and Professional Development School Partnerships – reveals that to a significant extent, inclusive education means 'doing what comes naturally' (Levin, 1997, pp. 389–400). This process of doing what comes naturally begins with the belief in inclusive education as a foundational precept behind everything that happens in schools.

Both of the ASP and PDS schools' processes of change consisted of comprehensive, thorough approaches to reform in all aspects of school organization, teaching and learning. Both involved a focus on individual teachers and students as well as on whole-groups or school-as-a-whole processes of decision-making, dialogue and innovation. Over all, the processes of change involved in both schools included creating a school culture that adhered to constructivist principles of 'educative change' in tandem with standards of excellence. The resulting combination of social justice and equity with 'standards' reform proved essential factors for effective inclusive education to take place.

Finally, both schools' reforms demonstrated increased capacity to accomplish the successful inclusion of SEN students socially, physically and academically. The complex approaches to the processes of change supported and developed teacher leadership and empowerment with responsibility in both schools. Combined with a core philosophy that drove their initiatives and a critical reflective spirit of inquiry, the results for SEN students meant doing what comes naturally: inclusive education. These two schools demonstrate that school reform efforts and inclusive education *can* be mutually 'inclusive'.

The results of this comparative study suggest that the 'gap' between school reform and the movement toward inclusive education may not be as wide as it is perceived by many in the field of education. The forces against educational change have deep roots in the traditional bureaucratic organization of schools and in the national push for standardization of curriculum and academic outcomes. Teachers in individual classrooms still struggle with the challenges of teaching and learning to large groups of diverse students. Deeply held beliefs about 'special' students' perceived weaknesses and deficiencies, reinforced by the widespread practice of separate tracks for preparing 'special' and 'general' education teachers in university programmes, are difficult to change.

Developing beliefs, practices and organizational structures that support inclusive education for all children also takes energy, time and resources as well as commitment. Levin has said that ASP schools are continuously in the process of becoming and improving and that for an individual school to establish a strong foundation is at least a five-year undertaking. The hope for the future is that the growing efforts in support of inclusive education within the broader socio-political and constructivist school reform movements will become an influential counter-force for social justice and political action in schools everywhere.

Acknowledgements

The author is grateful to Hank Levin and Pilar Soler for their invitation and support during her sabbatical at the Accelerated Schools Project, Stanford University. The author also thanks the teachers, principal, staff and students at Holmes Middle School and 'Esperante' Elementary School. They gave full access to their classrooms, as well as sharing their expertise, concerns, hopes and dreams for the future. I have learned a great deal from them, as have the pre-service teachers in my own classrooms who have indirectly benefited from the critical grounding in school practice that I experienced.

References

— School District, An Operational Vision (January 1997) Unpublished draft for the Leadership Council, —Community Schools, —, Michigan.

Clark, R.W. (1999) *Effective Professional Development Schools: Agenda for Education in a Democracy* (San Francisco, CA: Jossey-Bass).

Finnan, C., St John, E., McCarthy, J. and Slovacek, S. (1996) *Accelerated Schools in Action: Lessons from the Field* (Thousand Oaks, CA: Corwin).

Holmes Group (1990) *Tomorrow's Schools: Principles for the Design of Professional Development Schools* (East Lansing, MI: Holmes Group).

Levin, H.M. (1996) Accelerated schools: the background. In C. Finnan, E. St John, J. McCarthy and S. Slovacek (eds), *Accelerated Schools in Action: Lessons from the Field* (Thousand Oaks, CA: Corwin), 3–23.

Levin, H.M. (1997) Doing what comes naturally: full inclusion in accelerated schools. In D. Lipsky and A. Gartner (eds), *Inclusion and School Reform: Transforming America's Classrooms* (Baltimore, MD: Paul H. Brookes), 389–400.

Lipsky, D. and Gartner, A. (1997) *Inclusion and School Reform: Transforming America's Classrooms* (Baltimore, MD: Paul H. Brookes).

NCATE (1998) *NCATE Professional Development Schools Standards Project.* Available at http://www.ncate.org/projects/pds/pdsdraft.html

Chapter 14

Building-based change

One school's journey toward full inclusion

Roberta F. Schnorr, Edward Matott, Michele Paetow and Priscilla Putnam

At the beginning of the year, I wasn't sure what school would be like with kids with special needs in my class. . . . I don't really mind having kids with special needs in my class. I especially like Juan because he makes everybody laugh and he never makes fun of anybody.

In the beginning, I was scared. I didn't know how to act with them. When Anna was part of my group, I didn't know what she could do or what she was interested in. I have changed with Anna. Now I know she is into sports and doesn't like social studies and more. They can come up to me now and I don't feel weird.

(End-of-year comments from two seventh graders who
were part of an inclusive seventh grade team)

In the fall of 1996, Juan, Anna and 38 other students with disabilities began seventh grade at Oswego Middle School (OMS). In former years, approximately 15 of these students would have been assigned to self-contained special education classes at the middle school or outside of the district. This change was part of ongoing, district-wide efforts.

By 1994, self-contained programmes in Oswego's three elementary buildings had been systematically replaced by inclusive programmes (e.g. consultant teacher and team-teaching models) for students with mild, moderate and severe disabilities. However, there were still self-contained special education classes for students with mild and moderate disabilities at the middle and high school. Also, like Juan, most secondary students who had severe disabilities were served outside of the district in a segregated programme provided by an intermediate education agency.

Using a strategic planning process, Oswego Middle School spent nearly two years immersed in building-based planning to prepare for this restructuring (Rigazio-DiGilio and Beninghof, 1994).

Year 1 – getting started

The district's director of special education initiated meetings with the middle school principal to discuss planning for future middle school students with severe disabilities. Elementary students with these needs were now served in inclusive programmes, and in two years, the oldest of them would move into the middle school with their peers. By mid-year, the principal invited all staff to create an 'inclusive education committee' to begin budding-based planning (Davern *et al.*, 1997) for including students with special needs. Besides volunteers, other key individuals were recruited by the principal and the director (e.g. 'teacher leaders', a parent of an elementary student who has severe disabilities, an inclusion consultant from the local teacher's college). At the first meeting, one of the middle school special education teachers and the college consultant agreed to become co-facilitators.

One of the committee's first steps was to explore how students with disabilities currently participated in typical middle school programmes. Barriers to inclusion at Oswego Middle School were identified and analysed (see Figure 14.1). Based on discussion of current practices and barriers, the committee recommended initial steps for fall 1995, to support increased general class participation of Oswego Middle

---

Many of the barriers identified by the team related to procedural, staff or curriculum and instructional issues

Procedural
Scheduling
Students from special education classes are not 'counted' in class totals when mainstreamed
Student grouping (e.g. students in special education classes are not grouped by grade)
No defined procedures for mainstreaming
Report cards

Staff
Availability of support staff (special education)
Communication
Unclear roles and responsibilities for regular and special education teachers

Curriculum and instruction
Special education teachers have limited knowledge of general education curriculum
Appropriate modifications for students with IEPs
Expectations and goals for students with IEPs
Teaching styles for diverse groups
Training for general education teachers
Grading and assessment for students with IEPs

Other
Physical layout/space in classrooms
Fears/reactions of students and parents to students with disabilities

---

Figure 14.1 Barriers: what makes it difficult to include students with disabilities?

- Developed a mission statement for the middle school
- Discussed and documented current building practices for Oswego Middle School students who have disabilities (i.e. students with mild disabilities)
- Identified and analysed barriers in the school to including students with disabilities. Barriers included issues related to procedures, staff roles, curriculum and instruction and others (e.g. space, attitudes)
- Brainstormed possible solutions to current barriers
- Made specific procedural recommendations to support increased participation of current Oswego Middle School students who have mild disabilities
- Compiled and disseminated a written summary of above to all middle school staff in June, 1995

Figure 14.2 Outcomes of inclusive education committee: Year 1.

School students with disabilities. Outcomes of the committee's work through June 1995 are noted on Figure 14.2.

Year 2 – focused planning

When the committee reconvened in the fall of 1995, several ideas were proposed by the co-facilitators to create a more action-oriented approach. First, the committee agreed to meet every two weeks instead of once a month, and all meetings were open to any staff. Second, the committee adopted clear goals with a focus on outcomes for June 1996:

- Increase staff knowledge of inclusion.
- Demonstrate and document successful inclusion with current OMS students.
- Identify staff–student assignments and inclusive schedules for all OMS students for 1996–97.

These goals were adopted at the second meeting of the fall, and became the framework for the Inclusive Education Committee's work for the school year. Soon after the goals were adopted, the committee brainstormed possible activities to address each outcome. Figure 14.3 provides an overview of the activities which were implemented for each of the goals.

Goal 1: increase staff knowledge of inclusion.   Both of the co-facilitators were knowledgeable about inclusive education and had experience working with other schools to develop more inclusive practices. Most committee members had limited knowledge of inclusion. By engaging in structured activities to share information with other staff, committee members had opportunities to discuss issues and raise questions about what quality inclusion was – and was not.

Goal: increase staff knowledge of inclusion

Related activities

- Solicit and respond to faculty questions and answers about inclusion
- Survey faculty for inclusion in-service needs
- Plan in-service for Summer 1996
- Visit and observe elementary inclusion
- Review readings and videos on inclusive education
- Arrange for panel presentation on inclusion from another middle school
- Faculty meeting presentations/updates
- Bi-monthly school newsletter on inclusion
- School booklet on inclusion

Goal: demonstrate and document successful inclusion with current OMS students

Related activities

- Regroup students in special education classes (by age and grade)
- Assign all students to regular teams
- 'Count' all students for class size
- Teacher initiated inclusion efforts (one fully inclusive eighth grade team: increased mainstreaming on one 7–8 team)
- School board presentation on middle school efforts and plans related to inclusion
- Examples of current practices which support inclusion from OMS faculty for booklet

Goal: identify staff–student assignments and inclusive schedules for all OMS students for 1996–97

Related activities

- Initial structure proposed by committee for re-assigning special education staff and grouping students who receive special education services for the 1996–97 school year as full members of regular teams
- Guidelines articulated which include full access to all general education classes for all students on each team for 1996–97
- Forms developed to assist with transition planning for students with IEPs for core teams and special area classes

Figure 14.3 Inclusive education committee activities: Year 2.

For example, the committee surveyed all teachers about staff needs related to inclusion. The survey elicited a wide range of responses and fears. Committee meeting time was devoted to discussing and responding to common concerns (many of which were shared by committee members). The committee also began disseminating a bi-monthly newsletter on inclusion, which often highlighted current middle school efforts and offered tips. Finally, the committee invested months in developing a school booklet on inclusive education at Oswego Middle School with contributions from many faculty. Committee meetings were devoted to discussing topics and revising drafts for the booklet, which was later disseminated to all faculty and staff. Planning and developing the booklet helped committee members learn more about inclusive education and its implementation.

Goal 2: demonstrate and document successful inclusion with current Oswego Middle School students who have special education needs.   Several changes were made as an outcome of the committee's first-year discussion of barriers. For fall 1995, two special educators who taught self-contained classes regrouped their students by age and grade. Previously, each had served both seventh and eighth grade students. Each was now officially aligned with a grade level interdisciplinary team. They would only 'mainstream' within their new team, allowing them to provide some in-class support. For the first time, students from these special education classes were 'counted' as class members for general education classes which they attended (i.e. mainstreamed students were not 'add-ons' to a full class). The eighth grade special education teacher took this plan one step further. She negotiated with her new teammates to allow her students full access to all academic classes with in-class support from herself or a teacher aide.

Both special educators and several general education teachers involved in these early efforts were members of the Inclusive Education Committee. Their students became the focus of the committee's look at successful inclusion of students with mild and moderate disabilities. Examples of effective strategies and practices were shared at meetings, in the newsletter and in the school booklet. By writing about what was working in Oswego and elsewhere, the committee validated these efforts and made them public.

Goal 3: identify student–staff assignments (general and special education teachers) and inclusive schedules for all Oswego Middle School students for the 1996–97 school year. Before this goal could be realized, the committee needed to create a 'picture' of how students and staff would be incorporated into the general middle school structure. Some committee members had seen this as the fiat step and had wanted to 'propose a model' for middle school inclusion during year one. The co-facilitators believed that members needed a clear understanding of inclusion and its underlying values to guide their development of an inclusive model. They made conscious decisions to focus on increasing knowledge of inclusion for a sustained time before proposing a middle school inclusion 'model'. In January 1996, the committee had a working meeting on possible models for including all students with special needs for Year 3 (fall 1996). Using large chart paper to record committee ideas, the following questions were discussed:

1   Who are the students who need special services? Resource students; middle school students with mild and moderate disabilities who were assigned to self-contained classes; sixth graders with mild, moderate and severe disabilities; students who receive reading services and students who speak English

as a second language. Charts reflected anticipated numbers for each group of students for both seventh and eighth grade for 1996–97.

2   Who are the staff who will be serving these students? Resource and other special education teachers, aides at each grade level and reading and ESL teachers.

3   How can these students and staff become an integral part of the existing middle school teams in an equitable way? Charts of two possible plans for students with IEPs were created by the committee. Considerations were discussed for each regarding feasibility for both core teams and special area teachers.

This January planning session provided the basis for more specific scheduling and staff assignments. The committee made it clear that this was a 'first-year' plan, rather than a 'building model'. Implementation would be necessary to determine revisions. The committee recommended that for 1996–97 students continue to be grouped according to the intensity of services (e.g. all students with severe disabilities would be on the same seventh grade team, resource students would be served on another team). It also clarified that all students would have full access to all grade-appropriate classes and that special educators would become full members of their new interdisciplinary teams. Figure 14.4 outlines the three-year planning process.

Given these committee recommendations, the principal was able to recruit and assign specific learns for all students with special education needs for fall 1996. Six of the building's seven teams would serve students with disabilities with full access to general education classes.

Beyond committee work: other activities.   While most of the activities related to planning inclusion were carried out by committee members, the principal pursued other key steps as well. The principal visited another district's middle school inclusion programme where he spent a day observing classes and talking with staff. In the fall of year two, the principal invited parents of sixth grade students with severe disabilities to visit the middle school and meet with him. Parents had a tour of the school while it was in session, and they shared their questions and concerns about their children's transitions to middle school. The principal followed up by meeting individually with each set of parents – some at their homes, others at school – to talk more about their children and their needs. These were the students who raised the most concerns. By investing time in getting to know all students and their families, the principal felt better prepared to plan for them. This also served to build trust with parents, who had concerns about the new programme.

The principal continued to discuss anticipated changes related to inclusion with the faculty as a whole, with interdisciplinary grade level teams, and with key individuals. He asked for teams to 'volunteer' to create an inclusive programme for seventh graders. One seventh grade team did volunteer to include students with severe disabilities. The eighth grade team which was 'including' the special education 'class' agreed to continue.

Fall, 1994

- Director meets with principal

    Principal visits and observes student in elementary inclusion programmes

May, 1995

- Middle school inclusion committee convenes
- Committee members visit elementary inclusion programme
- Committee identifies current 'mainstreaming' and participation for students with IEPs

June, 1995

- Committee identifies barriers to inclusion in this school
- Analyses barriers and recommends some procedural changes to support more inclusion for 1995–96

September, 1995

- Committee sets goals
- Students from special education classes re-grouped by grade
- Increased mainstreaming and one inclusive team formed

October–December, 1995

- Learning about inclusion (panel, visits, readings)
- Sharing about inclusion (newsletter, survey, minutes)
- Develop booklet

June, 1996

- Plan grouping and schedules for 1996–97 students with special needs
- Plan summer in-service

September, 1996

- All students with IEPs begin year as full members of regular seventh and eighth grade classes (three teams now fully include students who were formerly in special classes)

November, 1996

- Inclusion support team begins meeting

January, 1997

- In-service course repeated

April–May, 1997

- New eighth grade team identified to develop inclusive programmes for 1997–98

June, 1997

- All teams: self-assess
- Revisions suggested by inclusion support team
- In-service plans for summer

Figure 14.4 Three-year building-based planning process for implementing inclusion.

In April 1996, the principal approached another seventh grade team. He informed them that he had selected them to develop an inclusive programme for students with mild and moderate disabilities for the coming fall. He assured them that he would provide additional resources. He invited them to generate questions and identify what they felt they would need to do this. The principal had several follow-up meetings over the next few weeks with this team to discuss general expectations and resources as well as to answer this team's questions. A new special education teacher was hired that summer to join this team along with an aide.

With three teams identified for new inclusive programming during the spring of 1996, the principal encouraged team meetings to determine individual student schedules for fall for students with IEPs. The principal indicated that each team had flexibility to determine their own student groupings and staff schedules. Their only criteria were that all students would have access to all classes and decisions would be based on educational needs of students. These three teams were required to provide fall scheduling information for students with IEPs by June 1996.

While the principal was a regular member of the Inclusive Education Committee, he did not limit his role to committee work. These examples highlight some of the additional activities which paralleled and supported committee activities.

Year 3 – initial implementation

In September 1996 all students with disabilities entered Oswego Middle School assigned to typical teams with schedules for general education classes. Three teams now served students who would have been formerly assigned to special education classes, while three other teams continued to provide resource services. The seventh team would not serve special needs students for yet a year. Schedules for staff and students for 7 East, 7 West and 8 South had been planned in June to ensure that in-class support was available where needed.

One of the suggestions that emerged from the Inclusive Education Committee the previous year was the idea of a problem-solving team for issues related to inclusion. The committee anticipated that teams and individual teachers would experience challenges, particularly in the first year of inclusion. The 'Inclusion Support Team' was formed to assist with such challenges. An open invitation was sent to all staff in the fall of 1996. Many of those who joined were former members of the Inclusive Education Committee – individuals who were knowledgeable about inclusion and committed to its success. This committee included general and special educators, special area teachers, aides, the assistant principal, and the local college consultant. Many of the participants were serving students who would have formerly been in special education classes. Student members were recruited to assist with several student-centred issues. This team met every three weeks after school and adopted a formal problem–solving process to assist with any issues related to inclusion. The Inclusion Support Team responded to a wide range of issues and provided recommendations for building policies and practices which support the goal of creating an inclusive school.

Lessons learned

The purpose of this chapter was to describe activities from a building-based planning process. These are offered as examples to clarify what kinds of steps were taken and how different individuals and groups participated in the change process. In reflection, we would like to note several features of our experience which seemed to be important elements of our change process. These include the coordination of district and building-based change efforts, the need for long-term planning involving many stakeholders, the importance of administrative presence and participation on building-based committees, the use of specific outcomes and products to shape productive committee work and the need for ongoing self-assessment and programme revisions.

Coordination of district and building-based change efforts.   McLaughlin and Warren (1994) cited the advantages of a 'hybrid' approach which decentralizes authority and resources while maintaining centralized decision-making and budget control for all special education programmes. District level planning and commitment to inclusion is fundamental to change. In Oswego the sustained development of elementary level inclusion programmes set the stage for change in middle and secondary schools. There was an established district commitment to inclusion. The Director of Special Education and elementary programmes had successfully advocated for the necessary resources. However, each school had its own possibilities and barriers. District efforts supported school-based planning and facilitated active participation on the building level (Rigazio-DiGillo and Beninghof, 1994). Those that were to implement changes needed an active role in shaping their school's programmes (Hughes et al., 1996).

The need for long-term, intensive planning involving many stakeholders.   We believe that a large part of our success can be credited to the year and a half of intensive planning by the Inclusive Education Committee. The benefits of long-range planning with a diverse group of participants has been documented (Fullan and Steigelbauer, 1991; Davern et al., 1997). The investment in ongoing school-wide discourse and planning was critical to establishing building-level knowledge, commitment and ownership. The participation of many groups contributed to high quality planning by ensuring that a variety of perspectives would be considered (e.g. general educators, special area teachers, special educators, administrators and parents). Time together to grow and learn was a key ingredient. Meeting every two weeks was, at times, gruelling, but it helped the committee to develop a sense of 'group', to experience continuity and to maintain momentum between meetings. While critics remained, there were many middle school staff members who understood and supported the goals of inclusion.

Administrative presence and participation on the building-based planning committee. There is wide recognition that principals are key players in school change and the development of inclusive programmes (Biklen, 1985; Sage and Burello, 1994). The participation of the middle school principal and vice principal on the Inclusive Education Committee was beneficial in a number of ways. First, their presence and participation sent messages about their commitment to this change as a school-wide development, not just a 'special education' issue. Participation gave them opportunities to learn more about the issues and to examine their philosophy of education for all students. As participants, administrators could answer questions and provide information during meetings (e.g. staffing, budget, policies). From another perspective, administrators were able to 'keep a finger on the pulse of the staff' by hearing first-hand the reactions and questions that were coming up at meetings. This contributed to making and timing decisions regarding other planning activities.

Use of specific outcomes and products to shape productive committee work. Like many committees, this one started slowly. Some members expressed the need to 'get more done' during the first few months. By setting goals, which represented clear outcomes, and a timeline, the committee was able to bring focus to the work it was doing. At several points during year two, the committee reviewed each of its goals and listed activities (completed and in-progress) for each. This helped the group to see progress and to set priorities about how to spend remaining time. The use of some tangible products (Davern *et al.*, 1997) also contributed to a sense of accomplishment. The newsletter and school booklet on inclusion were concrete items which documented the committee's ideas and highlighted the school's efforts and progress.

The need for ongoing self-assessment and revisions. We learned many lessons during the first two years of implementation. There were issues which were not anticipated and features of the first-year model which created challenges. However, this effort is defined as a work-in-progress, not a finished programme. Rigazio-DiGillo and Beninghof (1994) point out the need to take a long-range view because substantive change does not happen quickly. They recommend ongoing monitoring with the purpose of programme improvement.

End of the year 'self-assessment and goal setting' meetings were carried out by each team in the school after the first year of implementation. These self-assessments identified what was working at the team level and where teams could improve. Some of the problems which were brought to the Inclusion Support Team represent school-wide issues and practices for consideration. Our experience indicated the need for school leaders to facilitate ongoing, constructive discussions about both successes and challenges and to use this information to revise and further develop programmes.

Summary

No significant change can occur without challenges. We have now completed our third year of serving all middle school students within inclusive teams. There are certainly issues that we continue to struggle with, as individuals, as teams and as a school. None of these are unique to serving students with disabilities. Rather, as our new structures redefine who our classes and programmes are for, we become aware of areas in which we need to improve for all students. Recent changes have increased student diversity and added new adult team members. Our successes and struggles have few new themes; they highlight the tenets which undergird middle school philosophy and practice. Having truly heterogeneous classes heightens the need for effective collaboration and student-centred curriculum and instruction. Additionally, we still have too few forums for sustaining a school-wide dialogue about our beliefs and practices for all students.

Collaboration.   Middle school interdisciplinary teams provide a structure for assimilating students and staff from programmes that formerly operated in isolation. However, individual teams vary in their response to new team members and roles. The most successful teams are those where there is a growing, shared ownership for all students. While the special educator has some distinct responsibilities, these are carried out within the fabric of the team. On these teams, it is apparent that the roles of both general educators and special educators are changing and continue to evolve. Special educators have an active voice in team planning – for curriculum as well as problem-solving. General educators incorporate accommodations into their instruction and assessment. Changes are likely to be seen as 'good instruction' for diverse groups, rather than special adaptations for a few students. Not surprising, such teams meet regularly and topics related to curriculum and instruction are often central to discussions.

At times, other teams continue to reflect more traditional (and very separate) roles and responsibilities for general and special education teachers. While students with special needs are present and welcome in regular classes, they remain the primary responsibility of the special educator. The development of new collaborative relationships which support the goals of inclusion is an ongoing process. Early planning and implementation must facilitate this goal. Overly simple explanations of inclusion (e.g. 'Don't worry, there will be a special educator to deal with those students.') can send the wrong message.

Curriculum and instruction.   The increasing diversity of these classes highlights the need for practices which can meet the needs of all learners. Here, too, teachers and teams differ in instructional styles and practices. As some middle school literature suggests, learning activities which utilize student-centred approaches offer meaningful opportunities for all students (including those with disabilities) to be active and successful learners. Integrated curricula (Beane, 1993), cooperative learning (Johnson *et al.*, 1988; Hicks, 1997), whole language (Reif, 1992; Atwell, 1998), and authentic assessments (Vars, 1997) are examples of practices which can actively promote learning for diverse middle school students. All of our teams utilize some of these approaches some of the time and have experienced exciting results in particular projects or activities with our most heterogeneous groups. Helping all teams to expand the implementation of middle school 'best practices' is fundamental to including all students in the curricular life of the school.

Ongoing professional development: creating school-wide dialogue about our beliefs and practices. Many benefits were realized from the multi-year, building-based planning process which facilitated discussion among many members of the school community. Exploring issues for students with disabilities often led to examining our beliefs for all middle school learners. During the first year of implementation, the Inclusion Support Team continued to provide a forum for discussion among teachers and staff who were engaged in implementing changes. Structured problem-solving for inclusion issues revealed both successes and challenges for many middle school learners and led to examining our values as a school. However, when the outside facilitator from the college could no longer lead the Inclusion Support Team, its meetings ceased.

We need to find ways for our school to help teachers and staff come together regularly for professional dialogue which can nurture and sustain our beliefs and continue to shape our practice. It is this discourse that will ultimately lay the strong foundation of values necessary to sustain the change that has begun. Without strong underlying beliefs that are shared by many members of the school, these practices remain fragile and far too dependent on the 'believers'. There is a danger that once the schedule and staffing changes are made, people think the change is finished, when indeed it has just begun. We are reminded that reform is more than structural change and that 'people are central to success' (York-Barr *et al.*, 1996, p. 102).

In spite of challenges, change has occurred in how teachers and students are defining and understanding inclusion. By focusing on a small group of students who had been systematically excluded, we began examining our own values about education and about people. As we struggled to identify barriers, create new practices, and deal with implementation challenges, we realized we were no longer talking only about a few students with severe disabilities. Increasingly, someone would point out how an issue that was raised for an 'inclusion student' (e.g. Ben seems to be socially isolated) is often a problem for other middle school students. More teachers are asking how we can ensure that all students are scheduled with supportive peers throughout their school day and how we can create a sense of community for everyone. Student members of the Inclusion Support Team brought up the issue of 'students getting picked on' – not only students with disabilities, but those with the 'wrong' sneakers – and or, girls who experience sexual harassment. As a result of planning for the inclusion of students with disabilities, we are now thinking and talking about all of our students, and the kind of school we hope to become.

References

Atwell, N. (1998). *In the Middle: New Understandings about Writing, Reading and Learning* (2nd edn). Portsmouth, NH: Heinemann.

Beane, J.A. (1993). *A Middle School Curriculum: From Rhetoric to Reality* (2nd edn). Columbus, OH: National Middle School Association.

Biklen, D. (1985). *Achieving the Complete School*. New York: Teachers College Press.

Davern, L., Schnorr, R., Erwin, E., Ford, A. and Rogan, P. (1997). Working toward inclusive secondary schools: guidelines for developing a building-based process to create change. In D. D. Sage (Ed.), *Inclusion in Secondary Schools* (pp. 195–232). Port Chester, NY: National Professional Resources.

Fullan, M. and Steigelbauer, S. (1991). *The New Meaning of Educational Change*. New York: Teacher's College Press.

Hicks, L. (1997). How do academic motivation and peer relationships mix in an adolescent's world? *Middle School Journal*, 28(4), 18–22.

Hughes, M.T., Vaughn, S. and Schumm, J.S. (1996). Schools restructure their special education programs for high incidence disabilities: issues and outcomes. *The Special Education Leadership Review*, 3(1), 15–28.

Johnson, D.W., Johnson, R.T., Holubec, E.J. and Roy, P. (1988). *Circles of Learning: Cooperation in the Classroom*. Reston, VA: Association for Supervision and Curriculum Development.

McLaughlin, M.J. and Warren, S.H. (1994). Restructuring special education programs in local school districts: the tensions and the challenges. *The Special Education Leadership Review*, 2(1), 2–21.

Reif, L. (1992). *Seeking Diversity: Language Arts with Adolescents*. Portsmouth, NH: Heinemann.

Rigazio-DiGillo, A. and Beninghof, A.M. (1994). Toward inclusionary educational programs: a school-based planning process. *The Special Education Leadership Review*, 2(1), 81–91.

Sage, D. and Burello, L. (1994). *Leadership in Special Education Reform: An Administrator's Guide to Changes in Special Education*. Baltimore, MD: Paul Brookes.

Vars, G.F. (1997). Student concerns and standards too. *Middle school Journal*, 28(4), 44–49.

York-Barr, J., Schultz, T., Doyle, M.B., Kronberg, R. and Crossett, S. (1996). Inclusive schooling in St. Cloud: perspectives on the process and the people. *Remedial and Special Education*, 17(2), 92–104.

Part IV

Challenging perspectives

'Valuing diversity'

A cliché for the twenty-first century?

Shereen Benjamin

Introduction

From 'inspirational' stories about pupils in inclusive schools learning to value their able and disabled friends (e.g. Alderson, 1999; Karpf, 2001) to statutory directives to teachers in all English schools (e.g. DfEE, 2000a,b), 'valuing diversity' narratives are increasingly evident in the educational landscape of the UK and elsewhere. Some have argued that the term 'diversity' allows for the reconceptualization of (pathologized) 'difference', and for the production of non-hierarchical plural identities (Ballard, 1995; Munro, 1997). The school that 'values diversity' does not separate or exclude anyone, but instead celebrates the plurality of its community, to the benefit and inclusion of all. However, there are several problems with this seemingly easy and unarguable terminological solution. Sedgwick (1994) has shown that the concept of 'diversity' is located within the politics of liberal pluralism: the same politics of 'equal but different' which underpins the 'special educational needs' (SEN) discourses that have been so robustly critiqued (e.g. Corbett, 1996). Valuing diversity also begs the question of what forms of 'difference' can be slotted into the normative framework of the standards agenda[1] (Visser, 1999), how they are to be slotted into it, and on what terms.

The meanings and practices associated with valuing diversity are undoubtedly able to produce a certain amount of reconceptualization of difference, and some strategic repositioning of those designated as 'different'. But the possibilities for such change are limited both by the term's political derivation and location, and by the context in which it has been taken up.

'Valuing diversity' in context

Attention has been drawn to the shifts of meaning around the terms that have been used from the eighteenth century to designate and define perceived intellectual 'ability' (Tomlinson, 1982; Slee, 1995; Corbett, 1996; Allan, 1999; Benjamin, 2001). The social, cultural and material practices associated with the official identification of specific individuals and groups as intellectually less 'able' than the socially produced norm have meant that there is a continuing absence of non-pejorative language for discussing the significance of this site of social injustice (Wilson, 2000a). What exists is a set of euphemisms, situated more or less comfortably within discourses of 'special needs' and 'inclusion' (Wilson, 2000b). Past centuries show that such changes in language, whilst they can be important, are not sufficient to shift meanings on their own (Cole, 1989; Potts, 1998): when material practices remain unchanged, and when relations of subordination and domination are relatively untroubled, then new forms of language can become co-opted into reactionary agendas (Helldin, 2000).

The politics of change and justice underpinning 'inclusive education' is arguably a case in point. In the transition of 'inclusion' from the radical margins towards the centre of debate, that politics of egalitarian change has in many cases been evacuated in favour of bland and unarguable assertions, and sugar-coated optimism (Lloyd, 2000; Thomas and Loxley, 2001). Arguably, some versions of 'inclusion' discourses (Armstrong, 1999) have been shifted into the territories occupied by the new managerialism of global capital (Levitas, 1998). As 'inclusive education' moves (sometimes problematically) into the policy space dominated in the UK and elsewhere by the standards agenda, it is taking with it a number of supposedly (or formerly) egalitarian concepts, of which 'valuing diversity' is a good example. Such concepts lend a veneer of social justice and moral authority to the standards agenda, and play a part in making the current drive to improve student examination performance levels appear both inevitable and unarguable (Morley and Rassool, 1999). But does the strategic deployment of particular terms indicate their loss of political edge, and with that loss, the co-optation of 'inclusive education' by new managerialist practices? Are we moving from the surveillant regimes often associated with 'special education' towards a differently configured surveillant regime framed by this co-opted version of 'inclusion'? Is 'valuing diversity' on its way to becoming a cliché: nothing but a euphemism for the enduring reproduction of oppressive social relations and consequent material inequalities?

In this chapter, I argue that 'valuing diversity' is becoming an increasingly empty term. Its location within liberal pluralism allows its users to think that they are reconceptualizing difference. But, as a means of reconceptualizing difference, it does not do the work of 'strategic essentialism' (Hall, 1992; Weedon, 1997): it does not enable us to hold on to difference as a means of illuminating present inequalities and imagining radical alternatives. It thus seeks to do away with 'difference' prematurely, and can become complicit in the work of shoring up existing relations of inequality. This chapter points to some of the dangers associated with the use of 'valuing diversity' as a legitimating and explanatory narrative. Using some of the findings from an ethnographic research project,[2] I will show how such usage can be complicit in, and can conceal, the reproduction of some very reactionary meanings and practices.

Meadway School for Girls (not its real name) is a London comprehensive school for girls aged 11–16. At the time of the study, I worked there as a part-time teacher of 'learning support', with Meadway's uncomfortably designated 'special needs students'.[3] Meadway is in many ways a successful school, scoring well in the local league tables, and with a high proportion of its 16-year-old leavers attaining the externally recognized benchmark of five good passes in the General Certificate of Secondary Education (GCSE) exams. It also prioritizes issues of Equal Opportunities, and staff at the school are concerned to facilitate the achievement of all students. The contradictory nature of these twin aims – of improving the school's overall score in terms of examination results whilst seeking to become more 'inclusive' – is partially resolved through the deployment of notions of 'valuing diversity'. This deployment, which is primarily benevolent in intention, also constructs a binary, based on the older charity/tragedy model of disability (Ervelles, 1996; Allan, 1999). The complexity of this slippage can be explored through looking at the experiences of two of Meadway's autistic students.

Cassandra and Cheryl, who have been formally identified as having Asperger's syndrome, are part of a small but growing number of students at Meadway who until recently would have been educated in local special schools. A distinct discourse of 'success' operates in relation to such students. Where the progress and 'success' of most of Meadway's students is calculated through their performance in examinations, a 'disabled' discourse of success operates for Cheryl and Cassandra and certain clearly defined 'others'. It is a discourse that simultaneously allows these students to be different by valuing non-academic (or non-credentialized) success, and re-inscribes them as different by exempting them from requirements relating to academic performance. This discourse produces what is in many ways the most progressive and humane of the formal versions of success in circulation at Meadway. Legitimated and explained by the notion of 'valuing diversity', it does indeed allow for the recognition and celebration of versions of 'success' that fall outside of those produced by the increasingly dominant standards agenda, with its emphasis on examination performance. But because it is only applied in relation to a group who have historically been marginalized and oppressed, one of its functions is to police the borders of a binary division.

Cassandra: a successful placement?

Cassandra is a young woman from a Greek Cypriot family. Her primary schooling and her first year of secondary schooling took place in a local special school. She entered Meadway in Year Eight (at the age of 12), and remained there until the end of her compulsory schooling, when she was 16. At the time of this study, Cassandra was in Year Eleven – her final year.

Cassandra is a gentle, timid young woman. She tends to act in ways that are likely to be read as endearing and charming, and are likely to evoke tender feelings in other people. The aspects of social life that often frighten and bewilder autistic people[4] – such as changes in routine, apparent rule-breaking and perceived unkindness – frighten and bewilder Cassandra. Her response is to cry quietly, with her fists jammed into her eyes in the attempt to stop tears running down her cheeks. She speaks in an untypical and stylized way, using a high-pitched, child-like voice, together with frequent reversals of noun and verb order. She likes cartoons, and can spend entire lessons drawing Pokemon characters. She thus tends to be inscribed into traditional discourses of hyperfeminity through which she can be read as a vulnerable and rather charming 'child' in need of help.

> I go to lunch. There's a huge crowd in the corridor, which I fully intend to ignore by going through the hall. But Cassandra comes up to me, with her mouth turned down at the corners. She tells me she is 'feeling sad'. I ask why. She can't get to the till to buy her lunch token. She asks if I will take her with me. I do. The crowd of Year 11 girls is almost impenetrable. There is no way Cassandra could have managed it on her own. We hold hands, and I make my way through, Cassandra behind me. I'm not sufficiently high in status for the young women of the crowd to melt away as I pass through. But I'm high enough for individuals to allow me to push them aside. And Cassandra is 'special' enough for them not to protest at her coming with me. I ask someone why the crowding is so bad. There are new staff on duty, who haven't got the hang of the system. We get to the till. There is a little corner behind it, where I install Cassandra while I buy her token. Again, there are no protests from any of the waiting young women in front of whom we have pushed. I don't think they would have been nice enough to let Cassandra through on her own, but Cassandra, who they know is vulnerable, plus me in my authorised position as her protector, evoke their 'niceness' sufficiently to allow us this special privilege.
>
> (Fieldnotes)

In many ways, this extract can be read as an instance of very good practice around disability. Cassandra has been correctly read as 'different', and because of that difference, we 'normies' (Institute for the Study of the Neuro-Typical, 1999) have modified our own actions so that the environment becomes more accommodating and less disabling for Cassandra. The situation, of the corridor being unwontedly crowded and a lunch token not being as readily available as expected, is one that could reasonably be expected to threaten the composure of an autistic student (Jones et al., 2001). The fact that Cassandra seeks help, rather than panicking, speaks well for the progress she has made at Meadway, and for the work that has been done with her. The other students' contingent willingness to make way for Cassandra indicates both their understanding of her difference, and points to the work that still needs to be done if they are to recognize and act on this understanding without prompting. Whilst there is undoubtedly much truth in this reading, there is more besides.

The Year Eleven students' recognition of Cassandra's 'difference' is not merely a response to diversity, but implies a binary 'Othering'. There are many students in the school who find jostling the crowds unpleasant. However, they are not deemed worthy of special recognition. Somehow, Cassandra has crossed the line between 'different but normal' and 'really different'. And it is perhaps impossible for that recognition not to contain remnants of the charity/tragedy model of disability (Stone, 1995), when what we are asking the other students to do is to suspend parts of their usual struggle for power in order to show special consideration for Cassandra. It is certainly possible, and very attractive, to understand the students in this extract as being 'nice'. Their actions do contain an element of just that: unselfish niceness, and the ability to consider someone else's needs. But doing 'nice girl' involves more in the way of identity work than is suggested by unselfishness, however problematized that notion becomes (Francis, 1997, 1998). It also involves, in this instance, a measure of distancing oneself from the identification with disability. Cassandra is not just positioned as different: she is positioned as 'Other', and such an act is charged with power.

In the student microcultures that operate in Year Eleven, it has become unacceptable for anyone to be seen deliberately to frighten Cassandra. She has become so established as 'not-like-us' that acts of meanness towards her have been ruled out. This could be said to have the much-desired effect of helping all members of the school community to understand and value diversity, to accept people for who they are, and to act towards them accordingly. And Cassandra is not just positioned as vulnerable: she is genuinely vulnerable, inasmuch as the social world operates according to rules that do not make sense to her. However, the effect seems to be to reify the students' (and adults') notions of what counts as real disability. Far from enabling everyone to benefit from a wider notion of what constitutes personhood, the discursive field that constitutes Cassandra as 'not-like-us' appears to demand that 'normal' students distance themselves from her. This is especially true of the Year Eleven 'special needs students', who are concerned to mark out the distinctions that constitute Cassandra as 'not-like-us'.

Suleika: Like, Ms Jordan, she's never helping people, and Cassandra, I don't want to be mean, don't get this wrong, but Cassandra she can't do nothing if Miss doesn't tell her what to do, and Miss never goes over to her, and Cassandra, like every lesson, she's just sitting there, [pause]. She's just sitting there, and she isn't doing nothing, and Miss doesn't even notice, she doesn't even see. . . . And, don't get this wrong, it's like some people they say, 'Oh, it's only Cassandra, it doesn't matter, she won't get no GCSE's anyway'. But that ain't fair, and when it was Ms Corby, Ms Corby was all the time, 'Are you OK Cassandra, do you understand, Cassandra?' and Cassandra she could do it, like she wasn't just sitting there, and you should've seen this – what did she make – what was it?

Amina: Oh, I know, I remember that – it was like this thing for a uniform, like a coat what you wear and it hasn't got no sleeves, and it was all red –

S: Yeah, right, and she made this coat thing, and it was really good, you should've seen it Miss, it wasn't like it was just good for Cassandra, it was really good –

A: And now, she don't make nothing no more, and she – erm – it's not like it's her fault, she doesn't understand what to do, how can she understand what to do? And Miss Jordan she don't care, just as long as Cassandra's not bothering her, she doesn't even care if she knows what to do, and I don't think that ain't even fair.

Suleika and Amina's principal intention in this extract might well be to attest to the inadequacy of the new Textiles teacher. Within the discursive field that constitutes meanness to Cassandra as unacceptable, this teacher's actions have crossed the boundary between what they see as ordinary, run-of-the-mill teacherly neglect, and absolute inadmissibility. The two young women are illustrating their own grievances against the teacher by referring to Cassandra. Ms Jordan has often left them 'just sitting there', which they resent. However, her actions in leaving Cassandra 'just sitting there' are qualitatively different in their account. Whilst it is reprehensible of the teacher to leave Suleika and Amina 'just sitting there', for her to leave Cassandra in this way is an act of particular cruelty. The depth to which this teacher has apparently sunk is illustrated by her lack of caring towards this most vulnerable of their classmates. What Suleika and Amina leave out of their account is that Cassandra herself always enjoys being left alone: she appears to be at her happiest when she is allowed to draw cartoon characters in her pocket notebook. However, they are concerned to monitor her learning. They adopt a caretaking role in relation to Cassandra, in which they can express outrage at the teacher's neglect of her curricular progress. This effectively establishes a distance between themselves and Cassandra.

Most of Meadway's curriculum does not appear to make sense to Cassandra. She does not make the linear progress which is the only kind of progress that a linear, developmentally based curriculum can make admissible. For Cassandra, a distinct set of stories about success has to be invoked, in order to keep the fiction of her success, and its underlying narrative of liberal pluralism, intact. The dominant version of 'success' at Meadway, according to which the achievement of most students is measured, stands in direct relation to the standards agenda, and relates to GCSE $A^* - C$ grades. A consolation/deficit version, deployed in relation to some of Meadway's students to whom $A^* - C$ grades are not accessible, validates individual (curricular) progress at individual rates, but seeks to reposition those students as 'slow learners' who will eventually reach normative standards. Neither version will work for Cassandra. Her 'special needs' must be further differentiated and delineated, and the discourse of individual progress similarly differentiated. The deployment of 'valuing diversity' narratives allows any concerns about Cassandra's academic progress to be judged to be of secondary importance to the opportunities she has had to 'socialize' with mainstream students. For Cassandra, it is enough to succeed on what one teacher called 'the social side'.

Sarah: I haven't given up on Cassandra, but I've more, I've more or less taking her, you know, trying to teach her social rather than Science now, because she understands, she's very limited as understanding's very limited but I think it's important that she gets relationships with adults. So I talk to her, and when she's doing a practical, I try and pair her up with someone who knows what they're doing, so that they can guide her, but I go over and I talk to her, and I ask her how she's doing. So I try to be a little bit more social with Cassandra. But it was really nice like when you came in and you did the experiment with her. Cause it took the pressure off – that class, there's just so many that need help, it took the pressure off me a bit, and let me go off with the other, the other students. Cause she is a real – she is someone who needs, who needs, [pause] well she really needs, she really needs somebody following her round the school, basically, in every lesson sort of.

Again, this teacher's position can be understood as modification of practice to take account of and value diversity. However, she is also positioning Cassandra as someone who, unlike the other 'special needs students', is really different. In some ways, the discourses deployed in relation to Cassandra are those I would want to support. Sarah has decided that relationships are an arena in which Cassandra can be helped to make meaningful progress, and in which she can be given an enjoyably successful experience. I would want to agree with her in this analysis. I would want to be able to deploy differing notions of what can count as success.

However, the problem is that, of all the students in Year Eleven, Cassandra is the only one in relation to whom this more flexible account of what counts as success is applied. Cassandra's presence does not appear to enable different versions of success to circulate to the benefit of all students. To the contrary, her presence, and the 'diversity' she supposedly brings to Meadway, establishes the borders of 'normal' success and of 'normality' and, in many ways, strengthens and preserves them. Meadway has to understand Cassandra as successful, because she is a diligent and hard-working student: or, at least, she is one who does not act in ways that can be configured as challenging. An earnest, well-meaning student has to be read as successful in order to preserve the story that hard work brings success. However, the version of success that is ascribed to Cassandra both allows her difference, and at the same time re-inscribes her distance from the norm.

Cheryl: an unsuccessful placement?

Cheryl is from an African-Caribbean family. She entered Meadway at the start of Year Seven, in the year this study took place. She has a long history behind her of what was, for a long time, considered as very difficult behaviour and attributed to family problems. She is the child of a 'feckless mother' (Goodey, 1998), and class and race, as well as disability were key determinants of the stories that could be told of her as a young child. It was not until she was nine years old that she was diagnosed as autistic. Her primary education was spent in a number of mainstream schools, at which she never remained long enough for a thorough investigation of her difficulties to be carried out.

Cheryl is a big, boisterous and energetic girl. She seldom sits still for more than a few moments. The aspects of the social world that typically frighten and bewilder autistic people frighten and bewilder Cheryl, as they do Cassandra. However, where Cassandra responds in ways that evoke 'maternal' feelings in those around her, Cheryl panics and tends to lash out. She usually shouts, often using abusive language, and sometimes hits and kicks, or runs away. Although she is not intentionally aggressive, her actions tend to be perceived as threatening, and are more likely to evoke anger than tenderness. Like Cassandra, Cheryl speaks in a stylized way. She uses the vocabulary and inflection of rap music, which also serves to position her (albeit problematically) within discourses of big, threatening African-Caribbean girl (Wright *et al.*, 2000).

Cheryl treads a much finer line than Cassandra when it comes to being positioned as recognizably disabled. As a big, athletic, African-Caribbean girl, she is likely to be read as naughty, not vulnerable. She towers over most of the Year Seven girls, and over many of the teachers. Her temper tantrums are frightening: although I know quite well that they are the outward sign of panic and not of aggression, I can find myself feeling afraid when they suddenly erupt. Many of the students find her very frightening, and others respond to her with anger, reading an intentionality into her perceived violence and aggression. However, perhaps what is most damaging is the day-to-day, unremitting sense of profound annoyance and apparent powerlessness which Cheryl's mode of operation tends to evoke in those around her.

> After break it is Humanities. Cheryl arrives late as usual. She sits down next to me, in her appointed place, but moves her chair as far away from me as possible. The others are already doing their work on their 'Castles' books. Cheryl hasn't brought hers. I give her a piece of paper, but it is not the kind she wants. She creases it up, and says she cannot use it because it is too creased. She goes to get some more. She biffs people hard on the head as she moves around the class. Most of the girls try to ignore her. A few say 'ow', some cringe, and Natelle whirls around as if to hit back, then thinks better of it. Cheryl returns with some paper. She does not want to do anything related to castles. She wants to draw a picture of Dana. I try to persuade her to copy a castles picture. She makes four false starts, each time crumpling the piece of paper. I feel bad about the waste. She decides she hasn't got the right colours, and grabs Dana's felt tips. Dana tries to take them back, but Cheryl at first holds onto them, then throws them to the floor. I give her 'first warning'. The others on the table know what is coming next, and hurriedly put their pens into their pencil cases, to hide them. Dana moves onto another table. Cheryl takes Esin's entire pencil case, laughing loudly. She opens it, and throws the pens, one-at-a-time, to the floor. Esin looks at me in desperation. I tell Cheryl she must give the pencil case back, or it will be 'second warning'.
>
> (Fieldnotes)

Cheryl presents much more of a challenge to good governance than Cassandra. Cassandra evokes feelings of tenderness, and members of staff typically find ourselves wanting to protect and look after her. By contrast, members of staff get drawn into another kind of protection discourse around Cheryl. We want to protect other students from her. At the same time, most of us feel as confused and unable to understand her mode of making sense of the world as she must feel in relation to ours. This profound confusion and complex discursive positioning leads often to an immobilization of other people around her. Her position as someone 'really different' implies that we should treat her with the tenderness that we show to Cassandra. However, this can be extraordinarily difficult in the face of her often disturbing effects on virtually everyone with whom she comes into contact.

> Cheryl and I have agreed that I will not sit next to her so long as she gets on with her work, but if she does not get on, then I will sit with her on her table. . . . I could probably get away with sitting with her, but I decide not to try it. I rationalize that I might wreck Martin's lesson if I try. But really, I think I'm taking the route of least resistance. And the other girls are so much nicer. Really, they are. Later . . . when I think back to the lesson, I'm ashamed of having 'betrayed' Cheryl by having felt so negative about her.
>
> (Fieldnotes)

The governmental procedures that are invoked in relation to 'special needs students' are in many ways the hyperrational ones of new managerialism. The SEN Code of Practice (DfEE, 1994) appears to construct a technorationalist reality in which struggles of any kind can be objectively qualified and quantified, and a solution found. If only we get the targets right, and the provision right, then the 'special needs student' will make the kind of linear progression that rational, developmental models demand. And so difficulties in learning are measured, mapped and evaluated and remedial measures put in place to alleviate the effects of those difficulties. Nevertheless, those of us in Meadway who carry out those governmental procedures and operationalize those remedial measures do not do so in a hyperrational way. We respond, as one person to another, in a relationship that is always changing and developing, and, in Cheryl's case, is characterized by heightened emotions in response to the relational and governmental difficulties she can embody. In deciding that Cheryl is to receive classroom support, her own preferences have been overridden. This is apparently necessary, as the procedures of identifying her support 'needs' and the means by which those 'needs' are to be met are presented as rational choice-making exercises in which costs and benefits are objectively weighed up. As an autistic student, this process does not make sense to her. But does it make sense at all?

> I tell Cheryl that I am there to help keep her on task, and that if she doesn't want me to sit with her, she must show me she doesn't need me by getting on with her work. I use the example of the first Humanities lesson, when I worked mainly with Sunna and Fosia, to illustrate what I'm saying. She doesn't want me in the same room. I say this isn't an option. Now, I'm thinking about all the disability theorists who might argue that so-called 'normal' children don't have to prove themselves in order to be left alone, so why should someone who's been labelled disabled have to do so? And the orthodoxy (which often is merely lip-service) that young people have choices and options in how their

'special needs' are to be met. In this instance, I'm taking away most of Cheryl's choices. But how is an autistic student to make those choices, when the nature of her impairment makes the rational, choice-making exercize something of a mystery to her?

(Fieldnotes)

Perhaps one of the discourses that needs interrogating here is the one that constructs 'special educational needs' according to a hyperrational framework. What was really at issue with Cheryl was not her autism per se, but the fact that she often acts in ways that renders the network of social relationships around her, including relationships of power, unviable. My first thought, that Cheryl was unable because of her autism to take part in the rational decision-making process at which she was apparently the centre, told only a fraction of the story. What was going on was much more than a rational decision-making process: it was a complex negotiation, and what (in my view, quite understandably) was at the centre of it was whether the other members of the school community would be able to coexist with Cheryl.

Versions of rights, entitlements and equal opportunities discourses were used in weighing up the tenability of Cheryl's placement (Corbett, 1998). These were posited in opposition to each other. On the one hand was placed Cheryl's entitlement to a place in a mainstream school, and the obligations of the school to provide an environment in which she could learn effectively. On the other hand was placed all the other students' rights to a schooling experience in which their learning would not be disrupted by Cheryl, and in which they need not fear her constant low-level and occasional high-level abuse. These discourses were very much configured in terms of curricular entitlements, as the other students' right to learn. Meadway's assessment procedures, enshrined in and made mandatory by legislation (Riddell et al., 2000) appeared to rule out discussion of what seemed to me to be at the heart of the difficulties associated with Cheryl – the realm of the non-rational. The 'valuing diversity' rhetoric cannot begin to untangle such complex discursive practices, nor the relational difficulties they contain. Neither will arguments of professional vested interests (Tomlinson, 1982; Skrtic 1991, 1995), appealing though they might be in this context, quite do the job.

The Annual Review of Cheryl's Statement of Special Educational Needs took place just before the summer half-term holiday, when she had been at Meadway for just under a year. Her continued placement was always in doubt: officially because she had not made sufficient progress in terms of the targets on her Individual Education Plan (IEP), and unofficially because she was ungovernable and because people's goodwill towards someone who enacted her difference in demanding ways had been exhausted. At her Annual Review, Cheryl's placement was formally terminated, and a placement in segregated special provision recommended. Mine was the only report to comment positively on her time at Meadway. In it, I referred to liking Cheryl, and to enjoying working with her. There was an overall truth to this, although it was far from an accurate representation of the emotional roller coaster that had been my working relationship with Cheryl (Jordan and Jones,

1999). None of the other reports made reference to personal feelings, but underlying all the rational comments about lack of progress and deleterious effects on other students' learning lurked a strong subtext of dislike and despair. That subtext spoke of wanting Cheryl to go elsewhere: of wanting her to become somebody else's perplexing, worrying and seemingly insurmountable problem.

Whose diversity can be valued?

Could there have been another way? Along with the relief that accompanied Cheryl's departure was a feeling that everyone involved had failed. It would be easy to slip into a critique of Meadway, and to suggest that it is the failure of mainstream schools to value diversity adequately that is the problem here. However, that apparent failure to value diversity has to be interrogated in the context of the schooling systems of the UK. It is very difficult to see a way in which Meadway, itself embedded in a techno-rationalist regime of surveillance, could have offered anything very different to Cheryl.

Some have argued that the job of inclusive schooling is to accept the 'differences' of autistic individuals, whilst also enabling them to develop strategies to help them manage a non-autistic and autistic-unfriendly world (Jordan and Powell, 1995). For Cheryl, the autistic-unfriendliness of Meadway lay less in the intentions of individuals, and more at the heart of its mission. As a successful school, it has to make dominant versions of success available and desirable to as many of its students as it possibly can. Moreover, those versions of success are underwritten by, and re-inscribe, the hierarchical, competitive and linear model of new managerialist rationality which itself shores up the inconsistencies and inhumanities of global capitalism. Meadway, like other schools, has to work a fundamentally inhumane system in the most humane way it can. It also has to present the complex and often deeply emotional processes of learning as if they were a single, simply understood, unitary process, reducible to targets set and met. The presence of both Cheryl and Cassandra flagged up some of the fundamental contradictions inherent in such an endeavour.

Cassandra does her autism in a way that can leave at least some of these contradictions intact. We (the staff) could feel that we were doing something compassionate and humane in relation to her, with that compassion and humanity framed as valuing diversity. And she made a version of progress, albeit not the dominant one, which allowed us to think that she was learning to manage her autism and learning to exist in a non-autistic world. As caring people doing a difficult job, the staff needed to feel this. And as young women with formal and microcultural struggles of their own, the other students needed to feel this too. However, Cheryl's mode of doing autism left none of the contradictions undisturbed. In the challenges she presented to both staff and students, none of us could feel that we were doing anything remotely humane in relation to her. The problems that were flagged up by her placement indicated, in a powerful, intense and often painful way, the limits and limitations of current notions of 'valuing diversity'. In the prevailing contexts, her diversity could not, apparently, be valued. That left everyone concerned – and Cheryl in particular – with a deep and abiding sense of failure.

Cassandra's version of apparent success at Meadway was configured both by current new managerialist imperatives and by the desire of the people – adults and students – who work at the school to recuperate some kind of humanity into a system dominated by the unyielding demands of the standards agenda. In many ways, she came to represent the feared Other of rational discourses: the student who does not make linear progress. However, as that Other, a version of progress could be constructed around her, so that she could be valued in a non-dominant way for the progress she appeared to be making in her social relationships. She was also a vehicle around which a discourse of caring and compassion could be constructed. As someone who was not going to make anything approximating to the dominant version of progress, Meadway's staff and students could relax our usual demands, and allow ourselves to look after someone who we had produced as vulnerable. In doing so, we did draw on the notion of valuing diversity, but we also drew on a long tradition of feeling pity and charity towards the child-like and not-quite-human figure of the irrational and therefore helpless 'defective' (Sidney, 1854; E.G., 1862; Greenwell, 1869; Lapage, 1911; Hollander, 1916).

Cheryl's version of apparent failure was configured by those same new managerialist imperatives. Like Cassandra, she was the student who does not make rational, linear progress. However, she was a student who cannot exist in mainstream schools today: she was a student who seemed to make no form of progress whatever. There were no reachable targets on her IEP. And, far from Cheryl's presence facilitating the deployment of a discourse of recuperated humanity, she found herself positioned as a very, very 'bad' girl, ungovernable in every sense. However, whilst Cheryl's 'failure' cannot be attributed to her 'inadequacy', neither is it fair to attribute blame to the staff and students at Meadway. The problem is much more systemic than that, and is embedded in a set of socio/political values and practices in which 'difference' is seldom neutral in its consequences. At the same time, Cassandra's apparent 'success' needs to be unpacked. What actually went on in lessons for Cassandra was often not successful, except in that she presented no problems to good governance. Again, I would not want to argue that this was the 'fault' of the staff and students at Meadway. The instances in which Cassandra's success was contingent, and Cheryl's nonexistent, are in fact pointers to how the schooling process could have been made more productive for all of Meadway's students.

One of the problems with 'valuing diversity' arguments as they are often deployed, is that 'diversity' is located within certain groups or individuals. The standards agenda demands a certain homogeneity in its construction of academically successful students. It implies that one curriculum can be made to fit everyone, and that, with the correct teaching, every student's 'needs' can be correctly assessed, measured and, if necessary, remediated. Students and teachers in schools struggle with the daily reality that this 'curricular fundamentalism' (Slee, 1998) is profoundly flawed, and that many students experience no success within it.

Meadway tries to reconcile the dilemma of a prescriptive set of curricular demands on the one hand and its commitment to equal opportunities and attainment for all on the other, by identifying a few students as 'really different' and then appearing to value the diversity they bring. However, only a few students can be allowed to be diverse, when diversity implies inability to access the dominant versions of success produced and required by the standards agenda. This means there is a real problem with diversity. If only specific students and groups of students are valued for diversity, whilst everyone else is valued for what essentially is a form of conformity with the hyperrational, new managerialist rules of the standards agenda, then diversity operates as yet another binary. It becomes another way of distancing a group from the norm, a means for eliding the word 'difference' and its consequences, and a device for establishing and reifying the boundaries of 'disability' as deviance.

Cassandra and Cheryl are profoundly affected by this. Their 'difference' cannot be understood in neutral terms. When difference, or particular versions of difference, are only permitted to a few, then that difference has to be understood in terms of social relations of domination and subordination. These social relations cannot be explored through the depoliticized narrative of 'valuing diversity'. Like the much-critiqued 'special needs' terminology, which has been shown to conceal much of the reactionary practice with which it colludes (Corbett, 1996), 'valuing diversity' has the potential to become the new orthodoxy through which the politics of difference continues to be concealed. It does not facilitate any critique of the standards agenda or its underlying assumptions, and it sidelines questions about the social and material consequences of failure to 'perform' according to normative levels. As a piece of explanatory terminology, and as a legitimating narrative, 'valuing diversity' is inadequate for the task of illuminating present injustices or producing radical alternatives. It is a cliché for the twenty-first century, and it has been thoroughly co-opted into the new managerialism of the standards agenda.

Notes

1 The 'standards agenda' is shorthand for the drive to improve students' performance in examinations. It is a global phenomenon, linked to the needs of nations and of global capitalism to produce adults who will have the skills and dispositions to contribute to national and global economies as producers and consumers. It is also linked to regimes of surveillance and regulation, through (for example) punitive inspection and information proliferation.

2 I am grateful to the ESRC for the award of a research studentship to fund this work, the findings of which are more extensively discussed in Benjamin (2002).

3 Like many schools, Meadway has difficulty in finding a way to categorize these students: a difficulty framed by the implicit knowledge that there is no way to talk about such students that does not connote deficit (Goodley, 2001). The designation 'special needs student' is never used in front of the students themselves, but it is common in staffroom usage. I would argue that, unspoken or not, it constructs a distinct subject position that certain students are required to inhabit. I have accordingly retained it here, for the purposes of illuminating some of the consequences of this particular 'difference'.

4 There is considerable debate within disability politics and disability studies about the usage of 'people first' terminology (Barton and Oliver, 1997; Corker, 1998). I share the concern that, as a professional working with people who have been categorized, it is all too easy for me to find myself colluding with practices that objectify the people with whom I work (Gillman *et al.*, 1997). However, Cassandra prefers to describe herself as an 'autistic person' not a 'person with autism', so I have respected her preference and used the term myself.

References

Alderson, P. (ed.) (1999) *Learning and Inclusion: The Cleves School Experience* (London: David Fulton).

Allan, J. (1999) *Actively Seeking Inclusion: Pupils with Special Needs in Mainstream Schools* (London: Falmer).

Armstrong, F. (1999) Inclusion, curriculum and the struggle for space in school. *International Journal of Inclusive Education*, **3**, 75–87.

Ballard, K. (1995) Inclusion, paradigms, power and participation. In C. Clark, A. Dyson and A. Millward (eds), *Towards Inclusive Schools?* (London: David Fulton).

Barton, L. and M. Oliver (eds) (1997) *Disability Studies: Past, Present and Future* (Leeds: Disability Press).

Benjamin, S. (2001) The micro/politics of 'Special Educational Needs' in a comprehensive girls' school. Unpublished thesis, University of London, Institute of Education.

Benjamin, S. (2002) *The Micropolitics of Inclusive Education: An Ethnography* (Buckingham: Open University Press).

Cole, T. (1989) *Apart or a Part? Integration and the Growth of British Special Education* (Buckingham: Open University Press).

Corbett, J. (1996) *Bad-mouthing: The Language of Special Needs* (Bristol: Falmer).

Corbett, J. (1998) *Special Educational Needs in the Twentieth Century: A Cultural Analysis* (London: Cassell).

Corker, M. (1998) Disability discourse in a postmodern world. In T. Shakespeare (ed.), *The Disability Reader: Social Science Perspectives* (London: Cassell).

DfEE (1994) *Code of Practice on the Identification and Assessment of Special Educational Needs* (London: Department for Education and Employment).

DfEE (2000a) *The National Curriculum Handbook for Primary Teachers in England* (London: HMSO).

DfEE (2000b) *The National Curriculum Handbook for Secondary Teachers in England* (London: HMSO).

E.G. (1862) *Narrative Poems* (London: Dean & Son).

Ervelles, N. (1996) Disability and the dialectics of difference. *Disability and Society*, **11**, 519–538.

Francis, B. (1997) Power plays: children's construction of gender and power in role-plays. *Gender and Education*, **9**, 179–192.

Francis, B. (1998) *Power Play: Children's Construction of Gender, Power and Adult Work* (Stoke-on-Trent: Trentham).

Gillman, M., Swain, J. and Heyman, B. (1997) Life history or 'care history': the objectification of people with learning difficulties through the tyranny of professional discourses. *Disability and Society*, **12**, 675–694.

Goodey, C. (1998) Learning disabilities: the researcher's voyage to planet Earth. In S. Hood, B. Mayall and S. Oliver (eds), *Critical Issues in Social Research: Power and Prejudice* (Buckingham: Open University Press).

Goodley, D. (2001) 'Learning Difficulties', the social model of disability and impairment: challenging epistemologies. *Disability and Society*, **16**, 207–231.

Greenwell, D. (1869) *On the Education of the Imbecile* (London: Strahan & Co.).

Hall, S. (1992) The question of cultural identity. In S. Hall, D. Held and T. McGrew (eds), *Modernity and its Futures* (Buckingham: Open University Press).

Helldin, R. (2000) Special education knowledge seen as social problem. *Disability and Society*, **15**, 247–270.

Hollander, B. (1916) *Abnormal Children (Nervous, Mischievous, Precocious and Backward)* (London: Kegan Paul and Trench, Trubner & Co.).

Institute for the Study of the Neuro-Typical (1999) What is NT? Available at [ISNT@grrltalk.new.http://isnt.autistics.org/index.html and case] (accessed 8 February 2001).

Jones, R.S.P., Zahl, A. and Huws, J.C. (2001) First-hand accounts of emotional experiences in autism: a qualitative analysis. *Disability and Society*, **16**, 393–401.

Jordan, R. and Jones, G. (1999) *Meeting the Needs of Children with Autistic Spectrum Disorders* (London: David Fulton).

Jordan, R. and Powell, S. (1995) *Understanding and Teaching Children with Autism* (Chichester: Wiley).

Karpf, A. (2001) Tailored to take in therapies. *Times Educational Supplement*, **6 July**.

Lapage, C.P. (1911) *Feeblemindedness in Children of School Age* (Manchester: Manchester University Press).

Levitas, R. (1998) *The Inclusive Society? Social Exclusion and New Labour* (London: Macmillan).

Lloyd, C. (2000) Excellence for all children – false promises! The failure of current policy for inclusive education and implications for schooling in the 21st century. *International Journal of Inclusive Education*, **4**, 133–151.

Morley, L. and Rassool, N. (1999) *School Effectiveness: Fracturing the Discourse* (London: Falmer).

Munro, R. (1997) Ideas of difference: stability, social spaces and the labour of division. In K. Hetherington and R. Munro (eds), *Ideas of Difference: Social Spaces and the Labour Of Division* (Oxford: Blackwell).

Potts, P. (1998) Knowledge is not enough: an exploration of what we can expect from enquiries which are social. Articulating with difficulty. In L. Barton and P. Clough (eds), *Research Voices in Inclusive Education* (London: Paul Chapman).

Riddell, S., Adler, M., Mordaunt, E. and Farmakopoulou, N. (2000) Special educational needs and competing policy frameworks in England and Scotland. *Journal of Education Policy*, **15**, 621–635.

Sedgwick, E.K. (1994) *Epistemology of the Closet* (London: Penguin).

Sidney, E., Revd (1854) *Teaching the Idiot. Lectures in Connection with the Educational Exhibition of the Society of Arts, Manufacturers and Commerce* (London: Routledge).

Skrtic, T. (1991) *Behind Special Education: A Critical Analysis of Professional Culture and School Organization* (Denver, CO: Love).

Skrtic, T. (ed.) (1995) *Disability and Democracy: Reconstructing (Special) Education for Postmodernity* (New York: Teachers College Press).

Slee, R. (1995) *Changing Theories and Practices of Discipline* (London: Falmer).

Slee, R. (1998) High reliability organizations and liability students – the politics of recognition. School effectiveness for whom? In R. Slee, G. Weiner and S. Tomlinson (eds), *Challenges to the School Effectiveness and School Improvement Movements* (London: Falmer).

Stone, S.D. (1995) The myth of bodily perfection. *Disability and Society*, **10**, 413–424.

Thomas, G. and Loxley, A. (2001) *Deconstructing Special Education and Constructing Inclusion* (Buckingham: Open University Press).

Tomlinson, S. (1982) *A Sociology of Special Education* (London: Routledge & Kegan Paul).

Visser, J. (1999) Placing value on inclusion. *Times Educational Supplement*, **29 October**.

Weedon, C. (1997) *Feminist Politics and Poststructuralist Theory* (Oxford: Blackwell).

Wilson, J. (2000a) Doing justice to inclusion. *European Journal of Special Needs Education*, **15**, 297–304.

Wilson, J. (2000b) 'Learning Difficulties', 'Disability' and 'Special Needs': some problems of partisan conceptualisation. *Disability and Society*, **15**, 817–824.

Wright, C., Weekes, D. and McGlaughlin, A. (2000) *'Race', Class and Gender in Exclusion from School* (London: Falmer).

Chapter 16

Migrant worker children

Conceptions of homelessness and implications for education

*Richard H. Kozoll, Margery D. Osborne and
Georgia Earnest García*

Introduction

> I would say most of the families where I'm from migrate.
>
> (Hector Castillo)

The life of the migrant worker has many aspects of homelessness: the family or individual is poor and rootless for much of the year. Social services such as health care and education are discontinuous and often of low quality. The people seem to fall between the cracks of our society because of their life on the road and the low level of interactions they have within the communities they work. It is tempting to ascribe their problems of health, educational attainment and crime to their homelessness for, in many ways, these *are* the result of the homeless life they appear to lead.

The word home, to many people in the United States, is a symbol of freedom, choice, and power. It is a physical place that one shapes the way one wants, reflecting the 'inner' person, and where individuals can act like they choose without pretence or role-playing. Often home signifies a commodity, an object of monetary value that reflects the owner's value. To others, however, home is a conceptual or an emotional space used to represent relationships. We believe migrant workers such as Hector also think of home in terms synonymous with the word family where it suggests a conceptual space that defines roles and relationships. Home in this sense is not a creation that reflects individuality but an institution that shapes the identities of those within it. In much of the rhetoric surrounding homelessness, the first conceptualization of home as a place seems to be dominant. In our work with Latina/o migrant agricultural workers, the second sense of the word is apparent. Home means family for many migrant workers and is, in part, detached from space and place and these families often choose to be 'homeless,' in the sense that we usually think of the term, in order to maintain their 'home' or family structure. In particular, choosing to be in the United States (for most are not US nationals) signifies choosing family over 'home'.

Migrating is a choice these families make to maintain their family structure. For these people homed–homeless is not a dichotomy. Rather the operative word to define home is 'family'. The structure of the family is analysed as a lifeworld (Habermas, 1984, 1987), or system of values and experiences, which defines choices and ways of acting.

Migrant farm workers: statistics and context

The United States currently is undergoing a change in its ethnic and linguistic make-up. Recent data in the Midwest, for example, have shown a change in agricultural farm workers who qualify as migrants from Whites, African-Americans, Mexicans and Mexican-Americans to almost exclusively Mexicans and Mexican-Americans (King-Stoops, 1980; Prewitt Diaz *et al.*, 1990). According to these authors the majority of these migrant farm workers travel in family groups with school-age children.

When discussions of homelessness occur at the national and state levels, migrant families are usually overlooked (Parsad *et al.*, 2000). Federal law defines migrant workers for educational purposes as agricultural workers or fishermen/women who migrate for employment purposes and who 'have moved from one school district to another within the preceding 36 months' (Public Law 103-382, 1994). Many of the families we interacted with in this study are 'homeless' for part of the year; however, many do return to a particular community in Texas to live during the winter months. Their lives on the road are oriented towards this return. In Texas, they live in homesteads, buildings that extended family members have erected on public land at the outskirts of towns. As the family grows, the building is added onto. Many other migrants, however, do not have such roots and 'follow the crops' for the entire length of time they live the migrant life.

Data and analysis

The data presented here are drawn from a larger study examining the public education experiences of migrant worker children. For this study, a series of interviews with college-aged migrant students from this population were conducted. These students were selected as part of a study of experiences and structures that allow a minority of migrant worker children to become successful in schools. In particular a series of six, two-hour semi-structured interviews were conducted with five freshman students at a college in Austin, Texas. All interviews were audiotaped for transcription and later analysis. The initial interview was devoted to gathering background information on the participants, while the last discussion was left open to elaborate on relevant aspects of our conversations in prior interviews and member checks. Time-in-the-field ideas, interpretations, and conclusions were tested and discussed with participants, allowing them to react, and thereby enhance the credibility of the study (Lincoln and Guba, 1985).

Interview guides were developed with several narrative points in mind: questions were developed to elicit stories rather than reports, and participants were always invited to tell stories about their experiences. We encouraged them to make the relevance of the storytelling clear in their own terms (Polany, 1985).

The migrant farmer worker experience

> After my dad's arrest things really changed. We went from having the money that drugs provided to having nothing. My mom proved strong though and went back to school, finished high school, got a nursing degree, and supported us on her own. But I could see it was a struggle for her. When I was 14, I began to migrate so I could help my mom out with money. She didn't want me to go. She thought that it might be too tough for me since I had never been exposed to such a thing. But I decided to go anyway. So when school let out I headed over to west Texas and the town of Loveland with some of my extended family and we would find jobs cleaning cotton and picking onions. But I would always leave after school had let out and return before school began. My mom insisted on that. She thought education was real important.
>
> It was during this time that my mom met my step-dad and my half-brother was born. Well he owned a car wash in Roma that wasn't doing too well and since my mom had gotten pregnant with my baby stepbrother, he decided that the whole family was going to migrate to work in the fields and earn some money.
>
> (Juan Escalante)

Few studies or descriptions of migrant workers' lives have been published. One ethnography, *Fields of Toil: A Migrant Family's Journey* (Valle, 1994), traces a family's 'migrant cycle' from when they leave Texas to 'follow the crop,' migrating through the northern states and finally returning to Texas. This work describes the different farm jobs members of the family obtain during a season, how the family returns to Texas, and the months they live in the valley through the off season until it is time for them to travel north. The book suggests that many of the hardships associated with the migrant cycle arise from maintaining the family, keeping everyone together as a unit. Troubles with transportation – multiple vehicles are needed for the numbers of people often working different jobs, driving through horrible weather to get north – for they have to be at particular places at particular times, long hours in the field, poor living conditions, and struggles with money arise because the family is maintained with everyone travelling together, everyone living together. All of these hardships threaten family survival, as the obvious answer to many of their problems is to break up the family. Finally all of the things that a migrant mother, father, son, or daughter must do to help get through these difficulties (quitting school to work, fixing a broken-down truck, visiting social and migrant services, etc.) reflects choosing to maintain the family as a whole. We suggest that, in this way, the family is not only a focal point but also the construct in which these hardships lie. For example, in Juan's narrative it is because social relations are prioritized that hardships occur. Juan begins migrating when he is 14 to help his mother. He continues to go into the fields to help the family. Juan's family migrates as a group. Juan makes sacrifices to help the family with everyday needs when in Illinois. The family makes sacrifices so that Juan can go to school, for when he goes to school, he is no longer contributing his paycheque to the family budget. To construct programmes and services to address these hardships as well as create access for migrants to aspects of mainstream American life (such as public schooling), it is important to acknowledge the logic of the actions that lead to the experiences.

Homeless and homeless again

> And, even when we started to migrate as a family, I didn't complain or refuse to help out like my brother and sister would. It was before my sophomore year and it had been like a half a year that my dad had been without work. So they told us that we were going to have to go up north because Dad wasn't making any money in the valley. I had no idea what it was going to be like. So we would clean up the house, put all the furniture in one room and cover it, and board it up. After making sure that the van would make the long drive we would head up north to Ohio. We would go up to Ohio for the pickle harvest but that didn't start until July so up until then we found work picking strawberries, raspberries, and cabbage. The work itself was hard enough. We were in the fields from six in the morning until noon and then again from four until nine-thirty or ten. Man it was back breaking and it was seven days a week. And when we weren't working in the fields there was always other stuff to be done. Like helping with the laundry, going shopping, cooking, and cleaning. By the time we got home from our second stint in the fields all we would want to do is head to the community showers to get cleaned up and head back to the little houses the ranchers provided for us. I called them matchbox houses. They were always freezing at night, hot as hell during the day and so small that no matter how much you cleaned it would still be cluttered. All in all I migrated up to Ohio for three summers before coming to college.
>
> (Clara Garcia)

In thinking about Clara's description of her life migrating, it might be helpful to envision the homed–homeless dichotomy through a lens analogous to the Foucauldian conceptualization of power–powerless. We suggest that such a dichotomy is an oversimplification. Rather, if homed and homeless are thought of as states reflecting different value systems, each can be understood as creating relationships that both enable and constrain choices and actions. The dichotomy of homed–homeless is supported by the white, suburban, middle-class worldview that many of us assume in which home is a commodity rather than a relationship and that is prevalent in the national policies around homelessness. There is much precedent, historically and socially, in American society for us to think in this manner. Historically, many rights we now take for granted such as voting and access to schooling were only available to those with property. There is an assumption, rooted in such history, that owning a home is a measure of success but there are larger social and historical institutional assumptions which support such images and which make it hard for us to think otherwise. There are those in social and public policy research and in educational research who value the construct of home for its physical commodity but who also look at the role of that commodity in relation to people, power, family and values. This is an important distinction that should not be overlooked. However, we concentrate here on the relational dimension of homed/homelessness to magnify for the readers the important place of this relational stance in the lives of many migrant families. For migrants, home, if we define home as relationships rather than a thing, carries meanings equivalent to the word family, and this, in turn, shapes priorities and actions. The system of values suggested here reflects a particular worldview or lifeworld to use the terminology of Habermas (1984, 1987).

If we think about both the family and the home as signifying systems of relationships, Michel Foucault's analysis of power becomes helpful to us in understanding the obviously painful choices Clara's family are making. Foucault's (1980) view is that power is not a commodity. It is 'neither given, nor exchanged, nor recovered, but rather exercised, and . . . only exists in action' (Foucault, 1980, p. 89). When people interact in relationships, power comes into existence. That is, power is a productive social dynamic. 'Individuals are the vehicles of power, not its points of application' (Foucault, 1980, p. 98). Where action is completely constrained, one may not talk of there being a relationship of power. As Foucault (1982) states, 'Power is exercised only over free subjects, and only insofar as they are free' (p. 221). The person over whom power is being exercised (e.g. the migrant worker) is also simultaneously a person who acts, and whose actions in the process transform the one exercising power. Thus, the exercising of power is never unidirectional. It is never the 'province of one group and not the other' (Kincheloe, 1997, p. xxiii). Power implies the capacity to act.

In the migrant's narratives, families act within external constraints imposed by economics and status and also internal constraints arising from their own values and goals. The choice to go homeless can be interpreted as the exercising of freedom (power) in the context of the dialectic power–powerless. Rather than acting within a dichotomy such as homed–homeless, these poles exist in a dialectical relationship, that is, they are relational. Seen in this way, one category is not privileged over the other as is the case under the ordinary binary system. We can then deconstruct the homed–homeless dichotomy so that the two end up, not as opposites, but as 'definitionally interdependent' (Anyon, 1994, p. 119). Choosing to migrate, to be homeless, is exercising power. This in turn infuses the family as a unit with power.

The goals and values that help to support the family arise from a systemic relationship, a lifeworld and are shared, understood but not always articulated by family members. Lifeworlds can be thought of as a 'medium of reference' (Fairtlough, 1991), a 'shared linguistic and cultural resource' (Habermas, 1984) or a 'collective consciousness' (Durkheim, cited in Fairtlough, 1991). Never in the migrant's narratives do we hear them question the basic assumptions behind migrating. The children express unhappiness with the effects of migrating and the conditions they experience but no one questions the correctness of maintaining the family. In one sense, then, lifeworld is the cement for social cohesion of a social group; a shared lifeworld ensures that interpersonal relations are ordered in a way that makes groups to function effectively. The lifeworld of the migrant family does not exist in isolation, however. Rather it exists in a larger world in which other systems of values and assumption are apparent. Returning to Clara's narrative we can start to interpret some of the conflicts that assault the family and how these cause the family to continually reassert its integrity – a process emotionally loaded and full of unresolved tensions.

It was not long before Clara had answers to the questions she was asking about the migrant life.

> I remember that first day I just sat down right in the middle of the road and I started crying. And to my mom I told her, 'I was not born to do this'. I remember telling her, 'I was not made to do this I don't deserve to be here'. And I remember that she started crying and she said, 'And you think I was'? She goes, 'You think all these people were made were born to do this'?

But the hardships of the work and Clara's inner conflict, between where she wanted to be and where she was, became only one of the difficulties Clara faced. The family was struggling as well. The first payday caused an argument between Clara's mother, who wanted everyone to sign over their checks to the family, and Clara's brother and sister who wanted to keep what they had earned. As the argument escalated, Clara's mother threatened to leave. She said she was not willing to put up with this every time they were to be paid and would rather just pack up and go back to Texas than suffer through such frustration. But Clara's father begged her to stay and eventually she calmed down. Losing a family member would have divided the family, disintegrating the unity that was the reason they were on the road.

Recognizing that these conflicts arise not purely as a confrontation between individuals acting out of their own interests but rather as responses to a threat, which would shatter a systemic network of values, is helpful. We can extend this to understand the hardships that occur when the family chooses to break its unity because of the incongruent demands of a discordant system. There is a sense that no choices are possible for the family that would allow them to serve their own values and goals and the individual's needs.

Clara's migrant status was not something that she was willing to share openly with others. Clara did not like people to know she was a migrant and judge her based on where she lived and what she and her family did. Clara saw education as the way to give something back to her parents, be the exemplary daughter and avoid the life of migrant farmworking.

> Well, I knew that if I wanted to make something of myself and not work in the fields, I had to continue my education. Actually it's kind of weird 'cause

mostly everybody you talk to, you know, wants to earn money. They want to be where the money is but not me. And it's actually, it's kind of, I don't know, I think it's kind of ironic – I come from a low income family so it would be [normal] for me to have, like, this dream of being someone important and earning money, something that my parents didn't have much of. But no, to me what's most important is doing something I like and helping people, you know. . . .

This notion of an education and all the power that Clara grants to it as the means to become 'somebody' creates further family conflict. As the time came closer and closer for school to start, all the members of the family knew that Clara would be leaving to return to Texas and study. For example, the second year Clara and her family were migrating, Clara's oldest half-sister had come with her family to visit and expressed her dismay about Clara's parents allowing her to leave the fields early to arrive at school on time.

Struggling to return to Texas in order to start school just a few weeks, rather than months, late involved facing the loneliness of being there alone – in effect returning 'home' to Texas meant becoming 'homeless' in the sense that now Clara was without her family. 'I would stay in their room I guess to feel closer to them, I would stay in their room.'

Clara acknowledges that 'making something' of herself through an education was not something she could do alone. On the side of home and family, it involved the conflict and sacrifice of letting an extra pair of hands, leave the fields early – hands that could provide needed income for the months when work would be scarce or non-existent. It left Clara alone and lonely when she did return to school. It caused Clara to feel alienated from both the institution of school with its impersonal, disembodied requirements and members of her own family – both those who disapproved of her 'selfish' actions, and those that approved but suffered for them.

The process of naming an experience is also a process of creating and re-creating meaning around those realities. Creating and re-creating experience allows the holder of that experience to 'theorize' her/his life in relation to others. So, for example, in Clara's narrative, naming her values and needs acknowledges the political dimension of her experience for it articulates the 'labels' attached to knowledge and their sources, and allows us to place different value systems in juxtaposition to one another to challenge and transform those labels. In Clara's story, we see the effects of a system of values in confrontation with another system of values. To address the problems of homelessness for migrant workers requires understanding this conflict.

Ideas concerning the education of migrant children

To craft successful educational experiences for more than a small minority of migrant children such as Clara, we argue an understanding of their circumstances and the values systems that lead to those circumstances is important. Recent research concerning educational programmes for culturally diverse and language-minority students gives us some clues. For example, Native American and Inuit children, often considered taciturn, became surprisingly animated when instructional activities paralleled those considered important within their communities (Lipka, 1991; McCarty *et al.*, 1991).

Other researchers, such as Lucas *et al.* (1990), tried to characterize what successful schools do when working with Latina/o immigrant children. Lucas *et al.* identified that successful schools eschewed deficit models of instruction, and set high goals and expectations shared by students and school personnel. The school provided a variety of programmes that integrated social and cultural knowledge.

A consistent finding in research that examines the academic achievement of language-minority students is that successful teachers and schools accept students as they are, with the language that they speak at home and the value systems they live within. We suggest this be extended so that schools accommodate the way children live rather than assuming they live in a particular way.

Current research in education concerning children in poverty and children from other cultures speaks to larger issues. To understand or characterize these cultures, or lifeworlds, as the everyday world of human experience we must acknowledge that these are intersubjective worlds of social action (Schwandt, 1997). To do otherwise, to attribute the less than successful educational experiences of minority students solely to a mismatch between the features of home and school, ignores the importance of these social structures as a significant factor in the education of these youth (Allen and Boykin, 1992; Ludlow, 1992). Recognizing the social turns the student into one point amidst an array of social intersections that begin and end outside of school rather than an individual residing on one side of a clear-cut boundary that is culture (Nespor, 1997). The most immediate branches of this social array begin with the family and for the migrant student it is the family moving together that constructs both conflict and harmony in an everyday world of instability and struggle that transcends any material conception of place. Home does not exist in physical or perhaps even conceptual space but rather within these familial relationships fluctuating geographically (space), emotionally (strength) and politically (power) that dichotomies such as home–school or homed–homeless cannot capture. It is a lifeworld that moves literally from state to state as well as more figuratively between homed to homeless amidst these relationships.

Far from being unconcerned with the learning of their children, we can see from our stories that parents are very concerned with the discordance between their systems of values and the assumptions of the surrounding culture. Researchers have reported that parents from minority communities, particularly immigrant families, are highly motivated to support their children's efforts in schools (Goldenberg, 1987; Goldenberg and Gallimore, 1991; Delgado-Gaitan, 1991, 1992; Vasquez *et al.*, 1994; Valdés, 1996) but to support their children in schools requires choosing one system of values over their own. Different views of what is proper or adequate involvement often separate teachers and parents. We suggest some sort of mutual negotiation and compromise. McConnell (1989), for example, demonstrated how migrant students in Texas were able to increase their academic achievement when programme administrators hired parents as teacher aids. Such a compromise addresses parental and family needs and seems a simple way to bridge the two worlds.

Lopez *et al.* (2001) have noted that schools that successfully involve migrant farmworking parents in the education of their children recognize the social and economic needs of this group. They attempt to meet these needs on a daily and ongoing basis rather than following a regimented list of parental involvement considerations. This involves a significant redefinition of parental involvement where the school and home come to each other and includes what is termed 'home involvement' which centres, in part, on helping better familial circumstances. Thus, 'home' turns into something synonymous with family and is not temporary or dissolving with a move north but extends beyond space, time, and the academic year. The school's involvement with the home, or family, is a continuous interaction allowing it to become aware of and meet the shifting needs of the family.

Conclusion

Theorizing family and home through the constructs, power and lifeworld enables us to see how family and home and the experiences that emanate from them are situated in a complexity of intertwining value systems. This situatedness leads to embedded relationships between human beings, their resources, perceptions and environment. If we move this discussion into the schools and the education of migrant worker children, we can understand that services and programmes should address the entire family and not look purely at the individual student.

In many ways migrant workers are forced into 'homelessness'. Many of them left home when they left Mexico. They leave 'home' again in a cultural sense when they leave the Spanish-speaking communities in which they have lived within the United States, and when we ask them to break the family structure to go to school or for some other purpose we cause individuals to become homeless in a most fundamental way – an emotional rootlessness. We think that once we acknowledge other images of 'home' and the values and priorities that follow, policies and services for migrant workers and their children might take a different form. These might then serve our purposes (such as education) and their purposes (such as preserving the family) better. When policies and institutions ask a migrant family to choose between what they value (family) and what we value any good intended is undermined.

References

Allen, B.A. and Boykin, A.W. (1992). African-American children and the educational process: alleviating cultural discontinuity through prescriptive pedagogy. *School Psychology Review*, 21(4), 586–596.

Anyon, J. (1994). The retreat of Marxism and socialist feminism: post-modernism and post-structural theories in education. *Curriculum Inquiry*, 24(2), 115–133.

Delgado-Gaitan, C. (1991). Involving parents in the schools: a process of empowerment. *American Journal of Education*, 100(1), 20–46.

Delgado-Gaitan, C. (1992). School matters in the Mexican-American home: socializing children to education. *American Educational Research Journal*, 29(3), 495–513.

Fairtlough, G. (1991). Habermas' concept of 'lifeworld'. *Systems Practice*, 4(6), 547–551.

Foucault, M. (1980). *Power/Knowledge: Selected Interviews and Other Writings*, 1972–1977 (C. Gordon, Ed.). New York: Pantheon Books.

Foucault, M. (1982). The subject and power (Afterword). In H.L. Dreyfus and P. Rabinow (Eds), *Michel Foucault: Beyond Structuralism and Hermeneutics*. Brighton: Harvester Press.

Goldenberg, C. (1987). Low-income Latino parents' contributions to their first-grade children's word-recognition skills. *Anthropology and Education Quarterly*, 18, 149–179.

Goldenberg, C.N. and Gallimore, R. (1991). Local knowledge, research knowledge, and educational change: a case study of early Spanish reading improvement. *Educational Researcher*, 20(8), 2–14.

Habermas, J. (1984). *The Theory of Communicative Action: Vol. 1. Reason and the Rationalization of Society*. Boston, MA: Beacon Press.

Habermas, J. (1987). *The Theory of Communicative Action: Vol. 2. Lifeworld and Systems: A Critique of Functionalist Reason*. Boston, MA: Beacon Press.

Kincheloe, J. (1997). Introduction. In I.F. Goodson (Ed.), *The Changing Curriculum: Studies in Social Construction* (pp. ix–xl). New York: Peter Lang.

King-Stoops, J.B. (1980). *Migrant Education: Teaching the Wandering Ones*. Bloomington, IN: Phi Delta Kappa Educational Foundation.

Lipka, J. (1991). Toward a culturally based pedagogy: a case study of one Yup'ik Eskimo teacher. *Anthropology and Education Quarterly*, 22, 203–223.

Lincoln, Y.S. and Guba, E.G. (1985). *Naturalistic Inquiry*. Beverly Hills, CA: Sage.

Lopez, G.R., Scribner, J.D. and Mahitivanichcha, K. (2001). Redefining parental involvement: lessons from high-performing migrant-impacted schools. *American Educational Research Journal*, 38(2), 253–288.

Lucas, T., Henze, R. and Donato R. (1990). Promoting the success of Latino language minority students: an exploratory study of six high schools. *Harvard Educational Review*, 60(3), 315–339.

Ludlow, S. (1992). Is cultural discontinuity an adequate explanation for dropping out? *Journal of American Indian Education*, 31(3), 21–36.

McCarty, T.L., Wallace, S., Lynch, R.H. and Benally, A. (1991). Classroom inquiry and Navajo learning styles: a call for reassessment. *Anthropology and Education Quarterly*, 22, 42–59.

McConnell, B. (1989). Education as a cultural process: the interaction between community and classroom in fostering learning. In J.B. Allen and J. Mason (Eds), *Risk Makers, Risk Takers, Risk Breakers: Reducing the Risks for Young Literacy Learners* (pp. 201–221). Portsmouth, NH: Heinemann.

Nespor, J. (1997). *Tangled Up in School: Politics, Space, Bodies, and Signs in the Educational Process*. Mahwah, NJ: Lawrence Erlbaum.

Parsad, B., Heaviside, S., Williams, C. and Farris, E. (2000). Title I Migrant Education Program Summer-Term Projects: 1998 (NCES 2000–061). Education Statistics Quarterly, online – available at: http://www/nces.ed.gov/pubs2000/qrtlyspring/4elem/ q4-11.html

Polany, L. (1985). *Telling the American Story: A Structural and Cultural Analysis of Conversational Storytelling*. Norwood, NJ: Ablex.

Prewitt Diaz, J.O., Trotter, R.T. and Rivera, V.A. (1990). *The Effects of Migration on Children: An Ethnographic Study*. State College, PA: Centro de Estudios Sobre la Migration.

Public Law 103-388 (1994). Improving America's Schools Act of 1994 http://www.ed.gov/legislation/ESEA/index.html (Accessed 26 August 2004).

Schwandt, T.A. (1997). *Qualitative Inquiry: A Dictionary of Terms*. Thousand Oaks, CA: Sage.

Valdes, G. (1996). *Con respecto*. New York: Teachers College Press.

Valle, I. (1994). *Fields of Toil: A Migrant Family's Journey*. Pullman, WA: Washington State University Press.

Vasquez, O.A., Pease-Alvarez, L. and Shannon, S. (1994). *Pushing Boundaries: Language and Culture in a Mexicano Community*. Cambridge, MA: Harvard University Press.

Chapter 17

'What are we doing this for?'

Dealing with lesbian and gay issues in
teacher education

Kerry H. Robinson and Tania Ferfolja

Introduction

This chapter is based on the experiences and reflections of the authors who, over the
past seven years, have repeatedly taught the course diversity and social justice issues
to pre-service high-school teachers. This 12-week course is a mandatory component of a teaching degree at a university in metropolitan Sydney. The chapter
highlights the perceived (ir)relevance of gay and lesbian issues to pre-service teachers, the belief that sexuality is not the concern of teachers or schools, pre-service
teachers' assumption of 'compulsory heterosexuality' in both the university and
school classrooms and the pathologising of perceived lesbian and gay identities as
the cause of individual discrimination. Such beliefs pose numerous pedagogical
concerns for the teacher educator, including the silencing by peers of students
interested in this social justice issue as well as varying degrees of student resistance
around issues of difference.

There is some indication that teacher educators in tertiary institutions do not
adequately prepare their students to incorporate issues of difference into their pedagogical practices (Hatton, 1996). While we generally agree with this criticism, it
is also important to highlight some of the difficulties faced by the teacher educator
who is attempting to deal with aspects of diversity and difference, including those
areas that are considered controversial or 'taboo' in some schools and communities. Gay and lesbian issues can be particularly controversial, and are often silenced
and marginalised in educational contexts (Goldstein, 1997), sometimes through
legislation. For instance, in Britain's Local Government Act of 1988, section 28,
as it passed into law prohibited local authorities from 'intentionally promote[ing]
homosexuality' by publishing material or promoting teaching in schools 'of the
acceptability of homosexuality as a pretended family relationship' (Epstein and
Johnson, 1998, p. 58). However, the need to address gay and lesbian issues is
paramount in the light of the homophobic violence, vilification and discrimination
experienced by individuals in educational contexts in Western societies, who are
perceived to be gay or lesbian (Khayatt, 1992; Griffin, 1994; Sparkes, 1994; Clark,
1996; Robinson, 1996; Epstein and Johnson, 1998; Ferfolja, 1998). The effects
of discrimination can be far reaching, for both male and female youth, affecting

their educational achievements, their social development and their health (Besner and Spungin, 1995; Denborough, 1996; Griffin, 1997; Irwin *et al.*, 1997). The urgency to address lesbian and gay discrimination is intensified by the rate of youth suicide in the Western world, where an estimated 30 per cent of youths who commit suicide are struggling with issues of lesbian/gay sexuality (Mac an Ghaill, 1994; Denborough, 1996) and where Australia has one of the highest rates in the Western world (Donaghy, 1997).

Research shows that schooling systems and teaching practices constitute and perpetuate discrimination towards gays and lesbians, through the policing of hegemonic discourses of heterosexuality and gender (McClean, 1996; Britzman, 1997). Contrary to the right of students to feel safe in schools, homophobic slurs often go unchallenged by school authorities (Mathison, 1998). Recently, in Australia, individuals have sought redress through the legal system for hate crimes and discriminatory practices in schools (Angelo, 1997; Passey, 1997), which demonstrates many schools are failing to adequately address homophobic behaviours. Students have the right to expect teachers to 'do something' about the harassment they face on a daily basis (Goldstein, 1997, p. 115). Consequently, dealing with gay and lesbian issues in schooling, including the ways in which schools and teachers themselves actively police the boundaries of 'compulsory heterosexuality' (Rich, 1980) in their daily practices, is imperative to teacher training courses.

Pedagogical context

It is important to provide a brief overview of the pedagogical context of the university course that students undertake in their pre-service teacher training on which this chapter is based.

Through the process of critical reflection, students map, analyse and theorise the construction of their subjectivity, which is the unconscious and conscious thoughts and emotions of the individual, one's sense of self and how one relates to the world (Weedon, 1997). This process is informed by understanding how one's subjectivity, including the knowledge or truths one holds about the world, and the various degrees of power one experiences at different points in life and in different contexts are all constituted in discourse. Individuals are considered not passive, but active agents in the construction of their own subjectivity who are influential in the development of the subjectivity of others (Sawicki, 1991). Pre-service teachers reflect on their life experiences in relation to gender, sexuality, 'race', ethnicity, class, ability and so on, across a variety of contexts including family, work, school and personal relationships. The intersections and power differentials associated with these various aspects of identity are critically explored, on a local and systemic level (Robinson and Jones-Diaz, 1999). Exploring and understanding the construction of one's own subjectivity is, as Davies (1994) suggests, crucial to teachers and students in order to see its effects on us and on the learning environments that we collaboratively produce.

Student's resistance levels around social justice issues

There are varying degrees of resistance around social justice issues and one's preparedness to relocate oneself in more equitable discourses around difference (Robinson and Jones-Diaz, 1999). Sexuality or, more specifically, gay and lesbian issues, always incur greater resistance, due to the controversy and cultural taboos surrounding non-heterosexual or minority sexualities. This is reflected in some pre-service teachers' attitudes, interests and willingness to participate in various topic areas.

For example, there is much less resistance among students when dealing with multiculturalism, which is high on students' agendas as an appropriate issue to be addressed in a teacher-training course. Students perceive cultural diversity as being synonymous with multiculturalism, which is understood in the context of 'ethnic diversity'. This hegemonic reading of multiculturalism reflects its popular definition in Australia, largely due to the way that this issue has been constructed and represented in the media, education and government policies (Rizvi, 1991). This legitimacy is increased by the fact that ethnic diversity is commonly perceived as inescapably visible, and pre-service teachers often feel culturally validated when deconstructing discriminatory discourses and social constructions of ethnicity. The perceived importance and relevance of multiculturalism is in stark contrast to the attitudes and beliefs that many pre-service teachers have towards anti-racism, particularly related to Aboriginal and Torres Strait Islander issues. The hegemonic discourse of multiculturalism, based on liberal humanist perspectives of tolerance and intercultural understanding, unlike anti-racist or anti-homophobia discourse, does little to disrupt the dominant power relationships or *status quo* of society. Multiculturalism celebrates ethnic diversity, 'but the ethnicity that is encouraged is apolitical ethnicity, divorced from the larger socio-political matrix in which it is embedded' (Rizvi, 1991, p. 183).

Similarly, gender, although still a controversial topic evoking strong differences in personal opinion, especially around understandings or misunderstandings of feminism and its impact, has been given the official stamp of approval by schooling and university policies since being placed firmly on the agenda in the 1980s. Consequently, despite individual resistances around dealing with gendered power relations, there tends to be an overall acceptance that this topic needs to be discussed in relation to the curriculum context and their future pedagogical practices.

Sexuality, on the contrary, is considered in a different light by many students, and does not have the same recognition or sense of legitimacy about it as many other issues that are dealt with in this course. This is primarily the results of prevailing moral and religious discourses that mythologise the gay/lesbian as among others, paedophilic, hypersexualised, predatory and mentally unstable who aim to undermine dominant heterosexual family values (Hinson, 1996; Britzman, 1997). These discourses are further reinforced through legislation that overtly and covertly discriminates against the sexualised 'other' (George, 1997).

Perceived relevance of lesbian and gay issues to teaching

Social justice issues generally are perceived by many pre-service teachers as irrelevant to classroom teachers for several reasons. These include the belief that the fundamental praxis of teaching is a more immediate and more important concern, the fact that social justice issues are generally taught in isolation rather than across the curriculum and the prevalence of discourses that define 'worthwhile' knowledge. Within these generalised concerns, sexuality is more specifically perceived to be even more irrelevant by many students as it is considered a private issue or the responsibility of personal development, health and physical education classes (Beckett, 1996). Also, gay and lesbian issues are considered 'minority issues' and are therefore irrelevant to the majority, or 'normal' student. Unless difference is obvious, that is visible and vocal, it is perceived as non-existent.

Many pre-service teachers are focused on the 'mechanics' of teaching, which is perceived to be quintessential to classroom management and is reinforced in teacher training generally. Pre-service teachers' insecurities often stem from the fear of losing classroom 'control'. Thus, pre-service teachers often do not see sexuality (and social justice issues more generally) as a priority in their learning. However, it is crucial to extend pre-service teachers' awareness that an understanding of the socio-cultural contexts of their students and of the everyday politics of schooling are as relevant and important to positive classroom management as the daily mechanics of pedagogy. This includes understanding their potential role in perpetuating 'problems' in the classroom through discriminatory and exclusive practices, and through a failure to recognise and adequately deal with conflicts among their students.

Many pre-service teachers are positioned within the philosophies of their specialist disciplines where, in some contexts, there is a lack of perceived relevance both traditionally and historically to broader social issues. Consequently, depending on the background of their discipline, teachers demonstrate conflicting perspectives of the need to understand their students within a socio-cultural context. On many occasions during our teaching, pre-service teachers have articulated that discussions not directly connected with their discipline, or social inequalities resulting in either overt or covert individual or institutional discrimination, will not arise in their classroom because 'lifestyle discussions' are not written into their course syllabus. However, as Malinowitz (1995, p. 23) points out 'Leaving sexual identity out of the classroom is not an accident, it is an expression of institutionalized homophobia, enacted in a classroom not randomly but systematically, with legal and religious precedents to bolster it and intimidate both teachers and students.'

The perceived irrelevance of social justice issues by some students is reinforced through the course's isolation within the overall structure of the teacher-training course.

Similarly, when students are on practicum, the tasks they are expected to fulfil generally do not require them to demonstrate an understanding of inclusivity in their practical experiences in the classroom. Social justice issues, particularly sexuality and its relevance to pedagogy, are not a consideration of classroom management. Lesson preparation often fails to acknowledge sexuality differences. This exclusivity is reinforced by supervisors who frequently overlook sexuality as well as other social justice issues. Yet, schooling should play the vital role of deconstructing and disrupting the power relationships of binary logics, including the heterosexual/homosexual dualism which dominates in schools. To some extent, this disruption has been articulated in departmental policy and resource development. For instance, the personal development/health/physical education syllabus stipulates that a range of relationships be examined and that personal differences be addressed. The policy *Girls and Boys at School – Gender Equity Strategy, 1996–2000* (New South Wales Department of School Education) encourages equitable and inclusive learning environments and pedagogical practices. Teaching resources on anti-discrimination, including anti-homophobia, have been developed by the New South Wales Department of Education and Training for use in public schools. However, monitoring the manner, effect and extent to which inclusion actually occurs, whether it be in site-based policies or practices, is logistically problematic and, ultimately, left up to the social justice consciousness of individual schools and teachers.

Broaching sexuality in schools is complex and contradictory. Pre-service teachers often consider sexuality, particularly lesbian and gay sexualities, as a moral, private, adult issue relegated to personal relationships and the family. This is reinforced for students who are positioned within conservative, cultural and/or religious discourses. The family, as a modern disciplinary state apparatus, is seen traditionally as the moral guardian of children's sexuality education. However, there is on-going debate as to whether schools or families should teach sexuality issues. In many situations, families have relinquished the responsibility of sexuality education to schools. However, the content of this teaching is still monitored by families, vocal community members, religious teachings, legislation and official school policies and guidelines.

Many pre-service teachers comment that, when sexuality issues are to be dealt with in schools, it should be the sole responsibility of the personal development and health curriculum teachers who are legally required to deal with these issues. This curriculum has traditionally operated within the discourse of heterosexual 'normalisation', reinforcing the pathology and problematic nature of homosexuality (Beckett, 1996), although a focus on empathy and personal relationships has been incorporated into the curriculum. However, teachers' attitudes often dictate the manner in which this content is presented and, consequently, many of the stereotypes and dominant discourses around homosexuality and lesbianism prevail (Robinson, 1996; Ferfolja, 1998). Thus, we are not arguing that all teachers need to teach sexuality as such, but rather need to have the knowledge and skills to redress the homophobic attitudes, harassment and violence that occur in schools daily. Teachers must address all student needs through the provision of an inclusive curriculum and through the development of positive and equitable teaching practices and policies.

Britzman (1997) found a common misconception among pre-service teachers that gay and lesbian issues have little to do with understandings of the constructions of heterosexuality. But Sedgewick points out the importance of incorporating a 'universalising' approach to sexuality in which the deconstruction of the binary, 'heterosexual us'/'homosexual them' is of benefit to all sexualities (Sedgwick, 1990). Many pre-service teachers unquestionably assume the heterosexuality of their students and consider learning about lesbian and gay issues irrelevant to their teaching to the 'majority' culture. Individual gender and sexuality 'differences' are policed by schooling institutions and force 'others' to conform to dominant constructions of masculinity, femininity and heterosexuality or suffer the consequences (Nayak and Kehily, 1997). Another discourse operating in schools is the notion that, unless an issue of difference is obvious, visible and/or predominantly the majority, it is assumed to be non-existent. Within this, if the perceived minority is silent, then often their needs remain unacknowledged (Ferfolja, 1998). These discourses serve to marginalise lesbian and gay students, through notions of assimilation and 'hiding one's difference', and through the often-absolute invisibility and silencing of lesbian and gay issues in secondary institutions.

Aligning oneself with the dominant school culture is expected of both pre-service teachers on practicum and practising teachers, and thus many individuals behave in line with what is perceived as 'appropriate within their particular school' (Sikes, 1993, p. 18).

'Serves them right, they ask for it': the construction of 'gay' as the problem

A dominant discourse operating for many pre-service teachers is that students who are perceived to be sexual 'others' are ultimately at fault for any harassment endured and have the ability, if not the desire, to change themselves to fit into the majority culture. Some pre-service teachers, although espousing equality, demonstrate negative attitudes towards people who take up the more overt stereotyped characteristics of being gay or lesbian, which challenge the boundaries of hegemonic gender constructions. Simplistically, being gay/lesbian is acceptable, within constructed gender 'norms' and where 'difference' is not 'flaunted'. A frequently espoused belief is that, if the harassed student 'changed themselves' in some way so that they did not stand out, if they looked, sounded or acted like their peers, they would be accepted. The 'problem' is perceived to be their 'gayness'. The individual is pathologised, rather than recognising the broader social inequalities, discrimination and power relationships existing around constructions of gender and sexuality.

It is common for pre-service teachers to 'gloss over' issues of homophobic/ lesbophobic harassment as something with which harassed students must contend. Harassment is normalised through discourses of 'growing up'. After all, we are told, the pre-service teachers also experienced various forms of harassment (although not necessarily homophobic) and they 'survived'. Pre-service teachers often justify inequities through their own lived experiences and 'filter' new information through this lens (Lundeberg, 1997; Smith *et al.*, 1997), rather than looking at why the inequalities originally existed. It is the latter that must be deconstructed and examined in teacher training.

Whose voices get heard when dealing with gay and lesbian issues?

Pre-service teachers' views about gay and lesbian issues reflect a complex and contradictory continuum of opinions and attitudes. These include total dismissal, resistance on moral or religious grounds, perspectives that 'they are OK as long as they keep away from me', through to recognition and understanding of difference within a social justice framework. Yet, the voice that most often dominates classroom resistance on this topic tends to be those who position themselves within moral and conservative religious discourses. Deconstructing the heterosexual/homosexual binary and examining the inequalities experienced by sexual 'minorities' is often resisted. This resistance is expressed through aggressive body language, feigned indifference or silence, or through the use of religious, cultural and moral discourses to counteract the deconstruction of dominant discourses around sexuality. The resistance that arises articulates many of the myths and stereotypes that frequently underpin discrimination. These are explored and challenged to highlight macro and micro power relationships.

However, resistance in the form of vocal homophobic sentiment can prove a moral dilemma for the teacher trainer because, undoubtedly, minority sexualities exist in the class population. Anti-gay and lesbian discourses that do start to arise that are based on stereotypes give the more vocal students the power and platform from which to voice discriminatory attitudes. This can marginalise pre-service teachers who are supportive of different sexualities and who, through challenging their peers' resistance, often run the risk of potential conflict.

Gay and lesbian pre-service teachers often fear being 'outed' in the process of counteracting their peers' resistance (Chasnoff and Cohen, 1996). Challenging the hegemonic position of heterosexuality potentially results in a questioning and scrutinisation of their discursive position. In the least, they witness lecturers and peers experience difficulties in trying to shift the central position of homophobic discourses that operate in the group. Within this contradictory and sometimes volatile environment of the university classroom, endeavouring to shift the power relationships within the heterosexual/homosexual binary can ironically result in those pre-service teachers who identify as gay or lesbian feeling marginalised (Herek, 1993; D'Augelli, 1994; Sparkes, 1994). Gay and lesbian identities are often homophobically read and essentialised by their peers through stereotypes, the experiences of others and representations in popular culture.

Pre-service teacher's resistance, when in the form of homophobic sentiment often based on religious and moral discourses, has been articulated in assessment tasks, where they frequently resort to personal beliefs and opinions rather than theoretically analysing and deconstructing the discourses operating. In this way, the resistance is an attempt to reassert the individual's challenged power and status. This form of resistance often results in a personalised attack on the lecturer who is perceived to be biased in their marking, and pushing an agenda when these personalised comments are questioned. This resistance shifts the focus from the deconstruction of discursive power relations on a micro and macro level to one based on personality differences.

Other pedagogical considerations

When dealing with difference, particularly gay and lesbian issues, assumptions are made about the teacher educator's sexuality and their reasons for broaching the issue. It is often considered that one has to be gay or lesbian to express an interest in these issues or to be supportive of sexual differences (Chasnoff and Cohen, 1996; Ferfolja, 1998). The assumptionist position in relation to the teacher educator's perceived gay or lesbian sexuality can potentially lead to harassment regardless of one's actual sexuality. Furthermore, giving a focus to sexuality and deconstructing and problematising heterosexuality in the process is often read by some students and colleagues as a means of pushing one's own personal agenda.

For those teacher educators who do identify as gay or lesbian, there is a heightened sense of vulnerability when students are critical of any (however limited this might be) inclusion of gay and lesbian issues in teacher training. This can result in some students taking their personal grievances to other lecturers who may or may not support the students' claims depending on their own subjective position within sexuality discourses. Consequently, in some instances, the lecturers teaching in this course have been questioned by peers about the relevance of incorporating (homo)sexuality, in particular, as an appropriate social justice issue relevant to schooling and to pedagogical practice, ultimately questioning their professionalism. Other areas of identity perceived to be less controversial, such as class, 'race' or gender have not been isolated for similar justification.

The pre-service teachers' resistance around issues of gay and lesbian sexualities has led to very careful consideration about where to locate this social justice issue in the structure and timeframe of the course. Sexuality, like other social justice issues dealt with in the course, is examined continuously in relation to its intersections with other sites of inequality and power. Each area is dealt with in depth, with sexuality placed towards the end of the course. This is done strategically in order to ensure that students have developed understandings of theoretical concepts around power and inequality, and their relevance to schooling, before embarking fully on this more controversial issue. Hatton (1996, p. 33) found similar approaches were required when introducing issues of racism because 'if we react too strongly or make people feel immediately threatened or guilty they will retreat'.

Conclusion

There is a growing awareness and concern about the social inequalities faced by minority sexualities, especially in regard to violence and youth suicide. Many of these inequalities are prevalent in schools in Australia, which are increasingly expected to address such social justice issues. Failing to do so undermines the quality of education for all students by limiting their options in life. Hence, pre-service teachers need to understand and be trained to positively deal with homophobia and its negative social and educational consequences. As Martindale (1997, p. 68) states, 'Attending to homophobic discourse, learning how to question and reply to it without getting caught within its limited and destructive focus' is crucial to effective intervention. However, homophobia is also a major issue among some pre-service teachers and, if not addressed adequately at the teacher-training level, will hinder effective intervention and the promotion of equality in schooling.

References

Angelo, J. (1997) Walk like a man, *Daily Telegraph*, 2 April.

Beckett, L. (1996) Where do you draw the line? Education and sexual identities, in: L. Laskey and C. Beavis (Eds) *Schooling and Sexualities* (Victoria, Deakin Centre for Education and Change, Deakin University).

Besner, H.F. and Spungin, C.I. (1995) *Gay and Lesbian Students. Understanding their Needs* (Washington, DC, Taylor and Francis).

Britzman, D.P. (1997) What is this thing called love? New discourses for understanding gay and lesbian youth, in: S. De Castell and M. Bryson (Eds) *Radical Interventions: Identity, Politics, and Differences in Educational Praxis* (Albany, NY, State University of New York Press).

Chasnoff, D. and Cohen, H. (1996) *It's Elementary: Talking About Gay Issues in School* (video) (San Francisco, CA, Women's Educational Media).

Clark, G. (1996) Conforming and contesting with (a) difference: how lesbian students and teachers manage their identities, *International Studies in Sociology of Education*, 6, pp. 191–209.

D'Augelli, A.R. (1994) Lesbian and gay men's experiences of discrimination and harassment in a university community, *American Journal of Community Psychology*, 17, pp. 317–321.

Davies, B. (1994) *Poststructuralist Theory and Classroom Practice* (Geelong, Deakin University Press).

Denborough, D. (1996) Power and partnership? Challenging the sexual construction of schooling, in: L. Laskey and C. Beavis (Eds) *Schooling and Sexualities* (Victoria, Deakin Centre for Education and Change, Deakin University).

Donaghy, B. (1997) *Leaving Early: Youth Suicide – The Horror, The Heartbreak, The Hope* (New South Wales, Harper Collins).

Epstein, D. and Johnson, R. (1998) *Schooling Sexualities* (Buckingham, Open University Press).

Ferfolja, T. (1998) Australian lesbian teachers – a reflection of homophobic harassment of high school teachers in New South Wales government schools, *Gender and Education*, 10, pp. 401–415.

George, A. (1997) The gay(?) victim on trial: discourses of sexual division in the courtroom, in: G. Mason and S. Tomsen (Eds) *Homophobic Violence* (Sydney, Hawkins Press).

Goldstein, T. (1997) Unlearning homophobia through a pedagogy of anonymity, *Teaching Education*, 9, pp. 115–124.

Hatton, E. (1996) Dealing with diversity: the failure of teacher education, *Discourse: Studies in the Cultural Politics of Education*, 17, pp. 25–42.

Herek, G.M. (1993) Documenting prejudice against lesbians and gay men on campus: the Yale sexual orientation survey, *Journal of Homosexuality*, 25, pp. 15–27.

Hinson, S. (1996) A practice focused approach to addressing heterosexist violence in Australian schools, in: L. Laskey and C. Beavis (Eds) *Schooling and Sexualities* (Victoria, Deakin Centre for Education and Change, Deakin University).

Irwin, J., Gregoric, M. and Winter, B. (1997) Violence against homeless young lesbians, in: G. Mason and S. Tomsen (Eds) *Homophobic Violence* (Sydney, The Hawkins Press).

Khayatt, M.D. (1992) *Lesbian Teachers: An Invisible Presence* (Albany, NY, State University of New York Press).

Lundeberg, M.A. (1997) You guys are overreacting: teaching prospective teachers about subtle gender bias, *Journal of Teacher Education*, 48, pp. 55–61.

Mac an Ghaill, M. (1994) *The Making of Men: Masculinities, Sexualities and Schooling* (Buckingham, Open University Press).

McClean, C. (1996) Men, masculinity and heterosexuality, in: L. Laskey and C. Beavis (Eds) *Schooling and Sexualities* (Victoria, Deakin Centre for Education and Change, Deakin University).

Malinowitz, H. (1995) *Textual Orientations: Lesbian and Gay Students and the Making of Discourse Communities* (Portsmouth, Boynton/Cook Publishers).

Martindale, K. (1997) Querying pedagogy: teaching un/popular cultures, in: S. de Castell and M. Bryson (Eds) *Radical Interventions: Identity, Politics, and Differences in Educational Praxis* (Albany, NY, State University of New York Press).

Mathison, C. (1998) The invisible minority: preparing teachers to meet the needs of gay and lesbian youth, *Journal of Teacher Education*, 49, pp. 151–55.

Nayak, A. and Kehily, M.J. (1997) Masculinities and schooling: why are young men so homophobic? in: D.L. Steinberg, D. Epstein and R. Johnson (Eds) *Border Patrols* (London, Cassell).

Passey, D. (1997) Schoolyard victims, *Sydney Morning Herald*, 5 April.

Rich, A. (1980) Compulsory heterosexuality and lesbian existence, *Signs: Journal of Women in Culture and Society*, 5, pp. 631–660.

Rizvi, F. (1991) The idea of ethnicity and the politics of multicultural education, in: D. Dawkins (Ed.) *Power and Politics in Education* (London, Falmer Press).

Robinson, K.H. (1996) *Sexual Harassment in Schools*. Unpublished PhD Thesis (School of Sociology, University of New South Wales, Australia).

Robinson, K.H. and Jones-Diaz, C. (1999) Doing theory with early childhood educators: understanding difference and diversity in personal and professional contexts, *Australian Journal of Early Childhood*, 24, pp. 33–39.

Sawicki, J. (1991) *Disciplining Foucault: Feminism, Power, and the Body* (New York, Routledge).

Sedgwick, E. (1990) *Epistemology of the Closet* (Berkeley, CA, University of California Press).

Sikes, P. (1993) Gender and teacher education, in: I. Siraj-Blatchford (Ed.) *'Race', Gender and the Education of Teachers* (Buckingham, Open University Press).

Smith, R., Moallem, M. and Sherrill, D. (1997) How preservice teachers think about cultural diversity: a closer look at factors which influence their beliefs towards equality, *Educational Foundations*, 11, pp. 41–61.

Sparkes, A.C. (1994) Self, silence and invisibility as a beginning teacher: a life history of lesbian experience, *British Journal of Sociology of Education*, 15, pp. 93–118.

Weedon, C. (1997) *Feminist Practice and Poststructuralist Theory*, 2nd edn (Oxford, Blackwell).

Chapter 18

The creation of learner identities as part of social inclusion

Gender, ethnicity and social space

Sue Clegg and Katie McNulty

Introduction

There is growing evidence that the provision of learning opportunities does not, of itself, create participants who want to engage in education (Coffield, 2000a,b). Government policies and education providers assume the value of education as a source of individual cultural capital and collective social capital (McClenaghan, 2000). However, individuals in targeted communities frame their orientation towards formal learning through their own social networks (Atkin, 2000). The creation of new learner identities cannot be assumed. This is particularly important in the area of policies to tackle social exclusion, which rely on ideas of lifelong education linked to employment. Yet, evidence on the ground suggests that people not engaged in education do not perceive this as a lack, and that policies designed to encourage participation are based on inadequate conceptualizations of the relationship between people's lives and learning (Bowman *et al.*, 2000; Coffield, 2000a,b). Moreover, many of the unemployed, including parents, do not feel socially excluded (Levitas, 1998; Watts, 2001).

Policy context and background

Lifelong learning forms a central policy focus for developing people's capacities for employment (Schuller and Field, 1998). However, critics have pointed out that inclusion works on a number of levels (Watts, 2000), and the creation of learner identities and dispositions as a route to inclusion involves more than just the provision of opportunities. Even when 'learning' opportunities are bolstered by the 'carrot' and 'sticks' of government policy they are not necessarily effective. Without an extended understanding of the meanings of learning and of what is involved in learner identities it is likely that lifelong learning will remain the preserve of those already in work or already benefiting from education. The view that sees non-participation (estimated at about 25 per cent) as irrational and attempts to instil the social desirability of learning into others is both illiberal (Ecclestone, 1999; Coffield, 2000a,b) and doomed to failure on any meaningful definition of learning (Eraut, 1997; Claxton, 1999).

Moreland and Lovett (1997) have argued that a community development model, which is issues based, action orientated and participative, can contribute to democratizing the meaning of adult education. The community model, which cuts across formal and non-formal settings, takes the participants' perspectives as the basis for knowledge (Kenny *et al.*, 2000). It also extends ideas about what counts as learning, for example, Moreland and Lovett (1997) describe the importance of women coming together in a 'Family Group' in breaking down the isolation women experienced as mothers and in providing the self-confidence that could lead to other activities. Andruske (1999) draws on the idea of situated learning (Lave and Wenger, 1996) in order to understand how a person's individual learning is located within a social and community context. The community development model and partnership working, despite their recent policy association with some of the more discredited versions of social capital theory (McClenaghan, 2000), therefore, continue to be of interest as a way of working on the ground.

The case study

Our case study was located in a multiply socially deprived and ethnically diverse area of a large northern English city. Much Single Regeneration Budget funding has been targeted in this way (Department for Transport, Local Government and the Regions, 2002), and the partnership we studied supported multiple projects embodying the partnership's overall strategy to tackle disaffection and underachievement, based on a model of inclusive education (Clegg and McNulty, 2002).

The parents and carers project aimed to encourage previously disengaged adults to access educational opportunities. Although the project was designed in partnership with schools, its aim was clearly focused on parents as individual learners not as a means to school improvement (Tett, 2001). The project outlined its aims as being to '(1) provide opportunities for family learning, (2) encourage groups of men who have traditionally not been involved in learning, (3) support parents and carers in working towards accreditation, (4) remove barriers of learning, such as provision of care for dependants and (5) take learning into the community and to make learning fun and relevant'. As with other projects aimed at encouraging men to identify as parents in school settings (Caddell, 1996), in fact only women participated. The project model incorporated some of the community development principles described by Moreland and Lovett (1997) and the main worker was a Community Education Worker (CEW). The CEW specifically targeted parents/carers in a number of key schools through informal contacts; for example, when parents were taking children to and from school. The CEW could put individuals directly in touch with other learning opportunities, but she usually arranged a meeting between parents/carers in a 'first steps' group. The emphasis was on parents/carers being given the opportunity to decide what they wanted to learn. A variety of classes were offered based on negotiations with the parents; for example, 'books for babies'. These were taught mainly by the CEW, although teachers took some classes. Other classes were made available at the local community education centre.

Case study methodology

Our case study of the parents and carers project was formulated in the context of an overall stakeholder evaluation of the partnership that adopted a process evaluation model (Clegg and McNulty, 2002). Our research design was largely qualitative, involving a multi-stage study, where issues were followed through from strategic to operational level and back up again. It was multi-method, consisting of interviews, observations and shadowing, focus groups and documentary analysis.

In this chapter, we have drawn on the wider fieldwork that covered a period of six months, and specifically on the sub-set of data focused on the parents and carers project. This involved observations of project classes, partnership project worker meetings and a 'regeneration through learning' conference at which project workers and participants were present. Considerable time was spent in the field in order to gain rapport with beneficiaries, teachers and the community worker. Taped interviews were conducted with the project manager, project worker, project deliverers (two teachers) and two beneficiaries. Informal interviews were carried out with other women participants as part of the shadowing process. The analysis was ongoing and involved detailed reading and re-reading of the extensive notes and transcripts in order to build a rich description of the case study site from the perspective of the participants. Where we identified gaps in our understanding, we collected further data. No attempts were made to impose categories on the data prior to our involvement in the field and the themes we identify emerged from our analysis of the data.

Gender, ethnicity and space: working from the inside

It rapidly became apparent to us that we were involved in exploring the relationship of women carers to their own and their children's learning. Gender was central to the way in which the category of parent was understood both by the schools and also by the women themselves. However, gender is neither fixed, nor its meanings singular. As our study was based in a multi-ethnic area with established white, Pakistani[1] and African-Caribbean residents, and new migrants and non-English speaking mothers, we could not assume that they shared common experiences or meanings attached to education or to their involvement as parents.

A crucial aspect of the project was the way learning was placed within the context of the learners' own lives. Community education development work started with the schools as familiar spaces located within the community and where mothers and other carers came with their children. This approach depended on the CEW finding out about the women themselves, rather than assuming that they were already potential learners waiting to be offered opportunities. The approach was informal and was important in establishing trust and rapport. It involved understanding the dispositions of the people she was working with, as well as locating structural constraints and possibilities in individuals' lives. It also created the possibility of organizational responses based on these understandings. Metaphorically, it involved building new learning spaces for parents/carers.

One teacher talked about the CEW creating a specifically parents' learning environment within the school. This contrasts with when the school is the dominant practice and parents are expected to conform to the school's understanding of social space and the dispositions appropriate to that environment. The teacher was aware of the difference and the constraints on her role and time. The observational data confirmed the difference in nature of the rapport and informality of the contact between the CEW and that achieved by teachers who were more constrained by their positions within the school.

The community worker's focus was on the individuals and their personal journeys. It was not specifically confined to the school setting, where the contact had been established, or to involvement with children. Parents were encouraged to go on from this and involve themselves in other opportunities at the local community education centre. Learning was presented as

> ...providing a route into education for parents through ways of helping children...a step through the door, to join a course for their own educational development.
>
> (Interview: CEW)

The importance of development work, as a vital component for parent/carers in the take-up of learning opportunities, was raised throughout our research. All parents stated they had heard about the accredited classes through the CEW. Her encouragement and skill were praised in highly personal terms – as an individual who showed particular warmth and concern, having a 'really nice' personality and knowing how to talk to people. Other studies, in different cultural contexts, have also commented on the importance of the personal.

When asked what they gained, many women talked about confidence and the collective nature of the experience and that learning was not 'split' from other friendships and networks. Despite the explicit but failed intention to include and encourage men, the spaces the women created for their learning remained women's spaces. The negotiations also encouraged women to express their specific needs. Starting within the particularly gendered world of childcare and school therefore opened up new possibilities.

Some men did bring their children to and from school, but they did not become participants in the classes. The classes took place in the school nursery and the nursery provided a general space for women to chat and discuss parenting issues. In one observation, a male entered the room to collect his child from the nursery, but he sat away from the group, head down, reading his paper. In an informal conversation, he discussed the importance of learning for parents to teach their children, but it was clear that he felt it would be difficult to enter the women's personal space. The gender of the teacher also had an impact. When a male teacher entered the room, the conversation between the women was interrupted as they turned to pay attention to him.

Space is, therefore, important in both positive and negative senses. It excludes those parents and carers who do not fit; mostly it appears by reasons of gender (Caddell, 1996). While both teachers and the CEW expressed regret at there being no men, the term 'parents and carers' and the aim itself expressed norms that are more prevalent in middle-class men's relationship to schools (Crozier, 1998). Creating spaces for working-class men – white, African-Caribbean and Pakistani – may involve different starting places and ones not so normatively overlaid with gendered expectations. The positive side is that creating learning in the real spaces of women's lives, Pakistani, African-Caribbean and white women were able to define what was appropriate to them. It created the conditions under which some of the women could begin to extend their identities as learners (Andruske, 1999).

Creating learning identities

There was considerable evidence from the data that women did gain a new sense of self-respect and recognition that allowed them to begin to think of themselves as learners. The project adopted a pioneering accreditation model (Davies and Bynner, 2000) based on the work of adult educators and others outside mainstream education who came together in a national organization: the Open College Network. Rather than the normal model, where the curriculum is pre-set, the accreditation worked by negotiating learning objectives and involving the women in how these could be demonstrated. The accreditation built on the women's own experiences, and they could use experiences outside the classroom as part of the accreditation process.

The approach also allowed for development rather than a pre-set agenda:

> Initially, it was helping the children but, as the course progressed, parents began thinking about themselves, to develop their own education.
>
> (Interview: CEW)

By starting with the participants' own worlds and validating them, the form of accreditation extended the scope of what was seen to be possible beyond the initial involvement with children's learning. The women in class also praised each other, one parent being constantly praised by other members of the group for her practical work. Without being prompted, two beneficiaries referred to the certificates they had gained for completing the course and spoke of their achievements. Several parents had later attended classes outside the school at a community education centre. This was particularly true for the Pakistani women taking up opportunities outside their home. Some of them attended a computer course with their children, and a weekly class of creative activities at the community education centre. Participation in the parents and carers project, therefore, appeared to create potential for longer term identities as learners.

Benefits of the community participation model

Project benefits were not just on an individual level but filtered out to the community and schools. Beneficiaries gave examples of their involvement with the school. One was a parent link worker, and another a dinner lady, another had become involved in the Parent Teachers Friends Association and one African-Caribbean woman was involved in becoming a Governor. This woman spoke out at the 'learning regeneration conference', where representatives of the project, local dignitaries, and other community workers from across the region were present. She argued the case for accreditation in a workshop and reported that she is intent on taking a course offered by the local university. She discussed how it was important for her as a black woman to be in school as a role model for other children and not just for her own children. Having a voice and breaking boundaries through experiences of learning are part of going beyond individual achievement (Benn, 1997; Hoy *et al.*, 2000). Other women asserted an increased personal sense of empowerment. One woman talks about giving and has a clear sense that she is contributing not just helping her own child. A second woman refers to her own achievements in the context of no longer seeing the school as a place of automatic authority. The model of partnership working with the schools also appears to have enabled the school to listen to these new voices and become 'approachable'. A group of parents from the classes formed a Parents Teachers Friends Association at the school and ran a school summer fair. Parents also felt they had a better grasp of the realities of school.

Social capital theorists are rightly open to radical critique (Schuller and Field, 1998; McClenaghan, 2000), but, in a small way, the aims of the partnership to 'support individuals learning and community development' do appear to have been successful. However, the development of this sort of social capital in multiply deprived communities does not come, as some have suggested (Evans, 1996, cited in McClenaghan, 2000), without the expenditure of additional resources. On the contrary, it is resource intensive and comes through providing resources tailored to local, and even individual, need with high levels of inter-personal support. The validation of skills among adult learners takes time and support for them to re-recognize their own capacities (Titmus, 1999). Even then, not everybody wishes to or is able to participate. Parents may feel that others see them and their children as problems and may not feel confident coming to a group, especially if they have a disruptive child. This view was reflected in the way participants talked about other women who were not involved but whom they felt could benefit. The project deliverers echoed these views:

> I really do worry sometimes that the one's we're really trying to get at aren't the ones who are actually doing it.
>
> (Interview: Teacher)

It appears that even community development relies on unevenly distributed social capital, since those women with already formed networks found it easier to participate. This appeared particularly in the case of the Pakistani women who already had their own community networks. Inclusion, and barriers to inclusion, operates at the micro level as well as in the broader sphere.

Discussion

We, like other commentators in the field of lifelong education (Andruske, 1999; Atkin, 2000), are drawn to Bourdieu's (1992) concept of habitus as a way of thinking about the embedded values and taken for granted assumptions underlying everyday practices. For Bourdieu (1992), the habitus is part of a theory of practice:

> ...the principle of this construction is the system of structured, structuring dispositions, the habitus, which is constituted in practice and is always oriented towards its practical functions.
>
> (Bourdieu, 1992: 52)

Bourdieu draws our attention to those aspects of organizational culture that are structured as dispositions, which dictate the ordinary ways of being distinctive to particular settings. We find the concept illuminating in thinking about the way the fieldwork highlighted the importance of the CEW working with the dispositions of the beneficiaries, which are in turn structured by broader social inequalities. Dispositions are not fixed, but provide a resource from which to build, so for example the Pakistani women's common experience of dealing with welfare and health agencies created the basis for coming together to learn more English, but also the possibility of other activities. The advantage of thinking in terms of the habitus is that it problematizes practices rather than taking them for granted. Atkin (2000) has drawn our attention to the ways in which the embodied structures of the habitus create dispositions towards learning are often incompatible with current government thinking on learning as a source of cultural and social capital (see also Coffield, 2000a,b). Making learning opportunities available does not create the structurally located dispositions involved in participation (Gorard et al., 1997, 1999). Bowman et al. (2000) have explored the ways in which, in some communities, people's ways of thinking about their 'successful futures' does not involve engagement with formal education beyond, or even including, schooling. They, like Atkin (2000), found that other practices within the habitus are more powerful than those associated with the often alien modes of formal education.

It is important, therefore, to focus on the dispositions of all the actors, not just participants, since otherwise it is only practices of beneficiaries that are the subject of scrutiny. This is particularly important for social inclusion partnerships that stress community development since empowered parents may, and often do, become more critical of the school and other institutional arrangements, rather than more compliant. Tett argues that

> If parents can be helped to challenge deficit views of the culture of their homes and communities then a small step has been taken in enabling their voices to be heard in the learning of their children and in their own educational development.
>
> (Tett, 2001, p. 197)

In a context where people's lives are difficult and 'an education course is not on people's minds', partnership members hope that 'the benefit of reaching a small group of people is that they will spread the word to others' (Project Manager). This may happen and our data left us in no doubt about the achievements of the women themselves. Of course, the poverty of the area is not affected by the undoubted successes of small projects such as these. Most of the project workers and the partnership management team had been involved in working in community development and education for years, and they recognized that the work is long term and does not result in short-term gains for whole communities. Like Tett (2001), however, they hoped to challenge deficit models of communities, parents and their children. An end to cross-generational reproduction of structural inequalities will involve major institutional change, but small-scale projects like this give insight into the personally liberating achievements of people who have come to recognize their own skills, capacities and identities as learners.

Note

1 We have used the term Pakistani here, as this was the woman's self-description.

References

Andruske, C.L. (1999) Exploring everyday spaces: women's transitions from welfare to paid work and education. Paper presented at the 29th annual SCUTREA conference, University of Warwick, 5–7 July.

Atkin, C. (2000) Lifelong learning – attitudes to practice in the rural context: a study using Bourdieu's perspective of habitus. *International Journal of Lifelong Education*, 19, 253–265.

Benn, R. (1997) Participation in adult education: breaking boundaries of deepening inequalities. Paper presented at the 27th annual SCUTREA conference, University of London, 1–3 July.

Bourdieu, P. (1992) *An Invitation to Reflexive Sociology* (Cambridge: Polity Press).

Bowman, H., Burden, T. and Konrad, J. (2000) Attitudes to adult education in disadvantaged areas. In *Successful Futures? Community Views on Adult Education and Training* (YPS). Available online: www.jrf.org.uk/knowledge/findings/socialpolicy/810.asp

Caddell, D. (1996) Roles, responsibilities and relationships: engendering parental involvement. Paper presented at the SERA conference, Dundee, September.

Claxton, G. (1999) *Wise Up: The Challenge of Lifelong Learning* (London: Bloomsbury).

Clegg, S. and McNulty, K. (2002) The creation of learner identities: gender, ethnicity and spatiality in a community based model. *Journal of Education Policy*, 17, 587–601.

Coffield, F. (2000a) *Different Visions of a Learning Society. Research Findings Volume 1* (Bristol: The Policy Press).

Coffield, F. (2000b) *Different Visions of a Learning Society. Research Findings Volume 2* (Bristol: The Policy Press).

Crozier, G. (1998) Parents and schools: partnership or surveillance? *Journal of Education Policy*, 13, 125–136.

Davies, P. and Bynner, J. (2000) Learning culture, learning age, learning society: turning aspirations into reality? In F. Coffield (ed.), *Differing Visions of a Learning Society: Research Findings Volume 2* (Bristol: The Policy Press), pp. 119–142.

Department for Transport, Local Government and the Regions (2002) Lessons and evaluation evidence from ten Single Regeneration Budget case studies. Available online: http://www.regeneration.dtlr.gov.uk/research/srb/index.htm

Ecclestone, K. (1999) Care or control? Defining learners' needs for lifelong learning. *British Journal of Education Studies*, 47, 332–347.

Eraut, M. (1997) Perspectives on defining 'The Learning Society'. *Journal of Education Policy*, 12, 551–558.

Gorard, S., Rees, G. and Fevre, R. (1997) Learning trajectories: predicting patterns of adult education and training. Paper presented at the 27th annual SCUTREA conference, University of London, 1–3 July.

Gorard, S., Fevre, R. and Rees, G. (1999) The apparent decline of informal learning. *Oxford Review of Education*, 25, 437–454.

Hoy, J., Kumrai, R. and Webb, S. (2000) Practitioner research with a difference: widening participation projects. Paper presented at the 30th annual SCUTREA conference, University of Nottingham, 3–5 July.

Kenny, M., Ralph, S. and Brown, M. (2000) The importance of reflection in experiential learning with community and youth workers for the learning age. *International Journal of Lifelong Education*, 19, 115–125.

Lave, J. and Wenger, E. (1996) *Situated Learning: Legitimate Peripheral Participation* (Cambridge: Cambridge University Press).

Levitas, R. (1998) *The Inclusive Society? Social Exclusions and New Labour* (Basingstoke: Macmillan).

McClenaghan, P. (2000) Social capital: exploring the theoretical foundations of community development education. *British Educational Research Journal*, 26, 565–582.

Moreland, R. and Lovett, T. (1997) Lifelong learning and community development. *International Journal of Lifelong Education*, 16, 201–216.

Schuller, T. and Field, J. (1998) Social capital, human capital and the learning society. *International Journal of Lifelong Education*, 17, 226–235.

Tett, L. (2001) Parents as problems or parents as people? Parental involvement programmes, schools and adult educators. *International Journal of Lifelong Education*, 20, 188–198.

Titmus, C. (1999) Concepts and practices of education and adult education: obstacles to lifelong education and lifelong learning? *International Journal of Lifelong Education*, 18, 343–354.

Watts, A.G. (2001) Career guidance and social exclusion: a cautionary tale. *British Journal of Guidance and Counselling*, 29, 157–176.

Watts, J. (2000) 'Dual Track' – combining 'inclusive' education for individuals with 'bottom-up' community regeneration initiatives intended to combat social exclusion. Paper presented at the 30th annual SCUTREA conference, University of Nottingham, 3–5 July.

Index

ability grouping 87, 147
Accelerated Schools in Action 151
Accelerated Schools Project (ASP) 144, 151, 152–5, 157–8, 159; classroom support for teachers 157; parental involvement 156–7; principles of 151–2
adult education 5, 214–17; advantages 218
adult learners 217; views on learning 8
African-Caribbean children: school exclusion 15, 131
Americans with Disabilities Act 37–8
anger management strategy 134, 138
anti-bullying 134
apartheid: impact on education system 47
'ascertainment' 93
Ashton, Baroness 6
Asperger's syndrome children 88, 89, 185; peer relationship 178–80; schooling 107, 108, 116, 177–8; teachers attitude 179–80
Australia: inclusive education 7; resource provision 16; special education needs 13
autistic student: and mainstream schooling 181–6

Black, Mr 153, 154
block-scheduling 146, 148
'books for babies' 214
Boulder choice system (BVSD) 42–4
BVSD's Montessori focus school 44

Case Conference system 105
charter schools 38, 42; accountability of 41–2; enrolment of disabled children 40–2; funding 41; legislation 39
Chavez, Mrs 152–3, 156, 157

children: Inuit 198; Native American 198
Children Act, 1989 (UK) 131
Children's Fund 127
choice schools 38, 45; admission criteria 39; intra-district 39; types 42
'Circle of Friends' 134, 138, 139, 141, 154, 156
classroom environment 31
Code of Practice on the Identification and Assessment of Special Educational Needs 112, 115, 183
collaborative planning support 88
collaborative teamwork 155
Colorado Student Assessment Program (CSAP) 43
community development model: for adult education 214–17, 219–20; benefits 218
Community Education Worker (CEW) 214, 215–16, 219
competence centres (Norway) 25, 26, 31
Connexions 127
Consultative Paper No. 1 on Special Education: Building an Inclusive Education and Training System: First Steps 53–5; language of 55
consumer centredness 62, 69
content-focused culture 91
cooperation 32
cooperative learning 147, 170
counselling 138, 139, 141
'curricular fundamentalism' 186
curriculum 91–2
'Curriculum 2005' (South Africa) 53

deconstruction 13–14, 16–17, 20
developing countries: inclusive education 2, 6
disability 17

disability studies 14, 20–1
disabled children 181–3; academic
    potential 114, 154; education 4;
    enrolment in charter schools 40–2; and
    IDEA 38; inclusive education 6; in
    mainstream schools 3; and QAA Code
    of Practice 17–20; right to education
    3–4; social integration 29, 33
Disabled Children's Action Group
    (DICAG) 48
dissembling 15–16
diversity 175, 187
Down's Syndrome South Africa (DSSA) 48
Down's syndrome: student with 153

EAZs 127
education 213; barriers 51–2; migrant
    workers 8, 192, 196–7
Education Act, 1986 (UK) 130
Education Act, 1993 (UK) 73, 130
educational equity 3, 121; and special
    education needs 123–4
educational goals 124–5
educational policy 4; delay in development
    process 52–3; South Africa 47–8
'education for all' 3
Education for All by 2000 (EFA 2000)
    programme 4
Education for All Handicapped Children
    Act, 1975 (US) 36
education officers 78
education system: South Africa 47; United
    States 36–7
electronic communication boards 148
emotional and behavioural difficulties 105,
    131, 135–6; effect of school
    environment on 131–2
emotional intelligence 132
England: parental involvement in
    assessment of SEN 75–6, 78–81;
    provision for SEN 75; SEN policy
    73–4, 83–4
enrolment: in charter schools 40–2
epilepsy 108
Esperante Elementary School (US) 152–8
Excellence in Cities 127
exclusion, educational 14, 15; in charter
    schools 40–4
exclusion, school 7, 96, 105, 107, 114,
    130; appeals against 97–8, 131; deterrent
    to bad behaviour 101; extend of 97;
    impact of 131; parental involvement in

prevention 100–1, 138; period of 96–7,
    130; prevention of 136, 137, 139–41; in
    primary schools 130, 132; punishment
    for wrongdoing 104; reasons for 97, 99,
    131; respite for excluded student 103–4;
    respite for teachers and other students
    101–3; 'unofficial' 114, 130
'Explorer II' school reform project 146
expulsion see exclusion, school

Fields of Toil: A Migrant Family's
    Journey 193
Firmament (middle school) 43, 44
fixed term exclusion 130
focus schools 42, 43; neighbourhood 42

gay and lesbian issues see
    homosexuality/sexuality issues
Girls and Boys at School – Gender Equity
    Strategy, 1996–2000 (New South
    Wales) 206
Guidance on Issues Concerning Exclusion from
    School: Circular 2/98 97

HAZ 133, 140
headteachers 133; responsibilities 112
'Holmes Group' 144
Holmes Middle School (Detroit) 146–51
homed/homeless dimension 194–5,
    198, 199
homeless 191, 195–6
homosexuality/sexuality issues: attitude of
    pre-service teachers to 202–3, 205,
    206–10; education 206

in-class support 87, 88
Including Primary School Children (IPSC)
    133–5, 138; parents attitude towards 135
inclusion 1, 2–3, 8, 44, 59, 60
inclusive education 1, 5, 6–7, 36–7, 59–61,
    92; Australia 7, 85; barriers to 1–2, 161;
    and Consultative Paper (South Africa)
    54–5; developing countries 2, 6; factors
    influencing 26–7, 30–3; ideology 27–9;
    implementation 29–30; India 3;
    instructional methods 170–1; Norway
    26, 34; and QAA Code of Practice (UK)
    17–20; resources 16, 33; and special
    needs education 14–15; teachers' views
    on 5, 92–3; United Kingdom 59–61,
    68–70; United States 7, 44–5
indefinite exclusion 130

Independent Centre for Special Education Advice (ICSEA) 81–2
Independent Panel for Special Educational Advice (IPSEA) 74
individualization 123, 125
Individuals with Disabilities Education Act (IDEA), 1990 (US) 36, 38
integrated curriculum 146, 148, 170
Integrated Language Arts Partnership (ILAP) 147–8
integration 59, 60, 68, 70
Integration in Victorian Schools 85
intellectual ability 175–6
intellectual disability 88
'internal' exclusion 130

Jomtien Conference, 1990 4

K-12 public schools 144, 145

language instruction: United States 147
'learner deficit' view 47, 52–3
learning 8; disabilities 47; lifelong 213; opportunities 213
legislation: anti-discrimination 85; charter schools 39; special education (Norway) 25–6; special education (US) 37–8
Levin, Henry M. 151, 159
Local Authority (Scotland) 97
local education authorities (LEAs) (UK) 16, 61; interaction with parents 74; and special education provision policy 61–2, 69
Local Government Act, 1988 (Britain) 202

magnet schools 39
Maine, Mrs 153, 154, 157
mainstream schools: Australia 85; and autistic student 181–5; inclusion of disabled children 3, 37, 59, 75; United Kingdom 63–7
market-driven education system 36, 37, 39, 41, 45
'MEAP' 149
Michigan State University (MSU) 146
migrant farm workers 191–2; lifestyle 193–4
migrant workers' children: education 8, 192, 196–8; parental involvement 198–9
minority students 198
multiculturalism: attitude of pre-service teachers towards 204

named person 76, 77
National Commission on Education Support Services (NCESS) (South Africa) 48–9; tasks of 49–50
National Commission on Special Needs in Education and Training (NCSNET) (South Africa) 48–9; tasks of 49–50
National Committee of Enquiry into Higher Education (UK) 17
National Council for Accreditation of Teacher Education (NCATE) (US) 145
New South Wales Department of Education and Training 206
Norway: factors influencing inclusive education 26–7, 30–3; ideology of inclusive education 27–29; implementation of inclusive education 29–30, 33–4; resources for inclusive education 33; social integration 29; special education legislation 25; special education reorganization 25–6

Ofsted school inspection 113–14
'open enrolment' system *see* school-choice system
Osler, Chay 108–11, 117; academic potential 111, 112–13; impact of exclusion 110, 114–15
Oswego Middle School (OMS) 160–1; goals 162–4; implementation of inclusive education 167–8; Inclusion Support Team 167–8, 171; Inclusive Education Committee 161, 169; planning process for implementation *166*; recommendations by Committee 164–5

parent centred organizations (PCOs) 72
Parent Partnership Officer 77
parents: attitude towards IPSC 135; interaction with LEAs 74; involvement in accelerated schools 156–7; involvement in prevention of school exclusion 100–1, 138; role in participatory policy development 7, 69–70; role in SEN policy and procedures 75–6, 78–81; role in SEN policy and procedures in England and Scotland 73, 74, 83; views on inclusion 65–7
parents, migrant: involvement in their children's education 198–9

participatory policy development 7
peer relationship 178–80
peer tutors 87
permanent exclusion 130, 132
Pinnacle (elementary school) 43
play therapy 134
power/powerless, Foucauldian
    conceptualization 194, 195
powerful learning 152–5
primary schools: exclusion 130, 132
problem-solving 147
Professional Development School (PDS)
    project 144, 145–9, 150–1, 158;
    goals 145
Project Choice 147, 148
prototype schools 150
psychologists 77, 78
public school academies *see* charter schools
public schools: enrolment of disabled
    children 40; school-choice system
    in 39; United States 36–7
pull-out programme 156
push-in programme 156

Quality Assurance Agency's (QAA) Code
    of Practice on Disability in Higher
    Education 13
Quality Assurance Agency's (QAA) Code
    of Practice for Students with
    Disabilities 17–20

racism in education 15; South Africa 47
reductionism *see* dissembling
Rehabilitation Act, 1973 (US) 37–8
'removed from the register' 96–7
resources: inclusive education 33; special
    education needs provision 122; United
    Kingdom 62, 69
right to education 4–5, 115; of disabled
    children 3–4

Salamanca Conference, 1994
Salamanca Statement 4–5; support of
    United Kingdom 6
school change: United States 8
school-choice system 36; in public schools
    39; types 42
school organization 32, 85
school-parent relationship 32
school reforms: United States 8, 158–9
Schools General (Scotland) Regulations,
    1975 96

Schools Plus 127
Scotland: appeals against school exclusion
    97–8; extend of school exclusion 97;
    period of school exclusion 96–7;
    provision for SEN policy 75; reasons for
    school exclusion 97, 99–105; SEN
    policy 73–4, 83–4
Scotland's *Manual of Good Practice*
    (SOEID) 73
Scottish Office Education and Industry
    Department 97
secondary schools: inclusive culture 86;
    traditional model 85–6, 93
SEED 98, 99, 104; guidelines 96
SEN and Disability Act, 2001 (UK) 116
SEN Tribunal Annual Report 75
'social inclusion' 60, 105, 127
social integration: Norway 29, 33
social justice issues: attitude of pre-service
    teachers to 205–7
South Africa: barriers to education 51–2;
    delay in development process 52–3;
    educational policy 47; post-apartheid
    policy 48; transformative view of
    education 53
South African Federal Council on
    Disability (SAFCD) 48
special educational needs coordinators
    (SENCOs) 112, 113, 133
special education needs (SEN) 4, 13–14,
    121–2; alternative approach 124–8;
    Australia 13; and inclusive education
    14–15; models of support 86–8, 89, 90;
    monitoring of alternative approach 127;
    provision 7–8, 75; reorganization 25–6,
    60, 68–70; resources 122; school
    exclusion 131; South Africa 47, 48–50,
    54; teacher's attitude towards 112;
    United Kingdom 61; United
    States 36–7
special education needs (SEN) policy:
    parental involvement 72, 73, 75–83
special education schools 28; advantages
    29–30; closure 61
special education teachers 87–8, 89–91
special education workers 13, 21;
    professional interest 16
'special needs' 123–4
St John, Edward 151
Standards and Framework Act, 1998
    (UK) 130
State Education Agency (SEA) (US) 38

strand schools 42, 43
student-focused culture 91
Sure Start 127
systemic dualism 61–2, 68–9

teachers: attitude towards inclusive
   education 5, 92–3; attitude towards
   SEN 112, 178–80, 180–1; certification
   39; characteristics of 31; classroom
   support 157; collaborative planning
   support 88; qualified 32; training 8
teachers, pre-service 202, 203; attitude
   towards homosexuality 202–3, 205,
   206–10; attitude towards
   multiculturalism 204
temporary exclusion 96
test scores: United States 41–2
training: teachers 8

United Kingdom: parental involvement
   75–6; reorganization of special education
   provision 61–2, 68–70; views of
   mainstream professionals on
   reorganization 64–5; views of parents on

reorganization 65–7; views of
   professionals on reorganization 62–4;
   views of students on reorganization 67–8
United Nations (UN) 3, 4
United Nations (UN) Convention on the
   Rights of the Child 3–4, 115
United States: education system 36–7;
   inclusive education 7, 44–5; public
   schools 36–7; school change 8;
   school-choice system 36; school
   reforms 8, 158–9; special education
   legislation 37–8

'valuing diversity' 175–6, 187

Warnock Report 73, 123
whole-group instruction 153
whole-language approach 153, 170
women, African-Caribbean: adult
   education 217, 218
women, Pakistani: adult education 217,
   219, 220
World Bank 4
worry boxes 139, 141

DATE DUE